SAVING GLOBAL CAPITALISM

Interrogating Austerity and Working Class Responses to Crises

Alternate Routes 2011
A Journal of Critical Social Research

Red Quill Books | Ottawa

© Red Quill Books Ltd. 2010
Ottawa

www.redquillbooks.com

ISBN 978-1-926958-01-9

Printed on acid-free paper. The paper used in this book incorporates post-consumer waste and has not been sourced from endangered old growth forests, forests of exceptional conservation value or the Amazon Basin. Red Quill Books subscribes to a one-book-at-a-time manufacturing process that substantially lessens supply chain waste, reduces greenhouse emissions, and conserves valuable natural resources.

Includes bibliographical references.
ISBN 978-1-926958-01-9

Also published as a serial:

"Alternate Routes"
ISSN 1923-7081 (online)
ISSN 0702-8865 (print)

Red Quill Books is an alternative publishing house. Proceeds from the sale of this book will support future critical scholarship.

alternate

published since 1977

a journal of critical social research

routes

Alternate Routes: A Journal of Critical Social Research

Editors
Carlo Fanelli, Chris Hurl, Priscillia Lefebvre, Gulden Ozcan

Editorial Board
Dave Broad, David Camfield, Wallace Clement, Simten Cosar, Simon Dalby, Ann Duffy, Bryan Evans, Andrew Jackson, Rianne Mahon, Radika Mongia, Justin Paulson, Govind Rao, George Rigakos, Herman Rosenfeld, Stephanie Ross, Arne Ruckert, Toby Sanger, Ingo Schmidt, Alan Sears, Vivian Shalla, Janet Siltanen, Susan Spronk, Donald Swartz, Mark Thomas, Rosemary Warskett.

Alternate Routes: A Journal of Critical Social Research is a scholarly, peer-reviewed journal published annually in the Department of Sociology and Anthropology at Carleton University by a collaborative editorial committee consisting of faculty and graduate-students. Established in 1977, *AR* has sought to provide an intellectual forum for engaging debate and interdisciplinary inquiry. In working closely with international scholars, labour organizers and social justice activists, the editorial emphasis is on the publication of non-traditional, provocative and radical analyses that may not find a forum in conventional academic or mainstream venues. *AR* seeks to cultivate a very 'public' academic journal and encourages submissions that advance or challenge theoretical and contemporary issues related to political, economic and cultural processes that shape and reshape social interactions, as well as works dedicated to progressive political interventions. In addition to full-length articles, *AR* welcomes review essays sparked by previously published material, interviews with academics or political figures, in addition to media analyses, artistic and cultural contributions, and book reviews. *AR* publishes primarily special-themed issues and therefore requests that submissions be related to the current call for papers. Submissions should be free of racist or sexist language, have limited technical or specialized terms and be written in a style that is accessible to our diverse readership.

Saving Global Capitalism: Interrogating Austerity and Working Class Reponses to Crises

Table of Contents

Introduction

Saving Global Capitalism: Interrogating Austerity & Working Class Responses to Crises

AR Editorial Collective

After a four-year hiatus, *Alternate Routes* (AR) is back. Published since 1977, AR has always emphasized cross-disciplinary collaboration, critical research dedicated to progressive political and academic interventions, as well as partnerships with community groups and labour organizations. AR has been central to many significant debates over the course of its history (see our Archives in subsequent pages). Likewise, AR has sought to be a springboard for scholars central to sociology and anthropology, but also for the social sciences more broadly. Articles from Wallace Clement, Michael Burawoy, Leo Panitch, John Porter, Pat and Hugh Armstrong, Eileen Saunders, Gillian Creese, Daniel Glenday and Sut Jhally, for instance, line the pages of AR's past contributing original and creative analyses that continue to play on the minds of readers today. AR seeks to cultivate a 'public' academic journal where discussions revolve not only around the classroom, but also at the water cooler, dinner table, coffee house, pubs and parks. With this re-launch issue, we hope that such discussions get under way.

What began as an unprecedented housing meltdown centered in the U.S. in the summer of 2007, quickly turned into a global insolvency crisis throughout 2008, and later the most significant economic crisis since the Great Depression. Many terms have come to describe the period 2007-2010: The Great Recession; The Great Financial Meltdown; The Global Slump; The Great Moderation; The Global Financial Crisis and so on. However, prior to the crisis capital was bathing in excess: balance sheets were positive, corporate profits neared the historic highs of the 1960s, governments had successfully waged a war against deficits and inflation-targeting was the dogma of central bankers worldwide. Paralleling the exorbitant growth in wealth was an inverse squeeze on the working classes locally, nationally and globally. The foundation for this class war was laid over the next three decades following the failure of the Keynesian welfare state to sustain profitability. What become known as neoliberalism, that is, class war from above, set in motion an unprecedented era of capitalist militancy.

Over this period in the advanced capitalist economies real wages have generally been stagnant, work and labour has increasingly become insecure and characterized by part-time, contingent and 'flexible' forms of workplace organization, work-life conflicts heightened and racialized and gendered forms of labour market segmentation all the more rigid. In the so-called peripheral nations much the same has taken place, however often much more extreme and brutal in form and function. Indeed, significant sectors of the working class have been thoroughly defeated, perhaps none more evident than the near collapse of organized labour as an organ of discontent. The above goes a long way in ascribing the current political-economic context in which crises occur. But the uncertainty and the impasse must also be understood as nothing less than a social and ecological crisis, in which the routes out of the crisis are still difficult to discern.

In fact, for all the exaggerated rhetoric of crises, the 'real' crisis is on the part of the working class, and not of capital or capitalism as a historically specific socio-economic mode of production. With the weakness of the working class so exposed, the plundering of the public purse to save global capitalism has become an international reality. In spite of monumental bailouts by all major capitalist countries, and the quite extraordinary coordination among capitalist states led by the U.S. Treasury, it is the public purse that salvaged the making of global capital that is now being undermined and subsumed by the very financial markets that were rescued.

The new enemies of the state and capital are public sector workers and the unions that aim to defend the inherently incompatible interests of labour. Amidst exceptional uncertainty and populist rage, neoliberals are regrouping in order to take advantage of this historic opportunity. A new wave of record national and sub-national budget deficits, having consecutively been undermined for over three decades of neoliberal fiscal and monetary policy, are sweeping the globe from Tucson to Toronto, Ankara to Bangkok and Rome to Johannesburg. Attacking the "lavish" lifestyles of "big labour" and "big government" has been a dishonest and insidious way of dividing public and private sector workers in what is an orchestrated assault intent on full-out privatization (Traub, 2010). Increasing aggressiveness against universal entitlements such as health care, education and pensions has become a conservative sport, while the selling of public assets at bargain basement prices the new orthodoxy. In fact, given the limited resistance from Left forces, populist Right coalitions from the Tea party in the U.S. to the Wildrose Alliance in Western Canada, Tea Party North in Quebec and the rise of new right-wing populist parties gaining significant momentum throughout Europe -- as in Belgium, the Netherlands,

Sweden, Italy and France, most often infused with nationalistic, pro-Christian and 'traditional' core values -- clearly suggests that capitalist forces are reasserting their hegemony and power. Rescuing capital, then, is leading to a new wave of austerity.

This round of austerity is dynamic and multidimensional. Manufacturers, oil companies, banks and corporate profits are equal to or higher than before the recession in 2008 (Petras, 2010). At the same time, millions of jobs have been shed, labour concessions extracted, social programs gutted, environmental protections rolled back, new tax cuts enacted for corporations and tax increases implemented for ordinary workers. Clearly, there is an exploitative class-based relationship at play as elites attempt to reconstruct the neoliberal order in a new form. In fact, according to the 2010 World Wealth Report by Capgemini and Merrill Lynch, millionaires' assets have rebounded close to pre-crisis levels. Last year, the value of Asia-Pacific assets grew 31 percent to $9.7 trillion (U.S.), while the number of millionaires rose 26 percent to 3 million. Assets in North America advanced 18 percent to $10.7 trillion, while the number of millionaires rose 16.6 percent to 3.1 million. Similarly, assets in Europe climbed 14.2 percent to $9.5 trillion, while the growth of millionaires increased about 13 percent. Even in China, hard hit from a drop in total world demand for commodities, increased its number of millionaires by 31 percent. Finally, the ultra-high net worth of individuals with more than $30 million to invest saw their wealth rise by 21.5 percent in 2009 purportedly due to a "more effective reallocation of assets" (Capgemini and Merrill Lynch, 2010). With a further slide into recession a possibility in 2011, especially amidst the organized "fiscal consolidation" (read austerity) of G20 leaders, weak investment and the retreat of credit, the social crisis is by no means over even as the economic crisis is shouldered disproportionately by the working class.

All things considered, then, it should come as no surprise to the reader that the content of this forum does not seek to 'save' global capitalism. Rather, this issue scrutinizes the austerity responses from governments' around the world, which are being used as a strategy to kick-start capital accumulation and recreate a suitable environment for business investment. In turn, contributors seek to critically dissect the impacts and various responses emanating from the working classes. The articles in this forum provide a snapshot of a new era of capitalist militancy as they manifest unevenly across the globe.

In the first of the forum's articles, Bryan Evans and Greg Albo suggest that although the global economic crisis is now contained, economic stagnation and political turmoil continues in the central economies of capitalism, including Canada. They argue that there remain palpable fears of a further slide into recession in economic forecasts for 2011. After providing an overview of the form the crisis has taken internationally, with an emphasis on the centrality of the US economy, Evans and Albo focus their attention on the transition from 'rescue strategies' to 'exit strategies' now underway in Canada. Contrary to conventional public policy, they argue that it is necessary to resist austerity and defend public services. For this to happen, they maintain that it is necessary to account for the class nature of neoliberalism in order to build new organizational capacities for resistance.

The following article by Carlo Fanelli and Chris Hurl, critiques the "Janus-faced" nature of Canadian Prime Minister Stephan Harper's austerity measures. They argue that the current round of austerity has a dual-character: on the one hand public services, social programs, labour and environmental supports and protections are rolled back for the working class, while new and revamped state supports rolled out to serve the needs of capital. After tracing the theoretical presuppositions of neoliberalism, they locate its integration into the material practices and arrangements of the 'competitive' Canadian state as is reflected in the federal government's most recent stimulus policies. Dovetailing with the analysis of Evans and Albo, they conclude with some thoughts for resisting austerity and strengthening the resolve of the Canadian working class.

The third essay in this issue, by Minqi Li, begins with a series of interrelated questions: What are the "normal conditions" required for capitalist expansion and survival? Under what historical conditions may capitalism cease to exist as a historically viable system? If it turns out that capitalism is no longer historically viable, what "exit strategies" may be available for humanity? After delving into the complexities of such questions, Li focuses his analysis on China as a key battleground for global class struggles and explores the relationship between resistance to austerity and ecological degradation.

In a following essay, Ingo Schmidt's article explores the dialectic between core and peripheral European Union (EU) countries. Schmidt explicitly rejects the notion that the so-called PIIGS (Portugal, Ireland, Italy, Greece, Spain) are prone to fiscal and sovereign debt crises because of reckless spending by governments' and the inability to cultivate a 'good business climate'. Instead, he argues that the EU periphery is prone to crises because of its inability to compete with exports from dominant countries, especially Germany. Furthermore, he suggests, world market integration amid economic stagnation, combined with growing debts, rampant speculation and recurrent financial crises, is no way to overcome a country's peripheral position.

The fifth article in this issue by Hugo Radice raises the question of whether or not cutting government deficits are an economic requirement or an act of class war? He contends "that cutting government deficits is not an economic necessity, but a strategy for justifying attacks on the living standards of workers and heading off reforms that might threaten the power of the dominant business and financial elites." In order to escape from such debilitating attacks, Radice argues that a rejection of austerity is necessary, and that a restoration of class politics with an eye to other forms of oppression is the basis from which a movement of universal appeal may emerge to challenge the rule of capital.

The succeeding analysis by Richard Wolff examines the widespread resurgence of Keynesianism amid faltering faith in neoclassical economics and neoliberalism more generally. He critiques the historical inadequacy of Keynesianism to reverse or prevent recurrent capitalist crises, arguing instead that they lay the foundation from which a new phase of accumulation may begin. In its place, Wolff stresses a new kind of Marxian response that focuses on micro-level transformations, complementing the traditional macro-level emphasis of Marxism, socialism and communism.

Two final articles explore more concrete issues of particular importance to economic equality and rebuilding a viable Left project. Rebecca Schein explores the movement-building potential of a recently launched campaign by the Greater Toronto Workers Assembly (GTWA) for free and accessible public transit. The aim of the initiative, Schein explains, is to de-commodify Toronto's public transit system, showing that the GTWA's campaign for mass transportation is a public good that should be paid for by mass transportation. She argues that the demand for free public transit may create inroads for broader public dialogue regarding public goods and services, as well as public control over resource allocation. The final article by one of AR's former editors, Dave Broad, revisits his original article published in 1988 titled "Peripheralization of the Centre: W(h)ither Canada?".

The remainder of this issue features insightful contributions from Aaron Henry reviewing the Ottawa Fringe Festival's Outstanding Award Winner "Multinational gRape Corporations", Bora Erdagi reviewing the Hollywood thriller "Eyes Wide Shut", a cultural tract by Lyle Daggett titled "Political Poetry", as well as critical reviews of a number of recently published books.

With this issue, AR would also like to thank the Department of Sociology & Anthropology, as well as the Sociology and Anthropology Graduate Students' Caucus at Carleton University for their continued support. Last and certainly not least, we at AR would like to acknowledge the dedication and commitment by AR's editorial advisors who lent us their time and energy in order to see this issue through. AR would like to encourage all readers to view our current Call for Papers and consider submitting an article.

Sadly, the Department of Sociology & Anthropology recently lost one of its beloved administrators, Joy Nelson, after a valiant battle with cancer. Joy's countless efforts on behalf of faculty and students are beyond measure. She will be dearly missed by all of us in the Carleton community and beyond. Joy's strength, bravery and fighting spirit lives on. To her memory we dedicate this issue.

References

Capgemini & Merrill Lynch. (2010). World Wealth Report. Available at www.trigoncapital.com/ upload/wealth.../World_Wealth_Report_2010.pdf

Petras, J. (2010). Crisis. What Crisis? Profits Soar! Available at http://lahaine.org/petras/index.php?p=1818&c=1

Traub, A. (2010). War on Public Workers. *The Nation*. Available at http://www.thenation.com/article/war-public-workers

Permanent Austerity: The Politics of the Canadian Exit Strategy from Fiscal Stimulus

Bryan Evans and Greg Albo[1]

Abstract: This paper fills a gap in the analysis to date in examining the political context of Canada's fiscal stimulus rescue strategy and the subsequent turn to exit. The central question in Canada, as everywhere else, has been who will pay for the economic crisis? Canada's federal and provincial governments have answered by signaling a sharp turn to austerity in targeting public sector workers and public services. While examples of resistance are noted, these remain far too limited to effectively challenge what is becoming a return to not just neoliberalism but a more authoritarian form at that.

Keywords: austerity, public sector, deregulation, fiscal crisis,

Since erupting across the world market in 2007, the global economic crisis has held political centre-stage in the core capitalist states. What began as a liquidity crisis in mortgage markets in the heartlands of neoliberalism in 2007 – the US, Britain, Ireland, and the Baltic countries – quickly turned into an insolvency crisis in 2008, and the worst economic downturn since the Great Depression in 2009. Although the downward spiral is now contained, economic stagnation continues in the central economies of capitalism – including Canada – across 2010. Indeed, there remain palpable fears of a further slide into economic recession in economic forecasts for 2011. And slow growth is projected for the foreseeable future.

The centre of the economic turmoil has been the US, the driving force of the world economy over the last century. As a small open economy with an overwhelming trade dependence on the US, economic conditions in the US have been a crucial determinant of prospects for accumulation in Canada. A register of key de-

---

[1]   Bryan Evans teaches public administration at Ryerson University. Greg Albo teaches political economy at York University, and is co-editor of Socialist Register, and author of In and Out of Crisis (2010).

velopments in the US (noted in US dollars below) is indicative of the breadth and depth of the financial crisis (IMF 2010; Office of Management and Budget 2010; Realtytrac 2010; Bloomberg 2009; ILO 2009; McKinsey 2008; Crotty 2009).

- At the height of the US housing market bubble in 2006, a startling one-fifth of new mortgages taken out are high-risk sub-prime loans, with total outstanding residential mortgages valued at over $10 trillion. But in 2007 things turned sour: foreclosure proceedings by lenders on mortgages increase by 79 per cent from 2006 levels on 1.3 million properties; they increase again by 81 per cent for 2008 over 2007 on 2.3 million properties; and in 2009, foreclosure notices on 2.8 million properties shatter records. Into 2010, the numbers of mortgages either delinquent or foreclosed continues to climb.

- From a mid-2006 peak, US house values decline by one-quarter by September 2008 at the peak of the financial turbulence– a stunning $15 trillion in asset value vanishing.

- In February 2007, HSBC, the world's largest bank, is forced to write-down $10.5 billion in US sub-prime loan backed securities. This begins a chain of write-offs and bankruptcies that will take down over 100 mortgage lenders in 2007. By 2008, the IMF estimates that over $1.5 trillion of sub-prime mortgage-backed securities have to be written-off in a total market valued at over $7 trillion.

- In March 2008, the US government mandates the shotgun merger of Bear Stearns with JP Morgan at a meager $2 a share after trading at $170 per share only one year earlier.

- In September 2008, global inter-bank lending completely freezes up on realization that the sub-prime mortgage meltdown is moving from the shadow banking system into the formal banking system risking complete financial collapse.

- As a consequence, in September 2008 the major US investment houses are eliminated virtually overnight with the collapse of Lehman Brothers, the forced merger of Merrill Lynch into Bank of America and the automatic regulatory conversion of Morgan Stanley and Goldman Sachs into commercial banks.

- As well, in September 2008 the US government is forced to takeover AIG, the largest insurance company in the world with assets of some $1 trillion and a yearly turnover in the order of $10 trillion. By May 2009, the government has provided credit facilities to AIG in the order of $180 billion, the largest bailout in history.

- The US government also takes over Fannie and Freddie Mac in September 2008, owners or guarantors of about half of the $12 trillion mortgage market.

- A cut in half of global stock market capitalisation from some $63 trillion to only $31 trillion by November 2008.

- In December 2008, the largest Ponzi scheme in history at $65 billion, and run by Bernard L. Madoff Investment Securities (Madoff being a former head of the NASDAQ), collapses.

- In February 2009, the Obama Administration gains Congressional support for an emergency economic stabilization package nominally figured at $787 billion, the largest such stimulus measure in history.

- By April 2009, estimates are ranging from $2.7 trillion to $5 trillion for potential losses to banks for collateralized debt obligations (CDOs) assets, with half this falling on US banks. It is also estimated that an astounding half of all CDOs will default.

- The filing for Chapter 11 Bankruptcy protection by General Motors on June 1, 2009, the largest such filing by an industrial company at $82 billion in assets and $173 billion in debt.

- The estimated costs to US taxpayers for the financial crisis are notoriously hard to come by from the government, but one official puts the figure at a possible $23.7 trillion dollars.

- By 2009, the numbers of officially unemployed in the US are over 15 million, or over 10 percent of the labour force, with over 20 million estimated global job losses since the onset of the crisis.

- The US budget deficit for fiscal year 2009 is estimated at a stunning $1.42 trillion dollars, and 12.3 percent of GDP, a deficit share last seen during WW II. Budgetary forecasts for 2010 are only slightly improved.

- For the first time since the Great Depression, world output as a whole declined by 0.6 percent in 2009, with the US suffering a slump of -2.4 percent, the advanced economies of -3.2 percent and the developing economies (including India and China) growing by only 2.5 percent.

With the US mortgage meltdown and liquidity crisis triggering a global economic crisis, Canada could not be insulated from the economic turbulence. Nor was Canada cut-off from the processes of financialization and credit bubbles that formed in the US. The crisis in Canada has not been as severe as in the US, but there are certain features that bear noting (Department of Finance 2010; Bank of Canada 2009; McNish and McArthur 2008; Baragar 2009).

- From budgetary measures introduced in 2006, state mortgage guarantees in Canada more than doubled by the end of 2008. This included the move by mortgage lenders into high risk mortgages of 40 years and no down payment (after prompting from US mortgage brokers, and notably AIG). The Canada Mortgage and Housing Corporation (CMHC) effectively carrying much of the foreclosure risk, with financial institutions reaping the rewards of high leverage. This has included the CMHC taking major swaps in mortgages for 'cash' for the Banks to help bolster their balance sheets.

- In August 2007 as problems in derivatives markets began to spread, the asset-backed commercial paper market (ABCP) in Canada froze-up with some $32 billion in paper not being able to be traded.

- After removing the 30 percent limit on foreign asset holdings in Canadian retirement plans in 2005, US bond placements in Canada increase from a mere $1.5 billion in 2004 to almost $27 billion in 2007.

- From the fall of 2007 through 2009, the Bank of Canada begins to take a series of measures to increase liquidity in the financial system. This included driving interest rates down to just 0.5 per cent, and injecting billions into the financial system through purchases of Government of Canada securities, but also extending to the purchase of private sector securities and commercial paper.

- While the lead Canadian financial institutions avoided collapse in 2008, Canadian equity markets more than matched the US decline, Government of Canada Treasury Bill yields collapsed, and spreads with commercial paper shot up. These indications of liquidity problems moved the Finance Ministry to implement an Extraordinary Financing Framework (EFF) with $200 billion in available funds.

• With the turbulence in world markets, Canadian growth rates fell sharply from average rates of about 3 per cent from 2004-2007, to just about 0.4 per cent for 2008, before tanking at -2.6 per cent for 2009. Positive growth is returning across 2010 but expected to remain sluggish. As a consequence, the official unemployment moved from 6.0 for 2007 to 8.3 in 2009, and has stayed in this range since.

• As a consequence of falling output and fiscal support for Canadian financial institutions, the budgetary position of the federal government moved from a surplus in 2007-08 of about $10 billion, to a deficit of $6 billion for 2008-09 and spiraling to $-54 billion for 2009-10.

From Financial Rescue to Public Sector Austerity

The severity of the economic crisis left little alternative to massive state-led 'rescue strategies' across the world market, although concentrated in the core countries, including Canada. The rescue had two overarching components: a series of measures to stabilize the financial system and enhance conditions for borrowing; and fiscal stimulus to offset the demand shock from the collapse of the financial system and the severe decline in world trade (Loxley 2009; Roubini and Mihm 2010). The first and most urgent measures were to address the insolvency crisis of specific financial institutions where firms were facing massive loan losses or runs on deposits. In an unprecedented number of countries, the actions included forced mergers, bank nationalizations and, in almost all countries, specific steps to bailout banks by offloading 'troubled assets' into the state sector or central banks. As well, governments established emergency credit facilities available to financial institutions (as Canada did with the EFF and the CMHC) and boosting guarantees on deposits. Second, governments (in the form of central banks like the Bank of Canada) undertook a number of policies to re-establish liquidity in financial markets. These included: extensive interventions and guarantees for inter-bank lending market; purchases of government and private securities and commercial paper; allowing banks to increase their borrowing leverage against high-quality assets; purchase of bank equity to boost cash on balance-sheets; and by directly purchasing government debt issuances and thus government cash deposits held in banks. Third, financial regulatory institutions moved to oversee directly the operations of specific markets, deploy emergency oversight of others and arrange extensive audits of financial institutions. Finally, central banks have driven down their key market-setting interest rate, often by 2009 to the point of negative real rates, to encourage lending and widen spreads for banks. As bank lending has remained sluggish and markets highly unstable, this has included central banks radically pushing down the yield curves on 5 and 10 year government bonds. These measures occurred, to various degrees and at different stages, across the core capitalist states from 2007-10 to 'rescue' the financial system from collapsing credit markets.

To address the shock to aggregate demand, a coordinated turn to emergency fiscal expansion was led by the US government and the G20 states, with governments adopting, in general, fiscal deficits in the order of 2-5 percent of GDP (although with the severe banking crises and recession, these levels were much larger in the US and Britain) (Stiglitz 2010; Onaran 2010). As a consequence, and after two decades of neoliberal efforts to enforce balanced budgeting doctrines, to lower government debt to GDP ratios, and to reduce overall non-military and non-debt servicing expenditures (in other words, to reduce programmed social spending and activist industrial policies), government debt levels rose dramatically. (By some measures, and despite no major collapse in financial institutions, Canada had one of the largest fiscal stimulus packages and one of the most supportive monetary policies. See TD Economics 3 August 2010.)

At the first sign of the crisis stabilizing in late 2009, a campaign began being waged for 'exit strategies' from the emergency measures. This has been led by neoliberal think-tanks, the financial sector, the wider business community and international financial institutions. One exit is to leave behind the emergency oversight of financial markets and complete the installation of a new regulatory structure so that full-blown derivatives trading, particularly in credit instruments and a fullrange of interest and exchange rate swaps, can be re-established. This exit includes the Dodd-Frank Wall Street Reform and Consumer Protection Act passed in July 2010, which focuses on increased transparency in derivatives trading, limits on bank proprietary trading, regulatory consolidation, financial products consumer protection, a 'resolution regime' for financial crises, and a new proposals for international financial rating and regulatory standards. The new Basel III accord agreed to in September 2010 among global bank regulators also sets higher reserves to be held against potential losses, and more than doubles the key capital ratio to 4.5 per cent from the current 2 per cent (*Financial Times* 13 September 2010). The widely discussed Financial Transactions Tax (a version of the Tobin Tax long campaigned for by progressives to slow financial speculation) has come to naught, although a few EU countries are imposing a tiny levy on certain features of financial trades. Canada, in this case, has viewed its financial regulatory regime as a success over the crisis and mainly undertook special policy measures rather than develop emergency regulatory machinery. The Canadian exit here will simply be to tail some of the international agreements as they proceed to implementation.

A second exit is to return to a 'normal' monetary policy focused again on an 'inflation-targeting regime', and away from overly stimulative interest rates being set by central banks to spur bank lending and profitability. The Bank of Canada, for example, has moved the bank rate up three times since June 2010 to 1.25 per cent in September, to signal a return to more normal credit conditions. However, this exit remains highly contingent and no further increases are suggested into 2011 given the fragility of the recovery and the depth of problems still pervading the financial markets. And a third exit – and the focus of the most heated political debate – is from deficit-spending fiscal policies toward public sector austerity. Although there is some caution on the rush to austerity, notably from the US government, the OECD, World Bank, and the IMF are all calling for austerity, with the last notably suggesting two decades of 'fiscal consolidation' may be in order; or, more or less, 'permanent austerity' (IMF May 2010: 30).

The first two exits attempt to return to finance-led growth and financial disciplining that have been characteristic of neoliberalism. That this approach is dominating banking and monetary policies suggests how little the ruling classes have been destabilized within states (and particularly in the US and Canada where it is easy enough to see the political right and business in ascendancy) or across states (where competitive rivalries over world market shares have intensified in conditions of stagnant growth, but no general challenges or alternative approaches can plausibly be pointed to apart from the US).

The fiscal exit to austerity revolves around 'who will pay for the crisis?' and reasserts the distributional and administrative dynamics of the neoliberal form of the state. This exit marginalizes attempts to move fiscal policy toward a 'green new deal' or rebuilding the welfare state and public infrastructure that fleetingly appeared on the political horizon in the midst of the crisis; and it insulates the financial sector and the capitalist classes for assuming the costs of the 'rescue strategies'. Instead, the fiscal exits are focused on: bolstering bank and corporate profits through further tax cuts and shifting away from taxes on property, income and capital; cutting public sector wages, pensions and employment levels; cutting welfare transfers; imposing user fees; and beginning another round of privatization and 'monetization' of public sector assets. The general notion, expressed at the Toronto G20 Summit and other international meetings, is cutting public sector deficits in half by 2013, and phasing in a reduction of debt to GDP rations after 2016.

Across the central capitalist states, the context of the exits to austerity and the political struggles they have invoked have been quite diverse (Panitch, Albo and Chibber 2010). In the Irish case, for example, a major banking collapse has led to a severe economic crisis. As part of the Eurozone, this has left Ireland without the possibility of resort to devaluation to aid adjustment and public sector restrain has been a central focus of restructuring. Three austerity budgets have been introduced in less than 2 years. The first two largely coped with the collapse of the housing market and the main banks, while the last Budget of December 2009 shifted the cost of the crisis onto the public sector. Expenditure cuts of more than $4 billion euros were made with $1 billion of that coming from pay. Public sector workers are to take an average 7 per cent pay cut, while there is a 4.1 percent reduction in social benefits including for unemployment. But after a number of public sector walkouts and threats of a general strike, the Irish Congress of Trade Unions and key public sector unions have attempted to maintain the 'Irish partnership' and negotiate austerity. This led to an agreement that may result in the loss of 18-20,000 public sector jobs, largely ends overtime pay, creates a two-tier workforce marked by lower wages and pensions for all new hires into the public sector, and prohibits any industrial action for three years.

Greece faces some of the same constraints as Ireland as part of the Eurozone, but did not go through the same banking collapse. Rather, the crisis in public finances has been a result of the general weakness of Greek capitalism and the Greek state. Its exit strategy, therefore, has been a more proto-typical neoliberal stabilization programme. For example, pay for public sector workers is to be cut by 7 percent and frozen for the next five years; the value-added tax increased from 21 to 23 percent; contract/temporary workers in the public sector are to be terminated; the retirement age is to be raised; pensions will be based on lifetime earnings which will result in a 45 to 60 percent cut; and everything from water companies, railways and airlines are being discussed for privatization. This has, in turn, generated mass class conflict with five general strikes already launched by August 2010. With the social democratic PASOK party in power, Greece has been a case of 'social liberal' austerity.

In contrast to these two cases, the US has had a massive financial crisis after years of credit-aided economic expansion as the world's dominant economic power and issuer of the key reserve currency. As the world market's 'consumer of last resort', the US government has played a key role in coordinating the rescue strategies of the financial system and of the stimulus measures. Indeed, its global responsibilities for managing the world capitalist system has made the Obama Administration the most reluctant of the core states to turn to austerity. Instead, austerity has been displaced to the state level. Thirty-three states, for instance, are facing budget shortfalls of 20 percent or more in 2010-11. Since the summer of 2008, 231,000 state and local government jobs have been lost. All states combined are running a deficit of 30.2 percent of total budgetary requirements. To deal with this public services are being cut: States have reduced health benefits for low-income earners; 25 states are in the process of cutting support to primary and secondary education; 34 states are cutting support to state colleges and universities; 26 states have implemented hiring freezes; 13 states have laid off workers; and 22 states have cut public sector wages and salaries. In California alone the governor has proposed cuts that will result in the loss of 331,000 jobs. But across the US only sporadic protests have erupted, with public sector coalition fightbacks forming, but soon faltering. Indeed, political space in the US is increasingly being taken up by the political right, most visibly seen in the emergence of the 'Tea Party' movement within the Republican Party. The US is a case where a defeated and traumatized working class is facing another period of punitive austerity in an effort to revitalize the American capitalist class and the delusions of the American Dream.

Canada: From Fiscal Orthodoxy to 'Rescue' and Back

Canada has neither had the severe financial crisis of Ireland, the UK and the US, nor the long-term competitiveness and financial problems of Greece or other countries in the European periphery. Canada's monopolistic financial sector has been protected by its market structure, the underwriting of high-risk mortgages by the state, and the support given by the Bank of Canada to the financial sector to maintain profit margins. There has been, moreover, a long-term pattern of fiscal austerity by the federal and provincial governments that dates back to the 1980s (Doern 2009; McBride 2005). Systematic reviews of programme expenditures were established in the last years of the Liberal Pierre Trudeau government, and given particular prominence in the Nielson Task Force on Programme Review of the Conservative Brian Mulroney government. These governments began the neoliberal restructuring of the Canadian state, in terms of programme administration and levels of support, shifting tax policies, and restraining expenditures and the deficit. It was, however, the Liberal government of Jean Chretien and Finance Minister Paul Martin that the deficit was reduced through a radical programme of cuts and a displacement of fiscal responsibilities through the inter-government system. The Canadian fiscal 'miracle' was founded upon the destruction of 50-50 cost sharing programs created in the 1960s to support health care, social services, income maintenance and post-secondary education. This programme spending was off-loaded onto the provinces. They, in turn, restrained expenditures and, following the same logic of displacement, dumped as much as they could onto municipalities and cities. Local governments in Canada are now entering a second decade of a fiscal crisis, of cutbacks and astonishing levels of unmet infrastructure spending. A Canadian strategy of punitive austerity for public sector workers and services, coupled with the inter-governmental displacement of obligations, established a pattern of federal and provincial government surpluses. In coming to power in 2006, the hard right government of Stephen Harper had only to build on this financial legacy. It shaped, as will be shown, both the 'rescue' and 'exit' strategies to the financial crisis of the Canadian state.

The 2008 Fiscal Update: Fiscal Orthodoxy

Rarely does fiscal policy become the source of high drama, but that is exactly what unfolded at the national level of the Canadian state over an 8 week period spanning 27 November 2008 to 27 January 2009. Within that short timeframe, the Harper government's fiscal policy lurched from an uncompromising commitment to balanced budget orthodoxy to Keynesian style emergency stimulus. The two forces behind the fiscal re-tacking were the severity of the economic crisis and Washington's call for a coordinated global stimulus package led by the G20, and the possibility that a vote of non-confidence would see the minority Conservative government replaced in government by a coalition of Liberals and New Democratic Party (NDP) backed by the Bloc Quebecois (BQ).

On 27 November 2008, Finance Minister Jim Flaherty delivered the annual Economic and Fiscal Statement, essentially an update of the previous budget. In his address to Parliament Flaherty acknowledged that this was a dire time of "unprecedented deterioration in economic and financial systems around the world" and that such "difficult times" would require "difficult choices" (Department of Finance 2008). While governments around the globe embarked upon unprecedented public spending programs to contain the damage to their imploding economies and financial systems, Canada's Conservative government announced that their anti-recession plan was to keep the budget balanced. They did cede, however, that they would re-assess the situation in the weeks ahead (Department of Finance 2008). Alongside Flaherty's out-of-step budget orthodoxy, the minister proceeded to lay down a series of political attacks that would, on the one hand, challenge the fund-raising capacity of the opposition parties to exist and, on the other, intensify the assault on federal public service unions.

Prefacing his first bombshell by saying that tax dollars should not be "spent frivolously", he announced that the $1.95 per vote subsidy parties received would be terminated. This would deprive the political parties of a major source of income. Based on the votes received for each party in the 2008 election this would result in a loss for the Liberals of $7.7 million, for the NDP $4.9 million, and $2.6 million for the BQ (CBC 26 November 2008). Second, he announced that legislation would be presented suspending the right to strike for federal public servants for 2010-11, and that the wages of public service workers would be constrained for four years at 2.3 per cent in the first year and 1.5 per cent for the subsequent three years. Third, in an effort to undermine the success of pay equity complaints filed against the federal government and adjudicated by the Canadian Human Rights Commission, Flaherty announced that legislation would be introduced to terminate adjudication by the Canadian Human Rights Commission. Instead, they would require that pay equity be dealt with only through the collective bargaining process – a process that could itself be uprooted at any time as he had just demonstrated (Department of Finance 2008).

In the midst of an exploding financial crisis, the Conservative Government appeared adamant that they would rather cut spending than engage in the type of massive stimulus spending programs that the US and others were embarking upon. Instead, their focus was on taking advantage of a Liberal party in disarray and attempting to bankrupt the opposition parties. The opposition response was rapid. NDP leader Jack Layton, responding to earlier rumours of what the update contained, had already asked former leader Ed Broadbent to call former Liberal Prime Minister Jean Chretien to discuss how the two parties might coordinate a response (Valpy 2009, 11). The Liberals had also announced that they would be moving a non-confidence motion on 1 December, three days hence. Harper's operatives and MPs were picking up news that the three opposition parties were rapidly moving toward some form of common front. Harper moved to delay the confidence vote to 8 December and thus began a series of government retreats from what they had just announced. On 29 November, the government announced it was dropping its plan to eliminate the subsidy to political parties. The next day, 30 November, the government retreated from the strike ban and announced that it would table a Budget on 27 January 2009 to respond to the economic crisis.

The opposition parties pressed ahead saying that Harper had revealed what his real agenda was and that he had to be stopped. On Monday December 1st, the Liberals, NDP and BQ unveiled their accord that would see the Liberals and NDP share cabinet seats with the support of the BQ which would remain outside cabinet (Valpy 2009: 11-13). The Accord ensured that the coalition would command a majority in Parliament until 30 June, 2011 (Dion and Layton 2008). Harper immediately said he would seek a prorogation of Parliament: on December 3rd in an address on national television Harper poured vitriol on the coalition arguing that it was a fundamentally undemocratic maneuver that did not respect the choice Canadians had made in the previous election. His government would "use every legal means at our disposal to protect our democracy, to protect our economy, and to protect Canada" (National Post 2008). The following day Harper met with the

Governor-General, who granted his request for prorogation. The Coalition was dead. The question now turned to whether the Fiscal Update was as well.

Budget 2009: Emergency Keynesianism

A new Speech from the Throne was delivered on January 26 and signaled that the Harper government was now going to set a more conciliatory tone and, quite remarkably given the remarks just a few months prior, a budgetary u-turn. The Speech noted that "the government's agenda and the priorities of Parliament must adapt in response to the deepening crisis. Old assumptions must be tested and old decisions must be rethought" (Clark and Galloway 26 January 2009). The Finance Minister's conversion from the most dogmatic of balanced budget conservatives to a deficit spending 'Keynesian' came the next day in the 2009 Budget Speech. At the core of "Canada's Economic Action Plan" was an emergency fiscal stimulus built on a budgetary deficit of $34 billion and then $30 billion over two years. Emergency stimulus measures were then to be terminated, with deficit spending steadily reduced. This included $12 billion for infrastructure projects (Department of Finance 27 January 2009: 4). In addition, other key budget measures included a $20 billion cut to personal income taxes, $50 billion to expand a government program to purchase mortgages from banks, and $13 billion in additional financing for several state-owned agencies concerned with insuring mortgages, export marketing and business loans (*Globe and Mail* 27 January 2009).

With the possibility of a Liberal-NDP coalition government all but gone, and with Michael Ignatieff, a reluctant supporter of the Coalition accord, replacing Stephan Dion as leader, the Liberals decided to support the budget if the Conservatives agreed to an amendment that required the government to a regimen of three updates on the implementation of the budget. Although the pettiest of symbols, Ignatieff characterized it as "putting this government on probation" (CBC 28 January 2009). As for the prospects of the Coalition, BQ leader Gilles Duceppe summed up: "It's dead. It's over. It's finished" (CBC 28 January 2009).

Budget 2010: Back to Austerity

On March 4, 2010, Jim Flaherty tabled his fifth budget as Harper's finance minister. The fiscal plan presented in Budget 2010 contrasts with the previous year's reluctant 'rescue' budget. 'Canada's Economic Action Plan' was born out of, on the one side, the efforts to coordinate emergency stimulus spending by the G20, and, on the other, the Coalition Accord challenging the political stability of the Harper minority government. In contrast, Budget 2010 assumed the corner has turned on the economic crisis and presents a plan for 'exit' from deficit financing and a return to balanced budget orthodoxy. Moreover, a 'crisis in public finance' is now assessed as the foremost problem to be addressed. The Conservatives are seizing an opportunity to deepen the neoliberalization of the Canadian state well beyond an exit strategy from the emergency fiscal Keynesianism.

Budget 2010 proposes an aggressive plan to bring federal public finances back to balance, although the actual state of the Canadian economy and public finances measures comparatively well against other large economies. For example, through the 'Great Recession' the Canadian economy contracted less than the average of the core economies at 2.5 per cent in 2009, and is expected to grow at a faster clip for both 2010 and 2011 (IMF 2010). In 2009-10, the combined federal and provincial deficits equaled -5.5 per cent of GDP. The federal deficit alone equals -3.1 per cent of total GDP. In historical perspective, this is modest given that during the Mulroney era in the 1980s, the Federal deficit stood between 5.6 and 5.8 per cent of GDP (TD Economics August 3 2010). In comparative perspective, the Canadian position is rather modest given that deficit to GDP calculations for the US is -11.0 per cent, in the UK -11.3 per cent, and for the OECD as a whole -7.9 per cent. Similarly, with respect to debt levels, Canada falls toward the lower end of the spectrum with debt accounting for 28.6 per cent of GDP. This looks rather manageable compared with 56.4 per cent for the US, 46.9 per cent for the UK, and 50.2 per cent for Germany (TD Economics August 3 2010, 4).

While the recovery is widely regarded as fragile and uncertain, the Harper government has with Budget 2010 declared the Great Recession a historical relic. The priority now is an uncompromising five-year march to a near balanced budget in the fiscal year 2015-16. A range of constraint measures are to be deployed but without question a big part of achieving that target is the winding down of stimulus spending as of March 31, 2011. In addition to the termination of this spending, the Budget plans to cap international assistance spending at 2010 levels, reduce defense spending by $500 million in 2012 through to 2014 as the Afghanistan mission shrinks, and a three year freeze on federal program spending that will see 11 thousand public service jobs disappear (Conference Board of Canada 2010, 11). These measures are expected to contain growth in program spending to 2.2 per cent per year. To place this in comparative perspective what this means is that within a five year frame, the federal deficit as a percentage of GDP will shrink from -3.1 per cent in 2010-11 to -0.1 per cent (TD Economics 4 March 2010, 2). One bank forecast even projects a surplus of $1 billion in 2014-15, although there is also the caution that the scale of the cuts may slow economic growth in Canada by 0.2 to 0.4 per cent (TD Economics 3 August 2010, 6). Another forecast suggests that the government revenue forecasts are set low based on exceedingly low growth expectations. The result is that revenues to the government will be better than expected and by 2013 these may be as much as $6.3 billion higher than forecast. If this proves accurate, a fiscal balance will be achieved a full year ahead of target (Browarski, Stewart, and Derby 2010, 1; Hodgson and Stewart 29 July 2010).

But even while a program for aggressively shrinking public expenditures was being presented, the Finance Minister boasted that Canada's federal tax-to-GDP ratio had dropped to its lowest level since 1961 (Budget 2010, 10). This is astonishing given that 1961 precedes the advent of the important redistributive cost-sharing programs of the late 1960s that enabled an expansion in public health care, post-secondary education, social assistance and a myriad of other services and programs. There is clearly the fiscal space in Canada to increase spending and taxation by at least two per cent of GDP to bring Canada's spending up to the level it was during a period marked by the most progressive innovations in redistributive policy in this country's history (Yalnizyan, 22 March 2010).

In short, the response presented in Budget 2010 to Canada's federal public deficit and debt is an exaggeration. However, other policies sprinkled throughout the budget suggest that this exit is about more than public finances. Budget 2010 includes a massive deregulation program, corporate tax cuts, and a further liberalization of foreign investment. With respect to cuts to corporate income tax, the Finance Minister noted that by 2012 "Canada will have the lowest statutory corporate income tax rate in the G7" (Budget 2010, 10). The goal is to reduce the federal general corporate tax rate to 15 per cent and to move toward a combined federal and provincial corporate tax rate of 25 per cent by 2012. To place this in perspective, in 2000 the federal corporate tax rate was 28 per cent and the combined federal and provincial corporate tax rates were 43.6 per cent. Within a 12 year span, taxes on corporations operating in Canada will have been nearly halved by a succession of Liberal and Conservative governments (Budget 2010, 47; Department of Finance 2003).

The deregulatory dimension of the Budget received scant attention despite the fact that these proposals seriously erode environment protection and open the door wide for mining and hydro carbon exploration in the fragile eco-systems of the Arctic. The Budget proposes a 'Red Tape Reduction Commission' involving both Conservative Members of Parliament and 'private sector representatives', to review and eliminate federal regulations that are seen to impede investment and development. This mimics the Red Tape Commission set up by the Harris government in Ontario in 1995 but goes even further. Business interests who had been subject to regulation can now advocate from within the Canadian state to terminate or change regulations to which their industries are subjected. In the absurdly named objective of 'green jobs and growth', environmental regulations that have served to at least assess and shape investment and development projects are undermined. Indian and Northern Affairs have been directed to 'accelerate' the process of reviewing resource extraction projects in the Arctic so as to 'remove barriers to private investment'. The regulatory system is to be 'modernized' by transferring responsibility for conducting environmental assessments of large energy projects from the Canadian Environmental Assessment Agency to the much more producer and investment friendly National Energy Board. And Budget 2010 furthers foreign investment liberalization by removing restrictions on foreign ownership in Canada's satellite sector (Budget 2010, 93-102). While the heavy hand of state regulation over the environment and economy is lightened, the Canadian Security and Intelligence Service will see its budget grow by $28 million (Budget 2010, 127).

The Harper government's 2010 Budget is leading an aggressive attack on the fiscal deficit engendered by the economic crisis and the bailouts of the financial system. In many ways Canada is at the forefront of the central capitalist states in undermining public services as it has been since the Chretien-Martin Budgets of the mid-1990s. The punitive austerity they imposed has been sustained across the last decade and the Harper government. The 'fiscal crisis' that has been sparked by the panic rush to exit strategies from the emergency fiscal stimulus is being used as a further opportunity to intensify the neoliberal restructuring of the regulatory and redistributive remnants of the welfare state. It would not be too far off to describe the evolution of Canadian fiscal strategy as a turn to permanent austerity, particularly when the constraints on provincial budgetary policies are also considered.

The Provincial Exits to Austerity

While the federal government is attempting to move methodically toward balance within five years, the budgetary position of the Canadian provinces is much more uneven. In fiscal year 2009, the ten provinces collectively ran the largest provincial deficit in history at $48.2 billion. This equals 3.2 per cent of provincial GDP. It is expected that a combination of improving economic conditions and the conclusion of provincial stimulus programs will help the provinces reduce this deficit to $34 billion in 2011 (Conference Board of Canada 2010). But beyond that, how some of the provinces, especially Ontario and Quebec, exit fiscal deficit without a radical reconsideration of how revenues are raised or public services are delivered is difficult to imagine.

The provinces diverge widely in their exit planning both in time frame and policy measures. Whether social democratic or conservative, they all share a fidelity to ensuring the cost of the crisis is borne by workers via tax shifting, declining levels and quality of public services and regressive user fees. For example, various new and higher consumption taxes have been introduced in Nova Scotia, Quebec, Manitoba and Saskatchewan. Quebec has further added new user fees and introduced a health 'premium'. All provinces have presented budgets that aim to keep program expenditure growth at or below 2 per cent per year; have cut or frozen operational budgets and introduced constraints on public sector compensation and the number of staff working in the core public services. Only Nova Scotia has introduced a tax on high income earners and only Manitoba has indefinitely postponed a planned 1 point cut in the corporate income tax rate (TD Economics 3 August 2010, 7).

Of all the provinces, Ontario's budget position is the most politically and fiscally complicated. Ontario's 'third-way' Liberals have reinvested in public services since arriving in government in 2003 after defeating a Conservative Party led largely by Mike Harris. However, they have also been committed to some of the key principles of the Common Sense Revolution—regressive taxation, a fidelity to balanced budgets, and an ongoing erosion of social assistance benefits. The finance minister, Dwight Duncan, signaled a new era of austerity in his 2010 Budget. First, the Public Sector Compensation Restraint to Protect Public Services Act was tabled and which froze the salaries and wages of 350,000 non-union public sector workers until March 31 2012. The second signal delivered was that the Liberal government would ask the unions representing 700,000 broader public sector workers to accept a minimum 2 year wage freeze. Such an agreement would yield an estimated $750 million per year in savings (Ontario Ministry of Finance 2010). Third, Ontario will continue with its ongoing plan to cut corporate taxes. This will cost the province $1.2 billion in each of the next three years resulting in an accumulative loss of $3.6 billion (NUPGE 31 March 2010). Fourth, the Budget contemplates a massive privatization of public assets including the liquor control board that regulates the sale of alcohol, the Ontario Lottery and Gaming Commission, public electricity producers and distributors among others as a means to generate a large amount of revenue. (However, the political focus appears to be on public sector wage cuts, with the privatization measures being delayed or shunted to the side.) As a whole, Ontario's 2010 Budget forecasts 7 years of austerity with a plan that extends to 2017-18 when a zero-deficit is achieved. This will result in a shrinking of Ontario's public economy from a current 19.2 per cent of GDP to 15.5 per cent in 2017-18 (TD Economics 25 March 2010, 1). This translates as a nearly 20 per cent contraction of Ontario's public sector, leaving it at a size that corresponds to that of the period of the Common Sense Revolution.

If the Ontario Budget was the most complex of the provincial budgets in the hardest hit economy from the financial crisis, the most draconian budget of all the 2010 provincial budgets was delivered by the Liberal government of Quebec on 30 March 2010. The more regressive measures include a health care user-fee that applies to all citizens 18 years of age and older. This user fee will reach $200/year in 2012; a $25 fee per visit with a medical doctor; a 17 per cent increase in electricity costs by 2018; a 2 per cent increase in the sales tax; the core public service is subject to a pay freeze until 2014; an ongoing shrinking of the number of public sector workers by allowing only one replacement hire for every two retirements/departures; a review of all government programs; and the closure or amalgamation of 30 public agencies (Quebec Ministry of Finance March 30 2010, Press Release #1). It needs noting that the measures directed at public sector workers is in addition to the Charest government's draconian Law C-43 passed in 2005. The legislation imposed a two-year wage freeze and restricted wage increases thereafter to 2 per cent. Moreover, the bill introduced anti-strike provision ensuring there would be no union resistance and backed this up with punitive provisions including a $500 fine for any worker defying the legislation in addition to a penalty for striking of two days pay for every day on strike. The combined effect of five years of frozen wages followed by increases falling below the rate of inflation resulted in a decline in real incomes for public sector workers of 4 per cent (Mandel 2010).

Resisting Austerity, Defending Public Services

The turn to austerity in the core capitalist states has generated general strikes, disruption of public service delivery and sustained protests. These will continue over the coming year as the cuts are only starting and the impacts of austerity more severe and inequitable through time. In all cases, the cuts are revitalizing anti-neoliberal movements, and leading to new attempts to forge coalitions between public sector workers and users. The form of these alliances, however, varies greatly: from the general strikes and fusion with an emerging socialist politics in the European periphery; to the contradiction between the community based anti-cuts alliances and the peak-union 'partnership' with the government in Ireland; to the surging then sputtering fightback campaigns at the state and local levels in the US under the shadow of an ascending hard right.

After a number of previous coalitions against neoliberalism—in the struggles against NAFTA, the Ontario Days of Action, the public sector common fronts in B.C. and Quebec, the militant walkouts by nurses in Alberta and other provinces—the union movement in Canada has retreated into a defensive posture and the social movements are in a sustained phase of disorganization and political uncertainty. The exit strategy of 'permanent austerity' emerging out of the Canadian state and capitalist classes provides a direct challenge to the Left in Canada at a moment of historical weakness. The federal 'exit' budget, for example, was met with criticism from the Canadian Labour Congress, the Council of Canadians, among others. They argued that it laid out a program for eroding public services, economic sovereignty, and environmental protections, as well as its targeting public sector wages and work. But there is little evidence of strategy for resisting the cuts, or of a broader campaign of resistance through grass-roots mobilization of union members, social movements and users of public services. There is little beyond the ad hoc negotiating fronts of public sector unions and the sectoral campaigns around specific policy issues—climate change, healthcare, erosion of public broadcasting, and so forth.

This is in part explained by Canada's decentralized federalism with the provinces delivering public goods, such as health, education and social services, which are a key terrain for struggles over cuts. In Quebec, for instance, there has been a measure of political mobilization in defence of public services and workers' rights. After five years of legislated wage restraint, Quebec's public sector workers formed a Common Front—composed of the Confederation of National Trade Unions, the Quebec Federation of Labour, and the Inter-Union Secretariat of Public Services, and representing 475,000 workers—in anticipation of Law 43's expiration in March 2010 and an austerity budget being delivered to the National Assembly. The Front's main demand was for an 11.25 per cent wage increase over a three year period. But the Common Front refused to join forces with the broad-based Coalition Against User Fees and Privatization that emerged in response to the 2010 budget. Instead, the unions signed a five year 'accord' with the government that falls far short of restoring public sector wages and working conditions. The five year agreement will provide a 7 per cent increase or 10.5 per cent if there is better than expected economic growth. Given inflation, Quebec's public sector workers are facing a further five years of declining income (Mandel 2010). The Quebec case bears parallels to the Irish unions negotiating to preserve the illusions of 'partnership' with the state at the expense of austerity.

In Ontario, the momentum for a similar union accommodation, in this case without any union mobilization at all, may well prove unavoidable. Since 2003, the Ontario Liberals have built something of the old 'Lib-Lab' alliance with several key unions that has filled the electoral vacuum left by much of labour abandoning the NDP after imposing a 'social contract' under the Rae government in the 1990s. The Ontario government has been holding preliminary talks on restraint with a wide number of unions with public employees. To date, most unions have walked away from the talks, and voiced opposition to the wage restraint. But it is not so clear that the unions will mobilize opposition to the wage restraint or the cuts to government services, and build toward the strikes that will be necessary to break the budgetary proposals to have workers and the poor pay for the crisis. It would be foolish to rule out a deal emerging between a number of unions and the McGuinty government and further consolidation of a 'Lib-Lab' alliance under the fear that a Conservative government would be even worse. It is completely delusional that such 'there is no alternative' politics challenges austerity or builds an anti-neoliberal political bloc.

There is, however, a number of campaigns in Ontario—notably, against welfare cuts to the special diet and for disabilities support, Indigenous peoples struggles around mining, demands for improved public transit, ecology fights about commodification of water and the boreal forest—that are illustrative of the anti-austerity politics forming in specific sectors. These need to deepen their struggles over specific state apparatuses and bases of support in local communities and develop the organizational linkages of a province-wide anti-neoliberal front. The Ontario Health Coalition (OHC) includes nurses, unions, progressive doctors, and a vast array of community organizations, and is part of the Canada Health Coalition network; it is a good example of the potential to build an alternate political campaign to defend public services. In response to Ontario's 2010 budget, for example, the OHC rejected the 1.5 per cent increase in hospital funding that budget provided. The OHC concluded that this created a "gap between hospital funding and inflation for the third year in a row" (OHC 25 March 2010). The OHC has also effectively opposed the Ontario government's policy of incremental privatization of health care institutions and delivery. Examples include the OHCs opposition to the marketization of home care where a steady increase in for-profit contracting has been observed and the government's policy of public-private partnerships (P3s) in the hospital sector. P3 hospital projects have been characterized by public healthcare advocates as 'pay more, get less' projects that fatten private profits at public expense. An analysis of four Ontario P3 hospital projects in Sarnia, Ottawa, Brampton and North Bay found that they were posting budget overruns of 75 per cent. They were costing not the planned $1.2 billion but rather $2.1 billion, and delivered less bed capacity than had been planned as well (Canadian Health Coalition March 2009). These campaigns have built up impressive community alliances between public sector healthcare workers, local health policy activists and the wider union and progressive movements in defence of public healthcare.

The campaigns to defend public hospitals and healthcare offer an example of popular resistance, and the potential to expand this mobilization to other parts of the public sector such as waste management, transit, and energy production. Opposition to workers bearing the cost of the crisis and defence of public expenditure is the beginning case to be made. This will require linking public sector 'producers' with 'users' of public services. The quality of these services is directly connected to public sector workers. And there is any number of areas where the quality of public goods and spaces—parks, welfare provision, public transit—needs democratization and expansion. However, it is increasingly clear that the 'exits' from the emergency Keynesian measures introduced at the height of the crisis are intensifying the market and class disciplines of neoliberalism. This does not mean less state, or even less regulation, but a particular form of state and regulatory policies that enhance capitalist class power. The political opposition to the austerity exits need to account for the class nature of neoliberalism in building new organizational capacities for resistance. The lines of social division and political conflicts forming at this phase of the crisis suggest that these will be struggles, in the first instance, against and within the neoliberal state and the politics in Canada of permanent austerity.

References

Bank of Canada, July 2009, *Monetary Policy Report*, available at www.bankofcanada.ca/en/mpr/.

Baragar, Fletcher, 2009, "Canada and the Crisis," in Julie Guard and Wayne Antony, eds., *Bankruptcies and Bailouts*, Halifax: Fernwood.

Bloomberg, July 20, 2009, "U.S. Rescue May Reach $23.7 Trillion, Barofsky Says", at http://www.bloomberg.com/.

Browarski, Sabrina, Matthew Stewart and Paul Derby, 2010, *Budget Report 2010: The Long Road to Fiscal Balance*, Conference Board of Canada, available at http://www.conferenceboard.ca/topics/economics/budgets/fed_2010_budget.aspx.

Canadian Health Coalition, 2009, "*P3s = Private Profits, Public Pays*", available at http://medicare.ca/main/the-facts/p3s-private-profits-public-pays.

CBC, 28 January 2009, "*Ignatieff puts Tories 'on probation' with budget demand*",   available at http://www.cbc.ca/canada/story/2009/01/28/ignatieff-decision.html.

Conference Board of Canada, Summer 2010, *Canadian Outlook,* available at http://www.conferenceboard.ca/temp/9e6cbdc6-81e8-4a33-b0c1-c33bf33dc455/11-022_CO-Summer10-OTLK_WEB.pdf

Clark, Campbell and Gloria Galloway, 26 January 2009, "*Harper's words carry softer tone*", *Globe and Mail.*

Crotty, James, 2009, "Structural Causes of the Global Financial Crisis," *Cambridge Journal of Economics*, 33.

Department of Finance, 27 November 2008, *The Economic and Fiscal Statement 2008*, available at http://www.fin.gc.ca/ec2008/speech-eng.html.

Department of Finance, 4 March 2010, *Budget 2010: Leading the Way on Jobs and Growth* available at http://www.budget.gc.ca/2010/pdf/speech-eng.pdf .

Department of Finance, August 2003, *Federal Corporate Tax Rate Reductions*, available at http://www.fin.gc.ca/toc/2003/taxratered_-eng.asp.

Dion, Stephane and Jack Layton, 1 December 2008, *An Accord on a Cooperative Government to Address the Present Economic Crisis,* available at http://www.liberal.ca/pdf/docs/081201_accord_en_signed.pdf.

Doern, Bruce, 2009, "Evolving Budgetary Policies and Experiments," in Alan Maslove, ed., *How Ottawa Spends, 2009-2010: Economic Upheaval and Political Dysfunction,* Montreal: McGill-Queen's University Press.

Financial Times, 13 September 2010, "Basel Deal Reached on Banks' Reserves."

Government of Canada, 3 March 2010, *Speech from the Throne, A Stronger Canada. A Stronger Economy. Now and for the Future,* available at http://www.speech.gc.ca/grfx/docs/sft-ddt-2010_e.pdf.

Globe and Mail, 27 January 2009, "*Tax relief and major spending projects: a plan for troubled times*", available at http://v1.theglobeandmail.com/servlet/story/RTGAM.20090127.wBudget_Highlights0127/BNStory/budget2009/home.

Hodgson, Glen and Matthew Stewart, 2010, *Canadian Feds Ahead of Plan on Fiscal Rebalancing,* Conference Board of Canada, available at http://www.conferenceboard.ca/economics/hot_eco_topics/default/10-07-29/Canadian_Feds_Ahead_of_Plan_on_Fiscal_Rebalancing.aspx.

ILO, 2009, *World of Work Report 2009: The Global Jobs Crisis and Beyond,* Geneva: ILO.

IMF, May 2010, *Fiscal Monitor: Navigating the Fiscal Challenges Ahead,* Washington: IMF.

IMF, July 2010, *World Economic Outlook,* Washington: IMF.

Loxley, John, 2009, "Financial Dimensions: Origins and State Responses," in Julie Guard and Wayne Antony, eds., *Bankruptcies and Bailouts,* Halifax: Fernwood.

Mackenzie, Hugh and Richard Shillington, 2009, *Canada's Quiet Bargain: The Benefits of Public Spending,* Toronto: Canadian Centre for Policy Alternatives.

Mandel, David. July 25 2010, *Fighting Austerity? The Public Sector and the Common Front in Quebec, The Bullet,* N. 396, available at http://www.socialistproject.ca/bullet/396.php.

McBride, Stephen, 2005, *Paradigm Shift: Globalization and the Canadian State,* Halifax: Fernwood.

McKinsey Global Institute, October 2008, *Mapping Global Capital Markets: Fifth Annual Report,* New York: McKinsey Global Institute.

McNish, Jacquie and Greg McArthur, December 13 2008, "How High Risk Mortgages Crept North,' *Globe and Mail.*

National Post, 3 December 2008, "*Stephen Harper's Dec. 3, 2008 statement*", available at http://www.nationalpost.com/news/politics/story.html?id=1028147.

National Union of Public and General Employees, 31 March 2010, "Public sector workers paying for corporate tax cuts", available at http://www.nupge.ca/content/public-sector-workers-paying-corporate-tax-cuts.

Office of Management and Budget, 2010, "The Budget" at www.budget.gov.

Onaran, Özlem, 2010, 'Fiscal Crisis in Europe or a Crisis of Distribution?' SOAS, Research on Money and Finance, Discussion Paper, No. 18.

Ontario Health Coalition, 25 March 2010, "*Ontario Health Coalition Response to Provincial Budget*", available at http://www.marketwire.com/press-release/Ontario-Health-Coalition-Response-Provincial-Budget-McGuinty-Must-Stop-Over-Top-Crisis-1138192.htm.

Ontario Health Coalition, 20 January 2006, "*Say No to Privatized Hospitals!*", available at http://www.web.net/ohc/P3s/p3UpdateJan06.pdf.

Ontario Ministry of Finance, 25 March 2010, *Open Ontario: Ontario's Plan for Jobs and Growth*, available at http://www.fin.gov.on.ca/en/budget/ontariobudgets/2010/statement.pdf.

Panitch, Leo, Greg Albo and Vivek Chibber, eds., 2010, *The Socialist Register 2011: The Crisis this Time*, London: Merlin Press.

Quebec Ministry of Finance, 30 March 2010, *Choices for the Future* Press Release # 1, available at http://www.budget.finances.gouv.qc.ca/Budget/2010-2011/en/documents/Communique_1en.pdf.

Realtytrac, 2010, "US Foreclosures Market Report," at www.realtytrac.com.

Roubini, Nouriel and Stephen Mihm, 2010, *Crisis Economics*, New York: Penguin.

Stiglitz, George, 2010, *Freefall*, New York: W.W. Norton.

TD Economics, 4 March 2010, *The 2010 Federal Budget,* available at www.td.com/economics/budgets/fed10.pdf.

TD Economics, 25 March 2010, *A Long Road Back to Balance,* available at http://www.td.com/economics/budgets/on10.pdf.

TD Economics, 30 April 2010, *Fiscal Green Shoots,* available at http://www.td.com/economics/special/db0410_fiscal.pdf.

TD Economics, 3 August 2010, *Special Report: Canada's Fiscal Exit Strategy,* available at http://www.td.com/economics/special/pg0810_fiscal_exit.pdf.

Valpy, Michael, 2009, *The 'Crisis': A Narrative*, in Peter Russell and Lorne Sossin eds., *Parliamentary Democracy in Crisis*, Toronto: University of Toronto Press.

Yalnizyan, Armine, 22 March 2010, *Now is the Wrong time for Fiscal Frugality*, Canadian Centre for Policy Alternatives, available at http://www.policyalternatives.ca/publications/commentary/now-wrong-time-fiscal-frugality.

Janus-Faced Austerity: Strengthening the 'Competitive' Canadian State

Carlo Fanelli & Chris Hurl[1]

Abstract: The global economic crisis has triggered a wave of stimulus spending throughout the world, with particular concentrations in North America, the Eurozone and China. This paper examines its Canadian context. Focusing broadly on the deepening integration of neoliberalism since the election of Stephan Harper in 2006 as well as federal Conservative fiscal and monetary policy, this paper delves into the Janus-Faced character of Canadian austerity measures. It is argued that while social services and spending are restricted for certain segments of the Canadian working class, new arrangements and spending initiatives are rolled out by the federal government in order to fuel enhanced capital accumulation. This paper concludes with some propositions for resisting austerity and strengthening the resolve of the Canadian working class.

Keywords: Canada; Austerity; Fiscal & Monetary Policy; Capital-Preserving Federalism; Neoliberalism.

Introduction

The times are tough, we are told. The grim economic climate appears unmatched in severity since the Great Depression. It is on this basis that social spending is being slashed and wage freezes are imposed on public sector workers across the country and around the world. In order to save a sinking ship, workers are asked to throw wages, benefits and social security overboard. However, the thin veil of collective belt-tightening, the attitude that we must all share the burden, belies an enduring project of class polarization. Hence, rather than viewing the current

---

[1]   Carlo Fanelli and Chris Hurl are PhD candidates (ABD) in the Department of Sociology & Anthropology with a specialization in political economy.

responses to 'economic' crisis as somehow marking a break with neoliberalism, government stimulus policies reflect a profound continuity and further entrenchment of past strategies of privatization, creating openings for capital and public sector spending restraint.

In this paper, we will argue that the current round of austerity measures advanced by the Harper Conservatives is Janus-faced: on the one hand public services, social programs, labour and environmental supports and protections are being 'rolled back' for the working class, while state supports are 'rolled out' to serve the needs of capital. In so doing, Harper is showing no hesitation to use the coercive power of the federal government to centralize policies and institutional arrangements that appease business interests. After briefly tracing the theoretical presuppositions of neoliberalism and the realignment of governance at intersecting scales of operation, we situate the continuing assault on public services and organized labour by drawing attention to what we refer to as capital-preserving federalism. As a political and economic strategy, capital-preserving federalism provides a means of imposing constraints upon newly elected federal governments and sub-national constituent-units' (e.g. provinces, municipalities) ability to bypass market access to goods and services, in addition to restrictions upon withdrawing or opting-out of trade and investment agreements negotiated supra-nationally[2]. In other words, successive federal governments have firmly fixed the parameters of reform to meet the needs of capital accumulation[3]. While this dynamic is advanced on a federal level, it entails the enforcement of market-dependence through multi-scaler, multi-spatial and multi-temporal institutional and legal arrangements, as well as corresponding shifts in socio-cultural and political practices. This entails the marketization of public goods and services, the re-regulation of capital controls such as foreign direct investment (FDI), and the creation of new institutional arrangements under the auspices of 'scarcity' and 'restraint'. What's more, this entails a missionary faith in balanced budgets, fiscal discipline and monetary policy.

---

[2] 'Capital-preserving' federalism represents an effort on our part to develop a corrective to the concept of "market-preserving" federalism. While we cannot enter into a full analysis here, we base our critique on three main propositions. First, the notion of market-preserving federalism reifies the 'market' as if functioning by autonomous laws of supply and demand disembedded from broader social relations. Second, this mystification serves to obscure fundamentally antagonistic class relations where the extraction of surplus-value takes place at the detriment of labour for the benefit of capital. Third, in naturalizing social relations of capital, takes for granted the liberal dichotomization of the economic and political spheres of social life, while--incorrectly we might add—treating the state and market as competitors as opposed to mutually reinforcing. See, for example, Weingast, 1995; Yingyi & Weingast, 1996; McKinnon, 1997).

[3] While not employing the notion of capital-preserving federalism, Anderson (2010) outlines similar processes at work. For instance, in 2000 Brazil adopted a fiscal responsibility law that constrains both federal and state governments, with limits on spending for government employees, public debt, expenditures and short-term spending in election years. The federal government can withhold transfers to states when they do not comply and criminal proceedings can be brought against elected officials. Similar examples include Argentina, Mexico, Nigeria, Russia, South Africa and Belgium for example. See Anderson, 2010.

As we will attempt to show throughout, this is reflected in the federal government's most recent stimulus policies. These policies impose restraint measures on the public sector while ceding fiscal control and authority over domestic policies away from local governments and communities toward political and economic elites. For this reason, the response to the current economic crisis entails the 'rolling back' of certain state activities, such as social programs and capital controls, and the 'rolling out' of new institutions and governmentalities that aim to stabilize neoliberal accumulation strategies (Peck and Tickell, 2002). While the federal government's Janus-faced strategy is significant, this by no means marks the beginning of a new era. As Thomas Workman (2009, p.7) has recently reminded: "These institutional constellations evolve very slowly over decades of class struggle." In fact, the adoption of federal stimulus policies should be viewed in continuity with past neoliberal projects. The issue, then, in our view is what these multi-level arrangements and institutions do and on whose behalf? In other words, it's a class question. In what follows, we argue that the federal Conservative government has taken advantage of the current economic crisis and the regulatory, administrative and institutional powers of the state in order to facilitate planning, underwrite expansions, take on liabilities and contain class conflict. In other words, political and economic agents, via institutional arrangements and socio-cultural practices (i.e. "the market"), work through the state utilizing their positions of power to simultaneously cut services, while extending others to suit the valorization needs of capital. While we focus our analysis on the federal government, as this special forum in *Alternate Routes* suggests, this is a pattern being generalized across the country and around the world.

Theorizing Neoliberalism: Realigning Governance to Facilitate Capital Accumulation

In the wake of the economic crisis of the mid-1970s, neoliberalism emerged as a response to the failure of the post-war Keynesian welfare state to sustain capital accumulation. With the unprecedented profit rates of the 1950s and 60s faltering due to the rebuilding of Western Europe's and Japan's productive capacities, increased competition from emergent economies in Latin America and Asia, rising militancy on the part of the working classes and especially trade unions, in addition to increasingly aggressive Cold War geopolitics, a ruling class *coup d'état* was launched to reestablish higher rates of profit. With an adherence to neoclassical economics and classical liberalism, neoliberalism emerged in the 1970s as a comprehensive set of political and economic practices intent on reordering state administrations, creating new profit opportunities for businesses, imposing labour market discipline and a prioritization of 'finance' capital over industrial or fixed capital[4]. A central aspect of this process has been the realignment of governance: unloading the costs of social services onto the individual and compelling diverse communities to compete with one another for 'scarce' resources under an institutional framework of private property, free markets and free trade, while continuing to slash taxes for the wealthy, marketizing all aspects of life, and selling off public assets at bargain basement prices.

This entails a variety of cross-penetrating strategies that reconfigure the jurisdiction of markets across intersecting scales of governance, revamp institutional responsibilities and encourage socio-cultural changes around four central processes. First, neoliberalism presupposes the ongoing and active separation of people from the means of subsistence, cultivating dependency on market mechanisms in areas of life previously outside of the market. Second, under neoliberalism, class solidarities are actively decomposed through the individuation of the labour process and service-provision, increasingly rendering individuals responsible for their own self-management and pitting them against one another for 'scarce' resources. Third, neoliberalism cultivates short-term speculation, aspiring to transform every aspect of life into an investment opportunity. Fourth, this entails the reconfiguration of the labour market away from a stable, skills-based labour force and toward temporary, contract-based labour arrangements that encourage competition between the private and public spheres.

Internationally, 'globalization' is the neoliberal face of a worldwide strategy that aims toward the creation of new zones of accumulation through increasingly authoritarian state apparatuses that seek to entrench market imperatives and reduce the power of labour (Saad-Filho & Johnston, 2005). This includes: lowering and eliminating tariffs on imported goods, the removal of restrictions on foreign direct investment, domestic quotas and monopolies, an export-led growth strategy, the re-regulation of domestic capital markets, as well as the weakening of environmental and labour laws, for example, which are seen as market impediments.

This does not simply entail deregulation and dismantlement of the institutions of the Keynesian welfare state. In fact, as Peck and Tickell (2002) note, there has been a shift from the 'roll-back' neoliberalism of the 1980s to an "emergent phase of

---

[4]   In our view, finance capital is not merely speculative or parasitic, nor the result of the stagnation tendencies of advanced capitalist economies. Rather, what makes finance unique in its neoliberal form is its coalescing with industry, as well as leadership role. In other words, financial volatility actually becomes a developmental feature of neoliberalism that reinforces, rather than undermines the central position of finance-led neoliberalism and capitalist power structures. For instance, while finance may speculate in global money markets or bundle and repackage a host of derivative trading forms, a good many transactions are more often than not based on some form of real assets and commodity production. Moreover, finance has been central to the disciplining of industry and the working class through the availability of credit and reinvestments in mortgages, pensions and loans. Though neoliberalism was from its very beginning a project intent on restoring ruling class power, it went beyond this thoroughly integrating and subordinating the working classes into its dependent orbit. For a fuller exposition, see Albo, Gindin and Panitch, 2010.

active state-building and regulatory reform" which they describe as "roll out" neo-liberalism through the 1990s. While the crisis of the 1970s entailed wages freezes and dramatic austerity budgets, over the past twenty years governments have moved toward a more proactive position in unfolding new institutional frameworks that facilitate a deepening project of class polarization under the rubric of 'scarcity' and 'restraint'. Despite the political and ideological antagonism toward state 'interference' in the market, state intervention is central to securing the political, economic and social conditions necessary for accumulation such as the privatization of state-owned industries and utilities, the opening of its banking, healthcare, education and telecommunications systems to private ownership, in addition to competing international pensions and mutual funds.

Domestically, neoliberalism seeks to deepen and intensify internal competition among competing business interests, thereby pitting workers and workplaces in competition with one another through ever-increasing market compulsions. This includes efforts to contract-out and privatize provincial and municipal services, extract concessions from its unionized and non-unionized workforce, in addition to an increased reliance on public-private partnerships (P3's). Central banks are envisaged as inflation fighters, with an inflation control regime of between one and three percent. Provincially, and as creatures of the provinces, municipally, neoliberal policies have sought to shift the burden of taxes from businesses to consumers for competitiveness, slash social services and liquidate assets. In order to become more 'flexible' and 'leaner' in a globalizing economy, provinces and cities have increasingly responded with attempts to move away from the universal provision of social services to marketized provisions with attached user-fees, enhanced inter-jurisdictional competition and sought a confrontational approach with unions, which have aimed to reorient accumulation strategies and to concentrate capital in metropolitan cores, which serve international markets (Albo, 1994; Kipfer & Keil, 2002; Tufts, 2004). The most recent emphasis on austerity and balanced budgets, however, is counter-acted by growing state involvement in creating new spaces for accumulation. In confronting the growing indebtedness of the state, an all out offensive is launched against remaining social provisions and universal entitlements, thereby tipping the balance of class forces away from labour and toward creditors and locally dominant capitalist coalitions with alliances to the US ruling-class. In this manner, politicians, economists and policy-makers ensconced in the neoliberal doctrine were successful in moving the terrain of debate from the realm of production whereby labour and capital struggled over the control of the working-day and the appropriation of surplus-value, to the terrain of distribution and exchange thereby strengthening the alliance between capital and the state.

As the always global scope of capital accumulation and the persistent need for more domestic and local forms of 'extra-market' (i.e. legal, juridical, political, repressive) supports enmeshed, rather than ceding power away from the nation-state neoliberalism created new and shifting scales of governance each with an historically unique dynamism. This includes, for instance, the devolution of regulating responsibilities onto local governments without matching fiscal supports or a proportional transfer of power, while also scaling regulatory capacities 'upwards' to regional or international institutions (Brenner, 2004). Likewise, efforts to extend and consolidate neoliberalism have centered on attempts to: reduce the power of organized labour through market disciplining; the commodification and marketization of the state through measures that promote 'competitive austerity'; reducing welfare disincentives to work; promoting the massive encouragement of part-time, precarious and contingent forms of service-sector employment; recklessly opening-up goods and capital markets to international competition; as well as disproportionately cutting taxes for higher-income earners and businesses, while moving-away from the social provision of universal programs to consumption-based levies (Albo, 1993; Clarke, 2005; Brenner & Theodore, 2002; McBride, 2005). For organized labour this has meant the institutionalization of policies that aim to make it easier to decertify unions, unilaterally proclaim them "essential" and thereby removing the right to strike, as well as the increased use of coercive back-to-work legislation. All things considered, then, the capitalist classes have used the economic recession and the rhetoric of 'fiscal consolidation', 'prudent business management' and 'government responsibility" as a strategic political opportunity to strengthen and expand processes of neoliberalism—from the urban to the international—through the state and market.

Under the guise of New Public Management mantras, there has been a retreat from the provision of social services through a stable, full-time labour force, increasingly toward part-time, seasonal and short-term contracts, which are seen as providing a more docile and globally competitive labour force (Ilcan et al., 2003). Likewise, through reduced social expenditures and long-term investments, all levels of government have sought to shed 'liabilities' through attrition, downsizing, leaving vacancies unfilled and retirements. By means of outsourcing, the government is increasingly advanced as a consumer that is responsible for purchasing services rather than actively producing them. This has served to weaken job security, seniority allowances, transfer and promotion opportunities, cost-of-living increases, erode pensions and benefits, in addition to increasing the absolute managerial control over the working-day. Indeed, a renewed assault on the public-sector, and in particular unionized jobs (as we argue below), will likely come down hardest on racialized groups and women since not only has this been where many have made the most gains but also because they are likely to see increases in the unpaid sphere of social life and reproduction. All things considered, we now turn to a discussion of the particular ways in which the election of Prime Minister Stephan Harper's federal Conservatives have acted to preserve the mobility and power of capital, while subordinating and intensifying pressures for the working-class.

'Constitutionalizing' Neoliberalism: Integrating the 'Competitive' Logic of the State

The current economic crisis has provided a calculated political and economic opportunity for the federal government to simultaneously 'roll back' its commitment to the provision of social services, while at the same time 'rolling out' institutions and social policies that are oriented towards the cultivation of new channels for accumulation. The measures advanced by the federal government are by no means based on austerity or restraint, but on expanding and deepening opportunities for capital valorization unburdened by the costs of social infrastructure. Welfare state retrenchment and tight fiscal constraints go hand in hand with irresponsible tax cuts and spectacular mega projects. As the immediacy of the financial crisis recedes and governments around the world restrict spending, with the most dramatic conflicts over public goods and services occurring in Europe, these so-called 'exit strategies' are attempting to re-establish liberalized financial systems and reconstruct the neoliberal policy framework and dominance of the market in regulating economic output and distribution. It is important, therefore, to begin by identifying some of the features of these so-called exit strategies being adopted by the Harper government in Canada, particularly with respect to fiscal policies, given that fiscal austerity is likely to be a flashpoint of political struggles in the coming period.

From his very first budget speech in 2006, titled "Restoring Fiscal Balance In Canada", Harper demonstrated his hard-line commitment to constitutionalism in the Conservatives proposal for a stricter separation of responsibilities by cutting federal social programs that would fall under the auspices of the provinces. Almost immediately after coming to power, Prime Minister Harper slashed the Goods and Services Tax (GST) from 7 percent to 6 and later 5 percent in an attempt to attract investment and spur economic development. The Conservatives devoted the Canadian state to "competitive and efficient" economic policies and proposed plans to harmonize the tax system. Meanwhile, they moved quickly to scrap plans for a non-profit, centre-based, affordable national child care program that had been negotiated by the Liberals with the provinces and territories and replaced it with the Universal Child Care Benefit that saw families on welfare, the working poor and modest-income families netting between $600 and $951 per annum; nowhere near close enough to cover the costs of child-care or to allow a parent to stay at home (Batte et al, 2006; Bezanson, 2010).

A short time thereafter, the 2007 global financial meltdown plunged the in-ternational political economy into the most significant crisis of accumulation since the Great Depression. In an act of political brinkmanship, soon after fixing federal election dates to every four years Prime Minister Harper called a snap election breaking his own election promise in the hope of gaining a clear majority. While this did not happen, the biggest losers in the election were the Liberals who had lost twenty-six seats; two-thirds of which were redistributed to the Conservatives and the remainder to the NDP. Meanwhile, governments of all stripes the world over responded with unprecedented levels of stimulus funding. The Harper Conserva-tives, long a sanctuary for fiscal hawks, likewise responded with stimulus spending. The centerpiece of the 2009 budget, titled "Canada's Economic Action Plan", in-jected $64 billion over two years toward infrastructure spending, personal income tax cuts and the 'securitization' (or preemptive bailout) of state-backed mortgage and insurance agencies. Harper's government, which since late-2006 required all provinces to consider the P3 route as a condition for receiving federal infrastruc-ture money and in 2007 created the aggressive Public-Private Partnerships Canada Crown corporation, was using its fiscal leverage as a source of cost-sharing and the economic crisis as a pretext to promote P3 projects nationally (see Loxley, 2010). This is in spite of the fact that a growing number of studies indicate that the priva-tization of formerly public services is often no more efficient or less costly than traditional approaches to service delivery (Loxley, 2010; Armstrong et al, 2001; Mackenzie, 2004). Despite exceptional amounts of stimulus spending, however, the Harper government has remained steadfastly committed neoliberals. With the two year stimulus spending coming to an end and economic "recovery" allegedly underway, Harper's Conservatives are looking to halve their deficits by 2013 under the euphemism of "fiscal consolidation", otherwise known as austerity. With an estimated deficit of nearly $56 billion for 2010-11 that is expected to remain well into 2013-2014, and a forecast debt-to-GDP ratio of about 34-35 percent, this is nowhere near the 25 percent threshold when the books were balanced. However, the state of the federal budget is by no means dire, when taking into consideration the record $14 billion surplus that Harper inherited from an earlier decade of Lib-eral austerity. In addition, prior to the onset of the current crisis, Canada's debt at 32.3 percent of national GDP was at its lowest in more than a quarter century given the largest payments in Canadian history and federal law that requires all surpluses to be used to pay down the national debt and not for new spending initiatives.

In an effort to rebalance the books, the most recent Speech from the Throne (March 3, 2010) suggests that, rather than depart from neoliberal austerity and monetary policy, Harper's Conservatives are seeking to further expand and intensify them. In other words, a private-sector crisis is being shifted onto the public sector and the power of finance capital is emerging stronger than ever. In their blatantly ideological quest to return to balanced budgets, Harper's Conservatives—no less aided by the Federal Liberals and New Democratic Party—have turned their attention toward an aggressive strategy premised on public sector austerity and private sector prosperity.

For instance, hidden deep in the 2010 budget is a technical change to tax regulations that aim to entice FDI through the weakening of domestic constraints. The budget removes restrictions that foreign investors, especially venture capitalists and private-equity funds, face in selling shares in Canadian firms. This change to Section 116 of the Income Tax Act effectively eliminates the need for tax reporting to the Canada Revenue Agency (CRA). Previously, the CRA required investors to disclose details of the sale for approval in the case that taxes needed to be paid. As a result, rather than repatriate any capital gains, investors kept the proceeds of the sale in Canadian accounts for fear of taxation. As of the Speech, these restrictions have been for the most part eliminated (Viera, 2010). Touting the alleged benefits of the change, Finance Minister Flaherty recently remarked, "[t]he best way to build a more competitive economy is to create an environment that allows the entrepreneurs who employ so many Canadians to succeed and expand—not an environment that stands in the way of their success with high taxes and red tape" (Department of Finance, 2010). Of course, Flaherty failed to mention that these changes are expected to cost Ottawa $130-million in lost revenue over five-years. Meanwhile, in all areas but defense spending which has increased 37% since 2000-2001, government operating expenditures have been frozen for two-years, which given inflation means real cuts. The Conservatives have recently pledged $9 billion to build jails for criminals who do not exist, spent $1.1 billion on turning Toronto into a militarized city for the recent G8/G20 meetings and promised another $16 billion for F-35 fighter jets for fighting 'terrorism' abroad. Finance Minister Jim Flaherty has also suggested that there are some opportunities for the privatization of crown assets, including real estate and the outsourcing of public contracts. In particular, the Conservatives are taking aim at Atomic Energy Canada Ltd., seeking to open-up Canada Posts' procurement of overseas mail, and grant the minister of the environment unilateral powers to waive environmental assessments. In seeking to create new clusters of accumulation, environmental regulations in the Arctic have been 'streamlined' for oil and mining companies to drill, while federal environmental assessment reports have been removed from the purview of the Canadian Environmental Agency to the business-friendly National Energy Board. This continues the removal of environmental initiatives by the Conservatives made most explicit by Harper's dismissal of the Kyoto protocol as a "socialist scheme" designed to suck money from the rich countries.

The weakening of social provisions, labour and environmental laws has been paralleled by new spending as Harper has further concentrated federal stimulus monies in the energy, resource and construction industries. Certainly new public spending is gravely needed given Canada's crumbling infrastructure (estimated at over $123 billion) and the fact that total public investment as a percentage of GDP has fallen from between two and three percent in the 1960s and 70s to about 0.5 percent by the 1990s (Mackenzie, 2004); however this spending has not been equally distributed among the various segments of the Canadian labour market, nor racial and gender neutral (Ontario Health Coaltion, 2008; Armstong et al, 2001; OPSEU, 2007). Attacks against the poor, refugee claimants, temporary workers, live-in caregivers, and non-status persons are increasing as the blatant power of the federal state is summoned to service capital, while abandoning any responsibilities to labour (Thomas, 2010; Hussan and Scott, 2009; Teelucksingh & Galabuzzi, 2005; Galabuzzi, 2006; Paz, 2008). Indeed, recent research by Kathleen Lahey (2009) suggests that women have received only about 7 percent to 22 percent of stimulus funding, since men tend to predominate in the construction, mining and forestry industries. The bulwark of stimulus spending has been untargeted without any long-term planning, community involvement or proactive infrastructural spending, going mainly toward existing backlogs as opposed to re-thinking development and the spatial development of where we live and work.

The federal Conservatives have continued to 'slash and burn' funding for equity seeking groups such as the Status of Women, or groups critical of Israeli state policies such as KAIROS, and have in the process punished those that dare to criticize their policies. For example, a short-list of recent Harper controversies includes what have (arguably) been labeled 'politically-motivated' removals such as the dismissal of openly critical and outspoken Veterans Ombudsman Pat Strogran, Chief Superintendent Marty Cheliak a strong supporter of the long-gun registry, former president of the Canadian Nuclear Safety commission Linda Keen who shut down the Chalk River nuclear facility over safety concerns, Chair of the Military Complaints commission Peter Tinsley who was investigating the controversial transfer of Afghan detainees and, most recently, Chief Statistician at Statistics Canada Munir Sheikh who resigned after the mandatory long-form census was scrapped in favour of a voluntary survey, which has been harshly criticized by a plethora of academics, think tanks, politicians, community groups and other levels of government. In addition, this includes last year's prorogation (the fourth time in three years) of parliament for more than two months amid speculation of a coalition Liberal-NDP, the Helena Guergis

affair, the dismissal of the arts and cultural community, alleged spending favourit-
ism for Conservative ridings, a foreign aid policy that denies funding for abortion
services, a bold-faced 802 page omnibus or "dumpster" bill bulging with disparate
issues, and public attacks targeting employment equity and affirmative action for
federal employees. Put into perspective, then, this can be understood as none other
than an act of capitalist militancy on behalf of and in accordance with the state.

A renewed round of austerity under the banner of "fiscal prudence" has led
new President of the Treasury Board, the main cabinet committee responsible for
the administration and operations of the federal civil service, Stockwell Day, to
suggest that public-sector unions need to 'share the pain'. This was a thinly veiled
reference to the concessions extracted by private-sector unions from GM, Ford,
Chrysler and Vale-Inco, for example, as well as the political failures and public
resentment of striking public-sector workers from Toronto and Ottawa to Windsor and Vancouver (Rosenfeld, 2009; Albo et al, 2010; Fanelli and Paulson, 2009).
Stimulus and restraint go hand-in-hand: capital-preserving tax cuts cause deficits
that then need to be resolved, which translates into social cuts and wage restraint for
the working-class and a vicious circle of more tax cuts to spur business investment
further eroding the fiscal base. For instance, over the next five years federal workers will subsidize corporate tax-cuts by $6.8-billion in transfers extracted through
wage-freezes and job cuts, which will total nearly $21-billion. Oddly, though, a
great percentage of Canadian Federal tax-cuts will flow directly right back into
the US Treasury, which taxes its companies the difference between foreign taxes
and domestic ones in order to stimulate internal production and slow outsourcing (Weir, 2009). The recently negotiated "Buy American" deal gives permanent
and unrestricted foreign access to publicly funded contracts. This is an historical
deed as it is the first time Canadian governments have agreed to open procurement contracts to bids by other World Trade Organization members since the
1988 Free Trade Agreement. This is particularly confusing as only about 2 percent of US federal stimulus funding, that is, about $4-5-billion of $275-billion,
remains. Still worse, Canada and the European Union are in trade negotiations
to enact what the Trade Justice Network, an alliance comprised of labour and
social justice groups, has argued would be the largest, most intrusive free trade
deal that Canada has ever entered into and is progressing quite quickly with little public scrutiny (Trade Justice Network). According to a recent study by Scott
Sinclair (2010, p.3) of the Canadian Centre for Policy Alternatives (CCPA):

> The CETA [Comprehensive Economic and Trade Agreement] also
> will have an adverse impact on public services, especially those pro-
> vided by local, territorial and provincial governments. The agree-
> ment would promote and entrench new forms of commercialization,

especially public-private partnerships. It would also prohibit governments from setting performance requirements that oblige foreign
investors or service providers to purchase locally, transfer technology or train local workers. The combined impact of its investment,
services and procurement rules would make it far more difficult to
reverse failed privatizations.

The austerity agenda of the federal government has entailed the drastic reconfiguration of public services as Canada is essentially offering to make commitments
at the federal, provincial and municipal tiers that go beyond NAFTA and the WTO,
opening up services and investments, domestic regulation and standards, public procurement contracts and intellectual property rights (McBride, 2005; Johnson and
Mahon, 2005). Foreign multinationals could potentially gain unprecedented access
to municipal water services, while the demand for local offsets, the most important
leverage that towns and cities have, such as local purchasing of goods and services or
labour reinvestments, may no longer be permitted. In seeking to 'constitutionalize'
neoliberalism, Canada is pushing to include a NAFTA-like investor-state dispute
mechanism that would allow European companies to sue any tier of government
should they enact policies that cut into profits. In effect this could nullify and void,
for example, fair wage policies and ethical strategies enacted by some provinces and
cities, in addition to ceding authority and control over domestic policies away from
local governments and communities to business elites whose profit interests trump
all others. The CETA, in particular, takes aim at Ontario's Green Energy Act, which
offers grants and exemptions for cleaner energy sources and local job creation. Toronto's "buy local" food policy which has committed to increasing the amount of
locally procured food served at city owned facilities and the celebrated 'living wage'
in New Westminster, for instance, could be prohibited.

For months ahead of the G8/G20 meetings in Toronto, the federal government had been lobbying world leaders to block proposals for a global bank tax for
G20 members to be used as a slush fund for expected future bailouts and to prevent
banks from shifting to jurisdictions with lower taxes. In an effort to convince G20
member states otherwise, Harper touted the stability of the Canadian banks, which
he misleadingly promoted as not requiring a bailout similar in kind to those in the
U.S. and European Union. This praise however is both unjustified and dubious,
when in fact Canadian banks received upwards of $200 billion—that is more than
the initial $700 billion bailout in the U.S. as a percentage of GDP—not to men-
tion a host of additional accounting trickery that kept the 'real' costs of the bank
bailouts out of the books (Dobbin, 2010; Stanford, 2010; Campbell, 2009). In
fact, Stephan Harper has recently gone as far as to say this would "punish" and be

"unfair" to Canadian banks that, in the midst of the crisis in 2007, racked in nearly $20 billion in profits, and which have since had a field day buying up insolvent American banks. Successful with their propaganda, the Conservatives managed to persuade G20 leaders to forego a bank tax and, instead, convinced them to commit to a unified push for austerity pledging to halve their deficits by 2013. In Canada, the potential class-based consequences are clear.

With tens of thousands of baby-boomers expected to retire in the next decade, dwindling revenues and rising social services costs are expected to compound the budget fiasco. Considering the twin perils of a falling birth rate and increasing retirements, Parliamentary Budget Officer Kevin Page has warned that a shrinking tax-base coupled with increasing usage of health care and service benefits will lead to higher government costs and therefore an uncertain fiscal future (Campion-Smith, 2010). The changing demographics of the Canadian labour market is expected to increase by 7 percent the number of retired people compared to those still in the workforce in the next ten years: that's nearly as much as it grew in the last forty years. Wait another ten years and the estimated cost to rectify this dilemma rises from $20 billion to $30 billion as nearly 40 percent of federal service workers are expected to retire in the next five years. In response, Page has argued that permanent fiscal actions are needed either through significant tax-hikes, serious cuts in social spending, or some combination of both. Unfortunately though, while understanding and analyzing the changing demographics of the Canadian labour market is crucial, such uncertainty often invokes alarmist exclamations on the need to shrink the public sector and shed 'liabilities' (such as that which is currently happening throughout the Eurozone, especially around health care and pension reform). True to form and typifying the inherent short-sightedness of neoliberal ideologues, Finance Minister Flaherty's spokesperson, Crisholm Potheier, called Page's warnings an "academic exercise" before dismissing it by replying that "Canadians expect the Government to focus on today's fragile economic recovery".

Despite Harper's dutiful allegiance to capital-preserving federalism, however, the Conservatives continue to remain under pressure from business interests and corporate lobbyists, such as Canadian Federation of Independent Businesses president Catherine Swift, to withdraw health benefits and pension supports. In a letter to the Federal Pension Review Panel, Swift stressed the need to do something about the "large and growing disunity between the pension benefits of private and public employees" stressing that the public sector should follow the lead of the private sector which the market will reward appropriately, in addition to urging the government to raise the retirement age beyond 65 (Whittington, 2010). In making these remarks, Swift was implying that unionized workers are overly compensated and to be blamed for causing the deep economic downturn. More to the point, it is likely that the key reason Swift was encouraging part-time seniors to re-join the labour force was because they remain one of the most 'easily' exploitable subsets in the labour market as they are often seen as flexible, part-time, easily disposable and unlikely to demand higher wages and benefits since many are under duress and relying on their meager earnings given inadequate pensions, social supports and rising living costs.

Contrary to Swift's exaggerated remarks, nearly two-thirds of all Canadian workers lack a workplace pension and over 1.6-million seniors get by on less than $15,000 per year. According to the Public Service Alliance of Canada (PSAC, 2010), in 2008 the average federal civil service pension was just over $23,000, which pales in comparison with the "diamond encrusted" pensions and retirement packages for C-level executives (e.g. chief financial and executive officers). Furthermore, as Toby Sanger (2010) of the Canadian Union of Public Employees (CUPE) has recently shown, total public spending dropped to its lowest since 1974 to about 36 percent of the economy in 2007 while total government revenues from taxes, on the other hand, dropped to less than 32 percent of the economy in 2009, its lowest since 1985. In fact, federal program spending fell from 17.2 percent of GDP in the early-1990s to 11.7 percent by the end of the decade (Loxley, 2010). Likewise, from 1990-2008, the share of total government spending in the economy has been reduced by 20 percent which, when considering that the federal government plans to cut its corporate tax on income from 18 percent to 15 percent leading to a decline in revenue by $20 billion over the next five-years, may spell long-term budget trouble. With inflation expected to rise 1.7 percent in 2010 and 2 percent or more in 2011, together with the ever-present fear of rating agencies downgrading the federal AAA status, which would lead to vast increases in interest payments and thereby increasing Canada's dependence on foreign capital injections, Canada is by no means out of the global slump.

As of January 2010, 380,000 more people are unemployed and 270,000 fewer people are employed than 15-months earlier. With the Canadian dollar near parity with the US dollar, Canada's manufacturing sector continues to suffer from both the increased penetration of imports and the difficulty of trying to compete in foreign markets, which are either strategically subsidized or draw their 'competitive advantage' by poverty-wages or externalizing costs onto the environment. Despite productivity output per employee rising by more than 37 percent between 1980-2005, real wages in Canada have been generally stagnant since at least 1982, despite the lowest levels of unemployment since the 1970s prior to the recent economic crisis. There has been an inverse relationship, then, between productivity growth and real wages. In an effort to maintain modest living standards workers have increased their hours of work, emptied their savings, added family members to the workforce, and took on huge debt loads by borrowing against their homes and accepting multiple credit cards. Recent job data suggests that a significant majority of newly created jobs are often 10 percent lower than the average wage of the jobs lost, with 20 percent having lost their pension plan by changing jobs (Bernard & Galarneau, 2010; Sanger, 2010b). Emerging amidst such blatantly Janus-faced austerity is a quest to return to the same old orthodoxy of neoliberalism. Under the auspices of 'spiraling' budget deficits, growing unemployment and low capacity utilization, Conservatives have used the crisis to attack the various segments of the working class, in particular those unionized, to lower wages, extract concessions and increase profits, thereby further indebting 'consumers' and leaving them more precarious and with less time to spare than ever. In turn, this further undermines federal fiscal capacities in an attempt to return to a mythical era of unbridled "free market" capitalism and proverbial small government.

The urge to curtail unsustainable spending, therefore, obscures capitalist militancy. While working class incomes have either stagnated or declined over the past thirty years, the wealthiest members of society have enjoyed unprecedented gains. While in 1995 the average executive compensation of the top 50 CEO's in Canada was eighty-five times that of the average worker, by 2007 it was two-hundred and fifty-nine times that (McNally, 2009). Likewise, the income share taken by the top 0.1 percent of income earners in Canada approached 5 percent by the mid-1990s, a level unseen since the 1930s and early years of WWII. The personal savings rate that was nearly 20.2 percent of disposable income in 1982 had plummeted to 2 percent by 2005 (Baragar, 2009). Indeed, 2009 marked the highest-ever debt-to-income ratio of 145 percent in Canada. The Vanier Institute of the Family found that the average Canadian household debt climbed to $96,000 while compared with 2008 mortgages 90-days or more overdue had risen by 50 percent, and the number of credit card holders at least 90-days arrears was up 40 percent. The report also went on the suggest that there is a looming housing bubble in Canada as prices toward the end of 2009 rose to about $340,000, which is about five-times the average after-tax income of Canadian homes. The long-term trend is just over three and one-half-times that (Sauve, 2010). A sudden rise in interest rates, changes in mortgage terms and the bitter realization that current prices are in the long run unsustainable may cause the bubble to burst. As 'exit strategies' come to the forefront, contesting the ruinous effects of these policies becomes a central imperative.

Where Do We Go From Here? Resisting Austerity, Reestablishing the Power of the Working Class

The capitalist classes have used the economic recession as a strategic political opportunity to strengthen and expand processes of neoliberalism through the state and market, and into every aspect of social life. While the federal government proclaims the need to impose wage freezes, sell off public assets, and restructure social services in the face of the baby boom generation's looming retirement, this is by no means driven simply by restraint. In fact, just as the federal government has advanced austerity in the face of new spending, it has also pursued massive tax cuts for corporations and the wealthy, rolling out new institutional structures that facilitate the increasing mobility of capital, and utilizing stimulus as a way of subsidizing the burgeoning construction and energy sector. In this context, new government spending does not spell out a return to Keynesian policies, but is rather symptomatic of a deepening program of class polarization. How can this be challenged? How may social movements adapt? Is the NDP a viable alternative? How can labour unions be pushed in a positive manner?

The struggle over austerity cannot be limited to its federal expression as issues related to service retrenchment and the increasing penetration of neoliberal policies manifests throughout the provinces and municipalities. Likewise, in an increasingly intertwined global political economy, national and sub-national decisions cannot be abstracted from their international context. While exit strategies targeting the public sector are emerging unconcealed in their aggressiveness and vigor, Canadian responses have so far been tepid. The capitalist class is recomposing and repositioning itself to make the public pay, spread the risk and hoard the gains. The shape taken by struggles over austerity and social services may very well dictate the next round of accumulation or, alternatively, lead to something historically unique. Indeed, a good many predictions already suggest a looming 'lost decade' of austerity. New alignments, coalitions and networks will no doubt emerge. More importantly, however, a frank and sober discussion will need to begin that seeks to move beyond the fractured coalition of network politics in hopes of creating something historically unique, all-encompassing and capable of challenging what the working class is collectively up against. The course of neoliberalism has thoroughly beaten down what vestiges remain of trade union militancy and existing social movements must come to the bitter realization of historical defeat. This is the only realistic starting point from which to move forward (Anderson, 2000).

Three decades of neoliberalism have eroded whatever 'progressive' remnants of social-democratic and labour parties that exist. The NDP is not an alternative and neither is, regrettably, the Green Party trapped in erstwhile eco-capitalist "solutions". Both parties have no transformative vision of society, adhere to the economic agenda of neoliberalism and display no interest in challenging the logic of capital or the democratic functions of the state. Moreover, they remain entrapped in top-down organizational structures with little interest in building mobilizational capacities at the community and grassroots level. Finally, when in power they have strayed little from Conservative and Liberal policies. This is demonstrated time and again in the countless cutbacks and repressive policies of a good many social democratic governments' over the past three decades (Caroll & Ratner, 2005).

Moreoever, organized labour bodies from the Canadian Labour Congress to the Ontario Federation of Labour, Canadian Auto Workers and Canadian Union of Public Employees, for instance, have increasingly shown signs of confusion having failed to break ideologically or politically with a social dependence on capital and by their inability to meaningfully intervene in recent battles. Great political and social divergences between Local's and their national or provincial affiliates continue to mar the collective bargaining landscape. If worker militancy as demonstrated by workplace stoppages is an indication of growing labour unrest, the 126 workplace stoppages in 2006 (its lowest since 1935) pales in comparison with the historic high of 1,173 in 1974, and indeed paints a grim picture of the state of labour militancy in Canada (Workman, 2009). By focusing narrowly on workplace gains such as, say, higher wages, the capitalist class and a good many politicians feed off the rhetoric that workplace gains undermine social services. This is a trap that labour gets caught up in when it focuses only on workplace benefits. Labour will need to develop counter-narrative strategies and seek to politicize their gains by rooting them in their communities and also in the form of non-economic improvements (paid leave, educationals, etc). Unfortunately, instead of inspiring new waves of mass protest, demonstrations and the spawning of new working class organizations, the current global economic insecurity seems to have weakened labour's resolve and risks signaling its ultimate class defeat.

To conclude, the power of capital and the state, as well as the impasse of both organized labour and many social movements to confront what the working class is collectively up against, belies the need for a new kind of radical, anti-capitalist political project suited to the current historical and social conjuncture. New political experiments will need to emerge that aim to incorporate the strongest elements of the traditional party, trade unions, social movements and community groups. In this regard, the Left may due well to study the growing brashness of political and economic elites as they reconfigure and reorganize themselves to seize the crisis. Nevertheless, the European anti-austerity protests and emergent anti-capitalist projects may provide a glimmer of optimism. What is certain is that the failure to take up such a challenge to reestablish the power of the working class in Canada would be to accept the existing social relations as unalterable and would therefore recognize the right of capital to exploit labour.

References

Albo, G. (1993). The Public Sector Impasse & the Administrative Question. *Studies In Political Economy*, 42, 113-127.

Albo, G. (1994). 'Competitive Austerity' & the Impasse of Capitalist Employment Policy. *Socialist Register*, 30, 144-170.

Albo, G., S. Gindin., and L. Pantich. (2010). *In and Out of Crisis: The Global Financial Meltdown and Left Alternatives*. Oakland, California: Spectre PM Press.

Anderson, P. (2000). Renewals. *New Left Review*, 2 (1), 5-24.

Anderson, G. (2010). *Fiscal Federalism: A Comparative Introduction*. Oxford: Oxford University Press.

Armstrong, P., Amaratunga, C., Bernier, J., Grant, K., Pederson, A., and K. Willson (eds.). (2001). *Exposing Privatization: Women and Health Care Reform in Canada*. Aurora, Ontario: Garamond Press.

Baragar, F. & M. Seccareccia. (2008). Financial Restructuring: Implications of Recent Canadian Macroeconomic Developments. *Studies In Political Economy*, 82, 61-83.

Baragar, F. Canada & the Crisis. (2009). In Guard, J. & W. Antony (Eds.), *Bankruptcies & Bailouts* (pp.77-106). Halifax: Fernwood.

Battle, K., S. Torjman, M. Mendelson, and E. Tamagno. (2007). *Mixed Brew for the 'Coffee Shop' Budget*. Ottawa: Caledon Institute of Social Policy.

Bernard, A., and D. Galarneau. (2010). Layoffs in Canada. Statistics Canada. Retrieved on August 7, 2010 from, http://www.statcan.gc.ca/pub/75-001-x/2010105/article/11161-eng.htm.

Bezanson, K. (2010). "Childcare Delivered Through the Mailbox:" Social Reproduction, Choice, and Neoliberalism in a Theo-Conservative Canada. In Braedley, S. and M. Luxton (Eds.), *Neoliberalism and Everyday Life* (pp.90-112) Montreal & Kingston: McGill-Queens University Press.

Brenner, N. & N. Theodore (Eds.). (2002). *Spaces of Neoliberalism: Urban Restructuring in North America & Western Europe*. Oxford: Blackwell.

Brown, L. (31, March 2010). Public Sector Workers Paying for Corporate Tax Cuts. *National Union of Public and General Employees*. Retrieved on April 12 2010, from, http://www.nupge.ca/content/public-sector-workers-paying-corporate-tax-cuts.

Campbell, B. (2009). The Global Economic Crisis and Its Canadian Dimension. *Canadian Centre for Policy Alternatives*. Retrieved online on June 7, 2010 from, http://www.policyalternatives.ca/publications/monitor/global-economic-crisis-and-its-canadian-dimension.

Campion-Smith, B. (19, February 2010). Aging Workforce to Drive up Debt: Report. *Toronto Star* [online]. Retrieved February 25, 2010 from, http://www.thestar.com/business/article/767833--aging-workforce-to-drive-up-debt-report

Carroll, W.K., & R.S. Ratner (Eds.). (2005). *Challenges and Perils: Social Democracy in Neoliberal Times*. Nova Scotia: Fernwood Press.

Clarke, S. (2005). The Neoliberal Theory of Society. In Saad-Filho, A. & D. Johnston (Eds.), Neo-liberalism: A Critical Reader (pp.50-59). London: Pluto Press.

Department of Finance. (2010). *Minister of Finance Highlights Budget Measure to Cut Red Tape and Boost Venture Capital for Canadian Firms*. Retrieved on September 9, 2010 from, http://www.fin.gc.ca/n10/10-079-eng.asp.

Dobbin, M. (24 May 2010). The Canadian 'Good Banks' myth. *The Vancouver Sun*. Retrieved on July 30, 2010 from, http://communities.canada.com/vancouversun/blogs/communityofinter-est/archive/2010/05/24/the-canadian-good-banks-myth.aspx?CommentPosted=true#comment ntmessage.

Fanelli, C., and J. Paulson. (2009). Municipal Malaise: Neoliberal Urbanism and the Future of Our Cities. *The Bullet*. Retrieved on July 1, 2010 from, http://www.socialistproject.ca/bullet/357.php.

Galabuzi, G.E. (2006). *Canada's Economic Apartheid: The Social Exclusion of Racialized Groups in the New Century*. Toronto: Canadian Scholars' Press.

Gindin, S. (2010). Working Peoples Assemblies. *Relay*, 30, 24-26.

Government of Canada. (2010). *A Stronger Canada. A Stronger Economy. Now and For the Future*. Retrieved on April 25, 2010 from, http://www.discours.gc.ca/grfx/docs/sft-ddt-2010_e.pdf.

Hussan, S.K., and M. Scott. (2009). Jason Kenney's Doublespeak Exposed: Tories Unleash Canada Service Border Services on Migrants. *The Bullet*. Retrieved January 8, 2010 from, http://www.socialistproject.ca/bullet/bullet207.html.

Johnson, R., and R. Mahon. NAFTA: The Redesign and Rescaling of Canada's Welfare State. *Studies in Political Economy*, 76, 7-30.

Kipfer, S., and R. Keil. (2002). Toronto Inc? Planning the Competitive City in the New Toronto. *Antipode*, 34 (2), p.227-264.

Lahey, K. (2009). Gender Analysis of 2009. *Progressive Economics Forum* [online]. Retrieved January 14, 2010 from http://www.progressiveeconomics.ca/2009/01/31/gender-analysis-of-budget-2009/.

Mackenzie, H. (2004). Financing Canada's Hospitals: Alternatives to P3s. Retrieved on June 2, 2009 from, http://www.web.net/ohc/P3s.htm#P3Reports.

McBride, S. (2005). *Paradigm Shift: Globalization & the Canadian State*: Halifax: Fernwood Press.

McKinnon, I. R. (1997). The Logic of Market-Preserving Federalism. *Virginia Law Review*, 83 (7), p. 1573-1580.

McNally, D. (2009). Inequality, The Profit-System and the Global Crisis. In Guard, J. & W. Antony (Eds.), *Bankruptcies & Bailouts* (pp. 32-42). Halifax: Fernwood.

Noonen, J. (2009). The Windsor CUPE Strike: Implications for the Labour Movement & the Left. *The Bullet*. Retrieved on October 23, 2009 from, http://www.socialistproject.ca/bullet/ bullet236.html

Ontario Health Coaltion. (2008). *When Public Relations Trump Public Accountability: The Evolution of Cost Overruns, Service Cuts and Cover-up in the Brampton Hospital P3*. Retrieved on July 14, 2009 from, http://www.web.net/ohc/jan08report%20final.pdf.

Ontario Public Service Employees Union Local 479. (2007). *Risky Business II*. Retrieved on April 7, 2009 from, http://www.opseu.org/bps/health/P3Report.pdf.

Panitch, L. & D. Swartz. (2003). *From Consent to Coercion: The Assault on Trade Union Freedoms*. Aurora, ON: Garamond Press.

Paz, A. (2008). Harvest of Injustice: The Oppression of Migrant Workers on Canadian Farms. *The Bullet*. Retrieved on May 2, 2009 from, http://www.socialistproject.ca/bullet/bullet117.html.

Peck, Jamie and Adam Tickell. (2002). Neoliberalizing Space. *Antipode*, 34 (3): 380-404.

Public Service Alliance of Canada. (2010). Seven Myths About Public Service Pensions. Retrieved on May 5, 2009 from, http://www.psac-afpc.org/petition-pension/mythes-e.asp.

Rosenfeld, H. (2009). The North American Auto Industry in Crisis. *Monthly Review*, 61 (2),18-36.

Saad-Filho, A. & D. Johnston (Eds.). (2005). *Neoliberalism: A Critical Reader*. London: Pluto Press.

Qian, Y. and R. Weingast (1996). China's Transition to Markets: Market-Preserving Federalism, Chinese Style. *Journal of Policy Reform*, 1, p.149-185.

Sanger, T. (2010). *Economic Climate for Bargaining*. Canadian Union of Public Employees, 7 (1), 1-15.

Sanger, T. (2010b). The New Grecian Formula: Still Toxic. *Progressive Economics Forum*. Retrieved on June 22, 2010 from, http://www.progressive-economics.ca/2010/06/18/the-new-grecian-formula-still-toxic/.

Sauve, R. (2010). *The Current State of Canadian Family Finances: 2009 Report*. Ottawa: VIF.

Sinclair, S. (2010). *Negotiating From Weakness: Canada-EU Treaty Threatens Canadian Purchasing Policies & Public Services*. Canadian Centre for Policy Alternatives. Ottawa: CCPA.

Speech from the Throne. (2006). *Restoring Fiscal Balance In Canada: Focusing on Priorities.* Government of Canada, Budget 2006. Retrieved on August 21, 2010 from, http://www.fin.gc.ca/budget06/pdf/fp2006e.pdf.

Speech from the Throne. (2006). *Canada's Economic Action Plan.* Government of Canada, Budget 2009. Retrieved on August 25, 2010 from, http://www.actionplan.gc.ca/grfx/docs/ecoplan_e.pdf

Teelucksingh, C., & G.E. Galabuzzi. (2005). *Working Precariously: The Impact of Race and Immigrant Status on Employment Opportunities and Outcomes in Canada.* Toronto: Canadian Race Relations Foundation.

Thomas, M.P. (2010). Labour Migration and Temporary Work: Canada's Foreign-Worker Programs in the "New Economy". In Pupo, N. & M.P. Thomas (Eds.), *Interrogating the New Economy: Restructuring Work in the 21ˢᵗ Century* (Pp.149-172). Toronto: University of Toronto Press.

Trade Justice Network. (2010). Fact Sheets: Overview. Retrieved on April 28, 2010 from, http://www.tradejustice.ca/overview?bl=y.

Tufts, S. (2004). Building the 'Competitive City': Labour and Toronto's Bid to Host the Olympic Games. *Geoforum,* 35 (1), p.47-58.

Veira, P. (5, March 2010). Budget Foreign Investment Shift 'Masterstroke'. *Financial Post* [online]. Retrieved March 6 2010, from http://www.financialpost.com/story.html?id=2647200

Warskett, R. (2007). Remaking the Canadian Labour Movement: Transformed Work & Transformed Labour Strategies. In Shalla, V. & W. Clement (Eds.), *Work In Tumultuous Times: Critical Perspectives (pp.380-400).* Montreal & Kingston: McGill-Queens University Press.

Weingast, B. (1995). The Economic Role of Political Institutions: Market-Preserving Federalism and Economic Development. *Journal of Law, Economics, & organization,* 20 (1), 1-31.

Weir, E. (2009). *The Treasury Transfer Effect.* Canadian Centre for Policy Alternatives, 10 (7), 1-8.

Whittington, L. (20, February 2010). Tories Target Civil Servants Pensions. *Toronto Star* [online]. Retrieved February 22 2010, from http://www.thestar.com/news/canada/article/768588--tories-target-civil-service-pensions

Wood, E.M. (2002). *The Origin of Capitalism: A Longer View.* London: Verso.

Workman, T. (2009). *If Your In My Way, I'm Walking: The Assault on Working People Since 1970.* Halifax: Fernwood.

Can Global Capitalism Be Saved? "Exit Strategies" for Capitalism or Humanity

Minqi Li[1]

Abstract: Global capitalism is currently recovering from the Great Recession of 2009. But the basic contradiction of neoliberalism has not been resolved. The fiscal deficits in the western countries and China's real estate bubble are setting up the world for a potentially more devastating crisis. China may emerge as the key battleground of global class struggle. As the global ecological system approaches total collapse, any further expansion of capitalism is now in fundamental conflict with the long-term survival of humanity.

Keywords: Global capitalism, crisis, class struggle, global ecological crisis

Introduction

In 2009, global capitalism suffered the deepest economic crisis since the Great Depression. In previous crises, such as in the early 1980s, early 1990s, 1998, and 2001, the global economy had managed to grow, though at comparatively slower rates. In 2009, according to the International Monetary Fund (IMF), the global economy as a whole contracted in absolute terms for the first time since the Second World War (see Figure 1). In response to the crisis, leading capitalist governments have thrown trillions of dollars to bail out the financial markets and kept the economies afloat through massive increases in fiscal deficits. Since then, the global economy seems to have recovered. The IMF now predicts the global economy to grow by 4.6 percent in 2010 (IMF 2010). Has global capitalism been saved, after all?

The question may be addressed at three different levels. First, there is no doubt that capitalism has survived the most recent economic crisis. However is the world

---

[1]   Assistant Professor, Department of Economics, University of Utah, Salt Lake City, Utah, USA. He is the author of *The Rise of China and the Demise of the Capitalist World Economy* (Pluto Press and Monthly Review Press, 2009).

back to some form of "normal conditions"? Capitalism is basically an economic system based on the pursuit of profit and capital accumulation. Saving capitalism, in this sense, has to do with securing the conditions that favor high profit rates and rapid capital accumulation (economic growth). Will these "normal conditions" required for capitalist expansion be reestablished in the foreseeable future? Second, there is the long-term, world historical question whether capitalism as an economic and social system can be saved in the long run. What historical conditions are required for capitalism to remain a "savable" system? Under what historical conditions may capitalism cease to exist as a historically viable system? Third, if it turns out that capitalism is no longer historically viable, in that case, what might be the "exit strategies" that are available for humanity? The following pages attempt to shed some light on each of these questions.

Figure 1. World Economic Growth
(Annual Growth Rate of World GDP, 1951-2009)

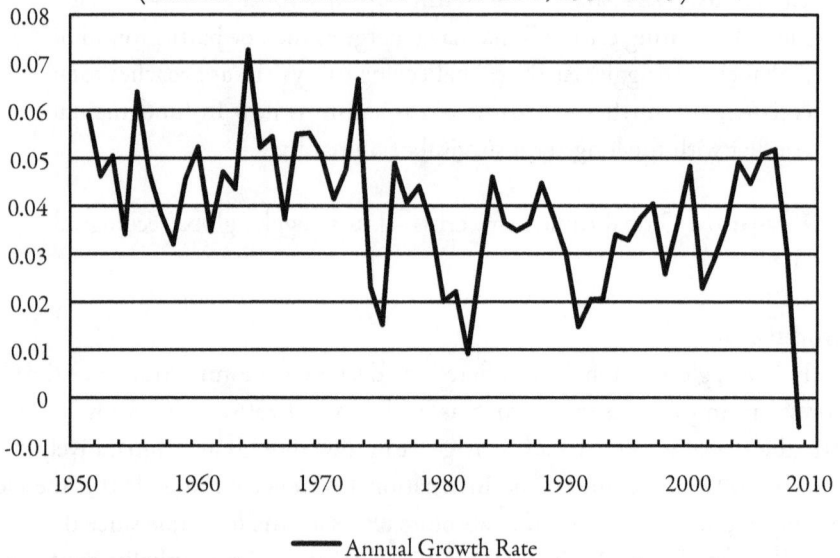

Annual Growth Rate

Sources: Maddison (2003); World Bank (2010); and IMF (2010).

Profit and Accumulation

Capitalist profit derives from the exploitation of workers' surplus labor. From this point of view, maximum profit requires maximum exploitation of labor. However, other things being equal, maximum exploitation is always beneficial for individual capitalists; it is not necessarily in the interest of the entire capitalist class however. Excessive exploitation reduces workers' purchasing power. Under certain conditions, it could also reduce the overall "effective demand" in the capitalist economy, thus lowering the total profits for capitalists. Successful capitalist accumulation requires an effective (though temporary) solution to this contradiction. This may be illustrated by the following formula:

$$W + \prod + T = C + I + G + NX$$

This equation shows that in a capitalist economy, the sum of wages (W), profits ($\prod$), and taxes (T) must equal the sum of consumption (C), investment (I), government purchases (G), and net exports (NX), that is exports less imports, or net purchases by foreigners. In other words, total incomes must equal total expenditures.

Rearrange terms and one arrives at the following profit determination formula:

$$\prod = I + (C\text{-}W) + (G\text{-}T) + NX$$

This equation illustrates that capitalist profits may increase if there is a rise in capitalist investment, or household consumption in excess of wages (which roughly corresponds to "household deficit"), government deficit or trade surplus.[2]

From the point of view of a national capitalist economy, the most ideal solution would be to keep wages and taxes low, while keeping profits high through large trade surpluses. However, this obviously cannot work for all national capitalist economies as some economies' surpluses have to be matched by other economies' deficits and, for the global capitalist economy as a whole, imports and exports by definition should cancel out. For the global capitalist economy or any national capitalist economy that has a trade account that is in rough balance, the "optimal" solution would appear to be keeping wages and taxes low, while solving the "effective demand" problem (also known as the "realization" problem) through high investment. This would maximize the rate of capital accumulation. However, capitalists would make large investments only when they expect high rates of return (the profit rate). But excessively high investment could lead to excess production capacity and higher production costs, leading to lower profit rates. Finally, there are the "second best" options such as household deficits or government deficits. The problem with these less than ideal solutions is that they will inevitably lead to unsustainable household or public debt, likely ending with devastating financial crises. How has capitalism historically managed to maneuver between these different temporary "solutions"? Figure 2 presents the historical trajectory of the profit rate in the US economy, a crucial indicator that represents the degree of "health" of a capitalist economy.[3]

---

[2]   This profit rate determination formula was first developed by Polish Marxist economist Michael Kalecki and later adopted by Hyman Minsky (Minsky 2008[1986]: 160-169).

[3]   The profit rate is defined as the ratio of the broadly defined profit (including corporate profits, interests, and rent) over the

The Great Depression marked the bankruptcy of free market capitalism and demonstrated that modern capitalism could not function without substantial government intervention. After the Second World War, capitalism underwent major institutional restructuring. Government spending now accounted for a substantial portion of the national economic output and Keynesian policies helped to stabilize the capitalist economy. Several factors contributed to comparatively high profit rates in the 1950s and 1960s. U.S. corporations benefited from monopoly over world industry in the early postwar years. On the other hand, in Western Europe and Japan, a large rural surplus labor force kept pressure on wages, thereby keeping labor costs low. All advanced capitalist countries benefited from cheap energy and raw materials imported from the periphery (the "Third World").

However, by the mid-1960s all of these favourable factors started to fade. Competition between the US, Japan and Western Europe in the world market intensified. After decades of economic expansion, strengthened by welfare state institutions, Western working classes enjoyed a period of rising bargaining power and wages started to grow rapidly. Finally, given the triumph of a good many national liberation movements, and politically strengthened by "cold war" geopolitics, peripheral states started to demand more favourable terms in the world division of labor.[4] The collapse of the profit rate led to the crisis of the 1970s and early 1980s. In response, the global capitalist classes undertook a counter-offensive in the form of neoliberalism which in effect amounted in a strategy to revive the global profit rate through global redistribution of income and wealth from labor to capital. "Globalization" was a key component of neoliberalism, which had to do with opening up the markets and resources of several large peripheral or former socialist states. The massive increase in the global reserve army of cheap labour turned the global balance of power decisively in the favour of the capitalist class.

As is presented in Figure 2, neoliberalism did succeed in reviving the profit rate. But by lowering the global wages, neoliberalism necessarily depressed the global mass of consumption. The neoliberal global economy was thus confronted with a serious problem of insufficient global effective demand. In this context, many capitalist economies (China, Japan, other Asian economies, and Germany) attempted to promote capital accumulation through expansion of exports (that is,

---

net stock of private nonresidential fixed assets. Ideally, if the purpose is to study the overall performance of global capitalist economies, one would like to examine the evidence of the global average profit rate. But reliable data on the subject is not available. Given the leading position of the US in the global economy, one may think about the US profit rate as representative of the profit rate in the global capitalist economy. The profit RATE trajectories of other advanced capitalist economies have been similar to that of the US in the postwar era and until recently the overall performance of the global capitalist economy had been largely determined by the performance of the advanced capitalist economies. For an attempt to study the "world profit rate", see Li, Xiao, and Zhu (2007).

4   For detailed discussions on the rise and fall of the postwar capitalist "social structure of accumulation," see Gordon, Weisskopf, and Bowles (1987).

through rising NX). However, as mentioned earlier, this meant that some economies would have to run trade surpluses, while others ran trade deficits. Since the
1990s, the US economy has consistently run large trade deficits, absorbing much
of the overproduction from the rest of the world. Within the US economy, demand
expansion has relied mostly upon debt-financed consumption (that is, through rising C-W). The situation was already unsustainable by the early 2000s. But the US
Federal Reserve attempted to prolong the expansion by fueling a massive housing
bubble, paving the way for the 2008-2009 economic crisis.[5]

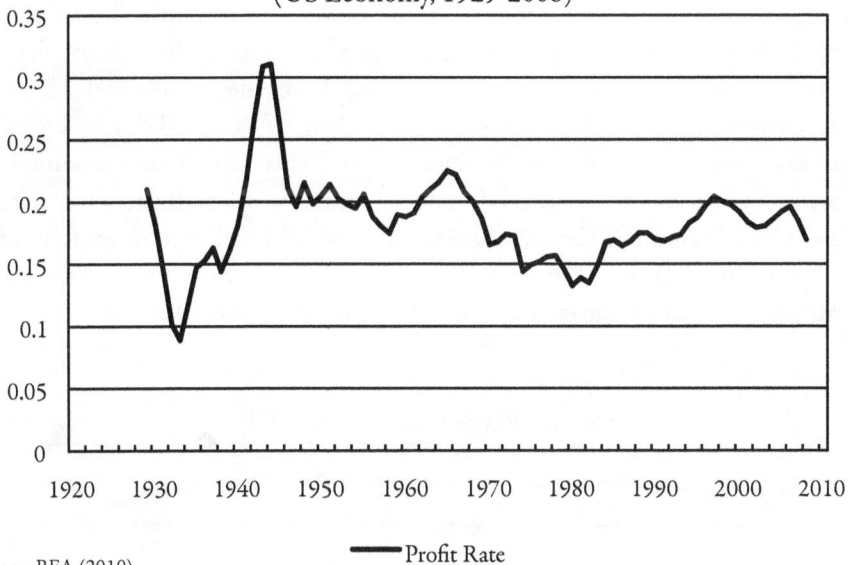

Figure 2. The Profit Rate
(US Economy, 1929-2008)

Source: BEA (2010).   ▬▬ Profit Rate

"Exit Strategies" for Capitalism?

To save global capitalism, all major capitalist governments have responded
with massive increases in fiscal deficits. In terms of the profit determination formula
discussed above, this amounts to an effort to substitute (G-T) for (C-W) to sustain
capitalist profits. The problem is that such a strategy will simply substitute fiscal
crises for private debt crises. According to the Bank of International Settlements,
by 2011 the general government debt to GDP ratio is expected to approach 100
percent in France, Portugal and the United Kingdom; 130 percent in Greece and
Italy; and exceed 200 percent in Japan (Cecchetti, Mohanti, and Zampolli 2010).
In fact, several Southern European countries (Greece, Spain, Portugal, and Italy) are

---

[5]   For detailed discussions on the structural contradictions of neoliberalism, see Crotty (2000) and Li (2009).

now threatened with imminent fiscal bankruptcy. In a few years, major capitalist countries such as the US and UK may have to confront an explosive fiscal crisis.

The current dilemma for Western capitalism, then, is the following. If Western capitalist governments respond to the fiscal crisis by imposing massive fiscal austerity programs (through cutting social spending and increasing taxes on the working classes), it would dramatically reduce global effective demand. This would, at best, result in a period of prolonged stagnation throughout the advanced capitalist world and, at worst, trigger a collapse of the global economy. On the other hand, if Western governments fail to address the fiscal crisis in accordance with the dictates of financial markets, financial capitalists may respond with massive sales of government bonds, leading to surging interest rates and economic collapses. In this context, the so-called "emerging markets" (such as China, India, Russia, Eastern Europe and Latin America and especially China), have emerged as a major pillar of global economic growth. Figure 3 presents the share of world GDP of the world's major economies. In 2008, the US, Eurozone and Japan combined accounted for 42 percent of the world's total GDP (and US accounted for 20 percent). The so-called "BRIC" countries (Brazil, Russia, India, and China) combined accounted for 22 percent of world GDP (and China accounted for 11 percent). Can China sustain global economic growth in spite of Western stagnation?

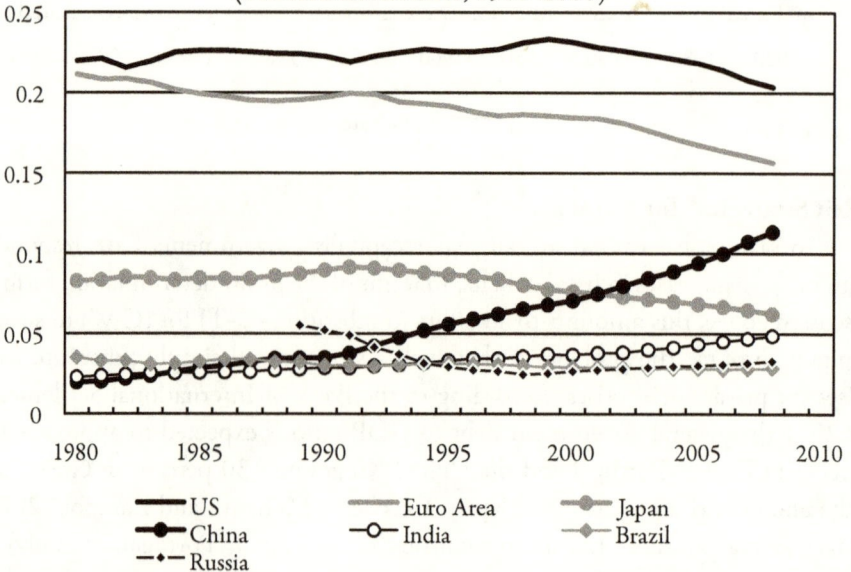

Figure 3. Share of World GDP
(Selected Economies, 1980-2008)

Source: World Bank (2010).

Figure 4 presents China's changing macroeconomic structure. Household consumption as a share of China's GDP declined from about 50 percent in the 1980s to about 35 percent by 2008 (by comparison, in the US household consumption accounts for about 70 percent of GDP). The relative decline of consumption reflects the fact that Chinese working class incomes have fallen behind the growth of GDP. According to the official Chinese General Federation of Labor survey, labour income as a share of China's GDP declined from 57 percent in 1983 to 37 percent in 2005. Further, according to the survey, in an economy with double-digit growth, about a quarter of the labour force has not seen any wage growth over the past five years. About 75 percent of workers believe the current income distribution in China is "unjust" and about 60 percent of workers believe excessively low labour income represents the greatest social injustice (Xin Jing Bao 2010). On the other hand, capital formation (investment) as a share of China's GDP increased from 35 percent in 2000 to 44 percent in 2008, and net exports as a share of China's GDP increased from 2 percent in 2001 to 8 percent in 2008. From 2001 to 2008, China's total merchandise exports (not subtracting imports) increased from 20 percent of GDP to 33 percent of GDP. Thus, before the recent crisis, China's economic growth was led primarily by investment and exports.

Figure 4. China's Macroeconomic Structure
(Share of GDP, 1980-2008)

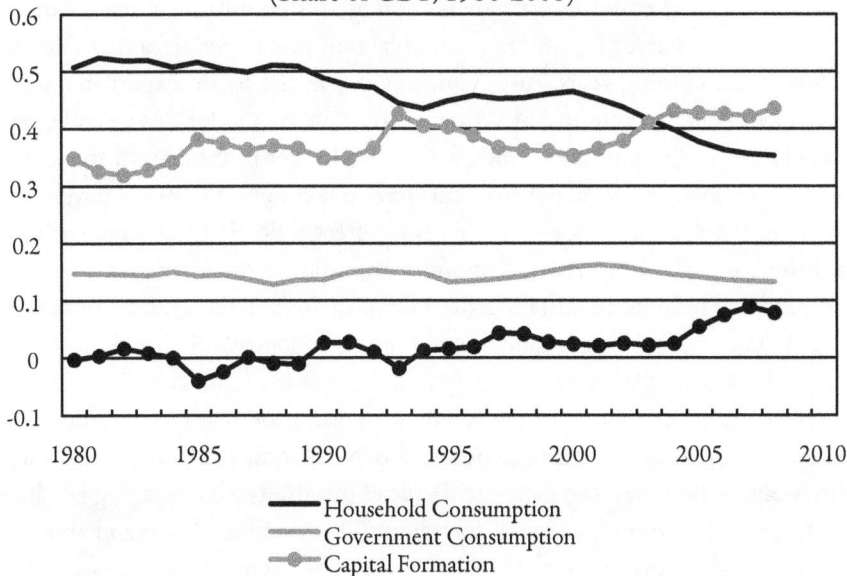

Household Consumption
Government Consumption
Capital Formation

Source: State Statistical Bureau (2009).

During 2009, in the midst of global economic crisis, Chinese exports deceler-
ated sharply. Total merchandise exports fell by 16 percent from 2008. China's trade
surplus fell from $196 billion in 2008 to $102 billion in 2009, falling by 48 percent. Investment emerged as China's only remaining engine of economic growth.
From 2008 to 2009, China's total fixed investments increased from 17.3 trillion
Yuan to 22.5 trillion Yuan (or an increase of 5.2 trillion Yuan). China's nominal
GDP increased from 31.4 trillion Yuan to 33.5 trillion Yuan (or an increase of 2.1
trillion Yuan). Increase in total fixed investments thus accounted for 240 percent of
China's economic growth in 2009 (that is, the increase in fixed investments more
than offset declines in consumption and net exports to have sustained economic
growth) (State Statistical Bureau 2010a).

In early 2010, China's economic growth continued to be led by investment.
Over the first four months of 2010, total urban fixed investments increased by
26 percent from the same period in 2009 (about twice as fast as overall economic
growth). However, excessively high investment has by now built up enormous excess capacity in productive sectors. Unable to profit from productive investment
any more, Chinese capitalists are shifting a growing proportion of capital into property and financial speculation. Over the first four months of 2010, about 21 percent
of the fixed investments went to real estate development, which increased by 36
percent from the same period in 2009 (State Statistical Bureau 2010b).

Andy Xie, the former chief Asian economist of Morgan Stanley, recently commented that China could face major economic and political instabilities in a few
years. It is likely that China will face rising labour, raw materials and environmental costs in the coming years. Also, China's share in the world export market may
shrink against the background of Western economic stagnation. As a result, capital
accumulation in the productive industries is no longer profitable. In this context,
Chinese capitalists and local governments have relied upon real estate development
to prolong the economic boom. China is in effect following the same path as Japan, Korea, and Southeast Asian economies once did. These Asian economies relied
upon property bubbles to sustain economic growth after the export boom ended.
Xie (2010) has argued that in a few years, China's property bubble will likely burst,
leaving China with a stagnant economy and threatening China's political stability.

The basic contradiction of the neoliberal global economy is that under neoliberalism, working class incomes and purchasing power tends to be depressed and liberalized capital flows tend to generate financial instability, discouraging productive
investment and government social spending. Global effective demand thus tends
to be depressed. Many national capitalist economies attempt to overcome this contradiction by promoting export-led growth. But for much of the world to pursue
export-led growth, there will have to be economies that are willing to run large

trade deficits. In the deficit countries, either the private sector or the government has to run large deficits, leading to rising private or public debts over time. Sooner or later, the deficit countries will be hit by financial crises as rising debts become unsustainable. During the current "recovery", this basic contradiction has not in any way been resolved. On the contrary, fiscal deficits in Western countries and China's real estate bubble are setting up the world for a potentially more devastating crisis. How will the evolving global capitalist crisis affect the conditions of global class struggle? This is the basic political question confronting global working classes.

What Has Happened to the Grave Diggers of Capitalism?

In the *Communist Manifesto*, Marx and Engels famously predicted that capitalist development would inevitably lead to the growth of the proletarianized working class and prepare the necessary conditions for the working class to organize economically and politically. As the organized working classes grow in size and strength, they argued, eventually they will prove themselves the grave diggers of capitalism (Marx and Engels 1978). Nearly one and a half centuries after the *Communist Manifesto*, what has happened? The late 19th and early 20th century saw the rapid growth of working class movements and socialist political parties throughout Europe. However, as Western working class movements gained strength politically, their stake in the existing capitalist system has also increased. Reformist tendencies (known as "revisionism") gradually became dominant within the European socialist parties (the "Second International" parties). After the Second World War, European socialist parties officially abandoned revolutionary objectives and committed themselves to incremental reforms within the capitalist system.

The Russian Bolshevik Party was the only major party within the "Second International" that remained committed to the revolutionary overthrow of capitalism. During the First World War, Lenin attempted to analyze and understand the phenomenon of "revisionism". Lenin argued that in the "imperialist" era, Western capitalism benefited from "super profits" exploited from the colonies and semi-colonies. The Western capitalists would then use a portion of the super profits to buy off the working class leaders, or the "labor aristocracies". Lenin argued that the colonial super profits constituted the material basis of revisionism (Lenin, 1916). After the Second World War, a growing Marxist literature followed the Leninist tradition and further argued that because of "unequal exchanges" and the operations of the "capitalist world system", Western capitalist wealth had been largely based on the exploitation of the peripheries. The so-called "technological revolutions" had basically been different ways to create world market monopolies that would allow a few "core" capitalist states to extract surplus value from the rest of the world (Emmanuel, 1972; Amin, 1974; Wallerstein, 1979).

However, neither the super profits nor the unequal exchanges had succeeded in maintaining permanent social peace in the West. Through long-term economic and political struggles, the Western working classes had been able to secure important concessions from the capitalist classes, winning a growing range of economic, social, and political rights. By the 1960s, these working class gains had begun to put pressure on capitalist profits, threatening to undermine the basic conditions of capitalist accumulation. Neoliberalism was the global capitalist response to this crisis. Neoliberalism is a significant world historical development. It clearly demonstrates that global capitalism has developed to such a point that it is no longer possible for capitalism to simultaneously meet the basic requirements of capital accumulation while accommodating the historically determined demands of the working classes in the core capitalist states. In other words, the second international reformism (or the social contract) that had secured basic social peace within Western capitalism since the mid-20th century has run into irreconcilable contradictions and is therefore historically bankrupt.

Another major development in the neoliberal era has to do with the changing balance of global economic forces. The relocation of global capital to exploit cheap labour forces in the "emerging markets" has been a major component of the neoliberal project. However this has led to the large formations of working classes in the "semi-periphery" (the geographical zone in the capitalist world system that has a position, in terms of the world division of labour and political strength, between the core and the periphery). Over time, the semi-periphery working classes will demand economic, social and political rights comparable to those enjoyed by the Western working classes. This development, once it happens, will presumably dismantle the global system of unequal exchange (which has been based on the super exploitation of the peripheral working classes) and therefore destroy the material foundation of Western labor aristocracies.

The current intensification of class struggles, such as in Europe, could thus mark the beginning of a new historical era. It is no longer possible for European capitalism to accommodate both the historically established "social contracts" (most importantly pensions and health care commitments) and the requirements of capital accumulation. This contradiction has manifested itself in the form of fiscal crises throughout Europe. The European capitalist classes are now attempting to impose the entire burden of adjustment onto the working classes in order to reestablish favourable conditions for capital accumulation by creating a new regime of cheap labour. The current struggle is therefore a life-and-death question for both the capitalist classes and the working classes. For the working classes, they will have to either fight back or eventually accept the loss of the historic gains made since the 19th century. Indeed, it is quite possible that the European working classes might lose the impending battle. The basic problem is that after a century of dominance of social democratic reformism, currently no effective revolutionary political force is playing a significant role in European working class politics. As a result, the European working classes have politically failed to break free from the historical limitations of capitalism, in the process coming to terms with capital. If the capitalist classes succeed in depriving the European workers of their historic gains, their "victory" could yet prove to be no more than a pyrrhic one. If the capitalist classes manage to impose massive declines of living standards onto the European working classes, this would dramatically reduce the European-wide effective demand and, in turn, reduce the export demand for "emerging market" economies. The decline of global effective demand could then lead to a global depression. As such, the economic crisis could then evolve into a general social and political crisis.

Under the second possible scenario, some effective revolutionary political forces may emerge in Europe in the next few years, breaking the current political stalemate. Under this scenario, the European working classes would undertake effective, unified struggles to make a decisive break with the existing capitalist order, moving towards the general socialization of the basic means of production and democratization of state power (in other words, establishing the "dictatorship of the proletariat"). The new socialist powers would then redirect the economy towards meeting peoples' basic needs and ecological sustainability. If such a scenario does unfold, Europe could emerge as the center of the 21st century global socialist revolution. The most likely scenario, though, is for Europe to repeat the pattern that has been established in the neoliberal era. The European working classes would wave off defensive struggles against capitalist attacks. As a result, the European working classes would suffer from some declines in living standards but manage to maintain most of their historic gains. The setbacks for the working classes, however, would prove to be inadequate to revive the European capitalism which would sink into an increasingly deeper accumulation crisis. In other words a slow motion, but increasingly deeper, vicious circle.

From a global perspective, under such a scenario, the European working classes would play an important role in weakening but not defeating global capitalism. The decisive battleground of global class struggle will then likely take place in other parts of the world. It is the global semi-periphery (China, India, Russia, and Latin America) that could prove to be the focus of global capitalist contradictions. Over the past two or three decades, capitalist development in the semi-periphery has depended upon (to different degrees) super exploitation of a cheap domestic labour force, intensive exploitation of material resources and the environment, based on exports to Western markets. These factors are no longer possible. In the coming years, the semi-peripheral capitalist economies will probably encounter shrinking

Western markets, rising tides of working class struggle, resource depletion and an increasingly devastating environmental crisis. The combination of these contradictions may lead to the breakdown of the semi-peripheral capitalist regimes and potentially a general revolutionary crisis. The surge of revolutionary struggles in the semi-periphery could decisively change the dynamics of global class struggle.

China: the Key Battleground of Global Class Struggle?

Within the semi-periphery, China may emerge as the key battleground. China is already the world's second largest economy and under the current trend will replace the U.S. to become the world's largest economy within a decade. In the neoliberal era, China has become the centre of global industrial production, playing a central role in the global division of labor. China has become one of the major markets of energy and raw materials for Latin America, the Middle East, Russia, and Africa. China is the main importer of capital goods from Germany, Japan and South Korea. China is also the leading supplier of low and medium-valued manufactured goods to the world market, especially to the U.S. market. In a way, then, the entire global capitalist market now works around China. Likewise, China is also at the very centre of global ecological contradictions. Chinese capitalist development has caused enormous devastation to China's own environment and China has overtaken the U.S. to become the world's largest energy consumer and greenhouse gas emitter. As China now accounts for fully one quarter of the world's total carbon dioxide emissions, it is virtually impossible to resolve the global climate change crisis without China being committed to large absolute emission reductions. How did China turn from a revolutionary socialist state in the 1960s and 1970s into a major pillar of global capitalism today? In short, after the counter-revolutionary coup in 1976 (when radical Maoist leaders were arrested), the emerging bureaucratic capitalist class took over and consolidated political power.

In the 1980s, the state sector working class continued to enjoy many socialist rights and remained strong at the factory level. Instead of organizing a direct, frontal attack on the working class that would be politically costly and might not succeed, the Chinese bureaucratic capitalist class adopted—in line with Mao's revolutionary approach—a strategy of surrounding the cities with the countryside. China's "economic reform" started with the privatization of agriculture. With the dismantling of the collective peoples' communes, hundreds of millions of "surplus workers" in the rural areas were made available for capitalist exploitation. Foreign and domestic capitalist enterprises grew explosively, profiting from China's cheap labor force, low taxes and lack of social and environmental regulations. By the 1990s, the capitalist sector has overtaken the state sector to become the dominant economic force. The Chinese government was ready to push for massive privatization in the cities. Tens of millions of state workers were laid off. Those who were employed were deprived of any remaining socialist protections. However, the very success of Chinese capitalism may have prepared the conditions for its eventual downfall. First of all, the state sector working class (including the laid off state sector workers) has developed political experience in both the socialist period and the capitalist period. This rich historical experience has contributed to a dramatic increase in class consciousness and organizational capacity among China's state sector workers. In recent years, the state sector workers have organized many anti-privatization struggles and many are led by activists influenced by Marxist-Leninist-Maoist ideas.[6]

By contrast, the migrant working class (the workers who have their origin in the countryside and work in the new capitalist sector) remains politically inexperienced. In recent years, however, migrant workers have also developed the consciousness to demand more economic and social rights (not yet political rights or socialism). As Chinese capitalist accumulation continues to deplete rural surpluses of labour and a new generation of migrants increasingly considers themselves as "workers" rather than "peasants", the objective balance of class power could increasingly shift in favour of the working class, encouraging migrant workers to get organized and fight for economic and social rights. In addition, under capitalist development, many among the petty bourgeoisie (or the urban "middle class") have also suffered from declining living standards. Many cannot afford to buy an apartment in the city. Several college graduates cannot find jobs and have to live in slum-like conditions. The proletarianization of the petty bourgeoisie has contributed to the rise of the intellectual left in China. A growing number of young people have turned into Marxist-Leninist-Maoists. The future of China depends on whether political unity can be developed between state sector workers, migrant workers and the proletarianized petty bourgeoisie. If such a unity does take shape, it may become a political force that the Chinese capitalist class cannot defeat. Is it conceivable that the Chinese capitalist class could undertake certain social reforms to accommodate rising class tensions and redirect Chinese capitalism onto a more "sustainable" path?

Over the past few years, the Hu Jintao-Wen Jiabao administration has been discussing building a so-called "harmonious society" with less inequality. In reality, despite some minor policy adjustments, economic and social inequality has continued to widen. For several reasons, meaningful social reform is unlikely to be achieved. First, much of the Chinese capitalist wealth has its origin in the theft of state and collective assets from the socialist era. The entire ruling class is thoroughly corrupt and, at the local level, political power increasingly rests upon cooperation

---

[6]   On the class consciousness and anti-privatization struggle of the state sector workers, see Weil (2010).

with local mafias. In this context, the central government has little ability to disci-pline the ruling class. Even if the central government cares about the long-term sus-tainability of capitalism, it does not have the ability or will to force any significant capitalist group to make major concessions. Second, despite the rapid growth of the Chinese economy, China has failed to make inroads into the truly high value added segments of global commodity chains. China now relies upon foreign capital for almost all key technological areas in industry. Without access to the monopolistic profits associated with the high value added activities, Chinese capitalism will have to rely upon cheap labour forces to maintain its global "competitive advantage". In the future, as the Chinese working class gets organized and demands a grow-ing range of rights, Chinese capitalism may no longer be able to maintain social stability without in some way undermining capitalist accumulation.[7] Third, and potentially the most important, both Chinese capitalist accumulation and global capitalist accumulation have rested upon the relentless exploitation of the environ-ment. As the global ecological system approaches total collapse, any further expan-sion of capitalism is now in fundamental conflict with the long-term survival of the humanity.

Global Catastrophes or "Exit Strategies" for Humanity?

In *Socialism: Utopian and Scientific*, Engels summarized the basic contradic-tion of capitalism as one between objective socialization of production and the capitalist system of private appropriation. This contradiction had led to increasingly more violent crises, demonstrating the inherent conflict between capitalist relations of production and the objective development of social productive forces. Such a contradiction could only be resolved through the establishment of a more demo-cratic and egalitarian form of social relations of production, based on social owner-ship of the means of production and rational economic planning. In other words, socialism (Engels, 1978 [1880]). For classical Marxists, socialism would prove to be a superior social system by developing social productive forces more rationally than capitalism. However, the greatest challenge confronting humanity today is no longer economic crisis but the fact that after centuries of relentless capital accumu-lation the global ecological system is now on the verge of complete collapse.

Consider the following aspects of the global ecological crisis (Climate Action Tracker 2010; Speth 2010; Wild 2010):

• According to the "Climate Action Tracker," the climate actions pledged by a good many national governments will commit the world to a warming of 3

---

[7] On how China has failed to rise to the technology frontier, see Hart-Landsberg (2010).

degrees Celsius by the end of the 21st century, steering the world onto a path of unprecedented catastrophes.

- According to the United Nations, by 2025 about 1.8 billion people will be living in countries with absolute water scarcity and about two-thirds of the world population could be under conditions of water stress.

- The world is currently losing soil 10 to 20 times faster than it is being replenished, threatening the very foundation of world agriculture.

- A recent Foreign Policy article argued that the world could face peak phosphorus production in the near future. Phosphorus is a key input in the production of fertilizers. The authors warned that "if we fail to meet this challenge, humanity faces a Malthusian trap of widespread famine on a scale that we have not yet experienced."

- About half the world's wetlands and a third of the mangroves are gone. An estimated 90 percent of large predatory fish are gone, and 75 percent of marine fisheries are now over-fished or fished to capacity.

- Twenty percent of ocean corals are gone and another 20 percent are severely threatened. Half the world's temperate and tropical forests no loner exist. Species are disappearing at rates about 1,000 times faster than normal.

How may the rapidly developing global ecological crisis be dealt with? Apologists claim that capitalism may be made "sustainable" or "green" by promoting "green technologies" or "eco-efficiency". This argument may be illustrated by the following "IPAT" formula:

$$I = P * A * T$$

The formula suggests that environmental impacts (T) are determined by population (P), "affluence" (A, that is, GDP per capita), and technology (T, which measures the environmental impact per unit of GDP). According to basic laws of ecology, ecological sustainability requires stable or falling environmental impacts. According to the IPAT formula, unlimited economic growth (that is, capital accumulation) can be made compatible with ecological sustainability if technological progress leads to increasingly higher eco-efficiency, that is, falling T, which presumably falls more rapidly than the growth of GDP. The fundamental problem with the "green capitalist" argument is that it fails to understand, on the one hand, why under capitalism there has been a powerful tendency towards endless accumulation of capital and, on the other hand, the insurmountable physical and political-economic limitations of "eco-efficiency" as a countervailing factor. All human civilizations have been based on the existence of a substantial surplus product (the part of total social product that is above the population's basic consumption and the means of production required to maintain society's simple reproduction). In pre-capitalist societies, the surplus product was used by ruling elites primarily for luxury consumption and various wasteful activities (such as war, religious rituals, or grand imperial projects), leaving little for the expansion of production.

Modern capitalism is unique in that it is the only socio-economic system that has ever existed in human history where market relations have become dominant in every aspect of social life. The dominance of market relations leads to universal and unending competition between producers, forcing every producer to use a substantial portion of the surplus-value (profit) to engage in capital accumulation and expand the scale of production. This dynamic, once it is dominant, becomes a self-sustaining economic force reproducing itself on increasingly larger scales. In the world market, world-wide competition forces all national states to pursue as much economic growth as possible. Those nations that fail to compete often suffer economic and political crises or are defeated militarily. Against this powerful tendency towards unlimited capital accumulation (represented by increasingly larger P and A), what has been the counteracting force?

Green capitalist advocates argue that market functions generate the most efficient economic system. For such a view, resource scarcity through rising prices will stimulate innovation leading to resource-saving technologies that can lower T and offset the growth of P and A. This argument, however, was found to be flawed as early as the 19th century by British economist William Stanley Jevons. Jevons argued that any resource-saving technology, by temporarily reducing the consumption of a resource, would lead to lower price, which would then encourage people to consume more of the resource. The perverse phenomenon was known as the "Jevons Paradox". Jevons' paradox could explain why in reality, despite improvements in resource efficiency (that is, falling resource consumption per unit of economic output), overall resource consumption keeps growing persistently.[8] Natural resources are, after all, "priced" in a capitalist economy, however flawed the pricing mechanisms might be. By contrast, generations of material waste from human activities or human pollutants are treated as "free" by capitalist markets. In economic terms, the ecological system is treated as an "externality" that is considered to have zero costs

---

[8]   For an explanation of Jevons' Paradox, see Orford (2010).

in a free market system. In a capitalist system, government regulations provide the only countervailing mechanism against externalities. However, as environmental regulations tend to increase the costs associated with accumulation, governments will typically only regulate those pollutants that do not significantly affect business profitability. Thus, even on national scales, government environmental regulations are often inadequate and ineffective.

On a global scale, any national capitalist economy that seriously regulates the environment will increase its own accumulation costs and suffer a competitive disadvantage in the global market. Thus, when the question concerns global environmental problems (such as climate change), few capitalist economies are willing to undertake the necessary actions. International agreements are supposed to help solve this dilemma by sharing the costs among national capitalist states. However, major capitalist powers rarely agree upon how the costs should be shared and few want to contemplate any restrictions on their own accumulation. The recent United Nations conference fiasco on Climate Change at Copenhagen demonstrates this clearly. In addition to the political-economic limits on "T", there are also fundamental physical-ecological limits. All human economic activities have to do with either physical or chemical transformations of the natural world, and thus necessarily require the consumption of material resources and lead to the generation of material wastes. It is therefore not possible to invent an economic activity with zero environmental impacts. Unlimited economic growth will inevitably lead to unlimited environmental impacts. In the long run, the only way to achieve ecological sustainability is to develop an economy with stable material flows (or a "steady-state" economy) that can meet the world population's basic needs and are consistent with the normal operations of ecological systems. The capitalist system is taking humanity down the path of global ecological catastrophe, which threatens the destruction of civilization. At this critical threshold of the early 21st century, what will be humanity's "exit strategy" for survival?

Under capitalism, society's surplus product is under the control of many big and small capitalists that engage in ruthless competition against one another. This competition generates an enormous, immensely irrational social force that is beyond any individual capitalist's control, forcing businesses to pursue ruthless exploitation of both nature and humanity. The only way for humanity to escape this ridiculous trap, an enormous irony of alienation (that the very social force created by human beings is now turned against humanity itself), is to establish society's collective and self-conscious control over the social surplus product—that is to say, over the economy and over the makeup of society itself. As classical Marxism argued, this control would in turn require social ownership of the means of production and the development of democratic, rational economic planning that determines the size, composition and use of society's surplus product. It is often claimed that the critics of capitalism have failed to provide a viable alternative to capitalism. This shortcoming is allegedly a fatal flaw that invalidates any attempt to move beyond capitalism. Such a claim, however, despite its vacuousness, only remains valid or legitimate so long as the capitalist system remains a viable historical option. Since the continued operation of capitalism is now in fundamental conflict with the survival of the ecosphere and humanity, the terms of debate have been fundamentally transformed.

References

Amin, Samir. 1974. *Accumulation on a World Scale: A Critique of the Theory of Underdevelopment*. New York and London: Monthly Review Press.

BEA. US Bureau of Economic Analysis. 2010. *National Income and Product Account Tables* and *Fixed Assets Tables*. Website: http://www.bea.gov.

Cecchetti, Stephen G., M. S. Mohanty, and Fabrizio Sampolli. 2010. "The Future of Public Debt: Prospects and Implications." Website: http://www.bis.org/publ/work300.pdf.

Climate Action Tracker. 2010. "High Chance to Exceed 3°C Despite Recent Developments." Website: http://www.climateactiontracker.org.

Crotty, James. 2000. "Trading State-Led Prosperity for Market-Led Stagnation: from the Golden Age to Global Neoliberalism." The Political Economy Research Institute of University of Massachusetts Amherst, Published Study 7. Website: http://www.peri.umass.edu/fileadmin/pdf/published_study/PS7.pdf.

Emmanuel, Arghiri. 1972. *Unequal Exchange: A Study of the Imperialism of Trade*. New York: Monthly Review Press.

Engels, Friedrich. 1978[1880]. "Socialism: Utopian and Scientific," in Robert C. Tucker (ed.), *The Marx-Engels Reader*, pp. 683-717. New York: W. W. Norton & Company.

Gordon, David M., Thomas Weisskopf, and Samuel Bowles. 2007. "Power, Accumulation, and Crisis: the Rise and Demise of the Postwar Social Structure of Accumulation," in The Union for Radical Political Economics, *The Imperiled Economy*, book 1, pp. 43-58. New York: Monthly Review Press.

Hart-Landsberg, Martin. 2010. "The Chinese Reform Experience: A Critical Assessment." *Review of Radical Political Economics* (forthcoming).

IMF. International Monetary Fund. 2010. *World Economic Outlook Update*, July 2010. Website: http://www.imf.org/external/ns/cs.aspx?id=29.

Lenin, Vladimir Ilyich. 1916. *Imperialism, the Highest Stage of Capitalism*. Website: http://www.marxists.org/archive/lenin/works/1916/imp-hsc.

Li, Minqi. 2009. *The Rise of China and the Demise of the Capitalist World Economy*. London: Pluto Press; New York: Monthly Review Press.

Li, Minqi, Feng Xiao, and Andong Zhu. 2007. "Long Wages, Institutional Changes, and Historical Trends: A Study of the Long-Term Movement of the Profit Rate in the Capitalist World-Economy." *Journal of World Systems Research* XIII:1: 33-54.

Maddison, Angus. 2003. *The World Economy: Historical Statistics*. Paris: Organisation for Economic Co-operation and Development.

Marx, Karl and Friedrich Engels. 1978[1848]. "Manifesto of the Communist Party," in Robert C. Tucker (ed.), *The Marx-Engels Reader*, pp. 469-500. New York: W. W. Norton & Company.

Minsky, Hyman P. 2008[1986]. *Stabilizing an Unstable Economy*. New York: McGraw-Hill.

Orford, Lionel. 2010. "Jevons' Law: Enforcing the Age of Energy Decline." Website: http://www.energybulletin.net/node/51158.

Speth, Gus. 2010. "Towards a New Economy and a New Politics." Website: http://www.energybulletin.net/node/53202.

State Statistical Bureau, People's Republic of China. 2009. *Statistical Yearbook of China 2009*. Website: http://www.stats.gov.cn.

____. 2010a. *Zhonghua Renmin Gongheguo 2009 Nian Guomin Jingji he Shehui Fazhan Tongji Gongbao* (Statistical Communiqué of the People's Republic of China on National Economic and Social Development 2009). Website: http://www.stats.gov.cn/tjgb/ndtjgb/qgndtjgb/t20100225_402622945.htm.

____. 2010b. *"4 Yuefen Guomin Jingji Zhuyao Zhibiao Shuju* (The Main Indicators of the National Economy in April)", May 11, 2010. Website: http://www.stats.gov.cn/tjfx/jdfx/t20100511_402641475.htm.

Wallerstein, Immanuel. 1979. *The Capitalist World-Economy*. Cambridge: Cambridge University Press.

Weil, Robert. 2010. "A House Divided: China after 30 Years of 'Reforms'," in Economic and Political Weekly (ed.), *China After 1978*, pp. 209-232. Hyderabad, India: Orient BlackSwan.

Wild, Matthew. 2010. "Peak Soil – It Is Like Peak Oil, Only Worse." Website: http://www.energybulletin.net/52788.

World Bank. 2010. *World Development Indicators Online*. Website: http://data.worldbank.org/data-catalog/world-development-indicators.

Xie, Andy. 2010. "Trapped inside a Property Bubble," January 10, 2010. Website: http://english. caing.com/2010-01-10/100106991.html.

Xin Jing Bao (New Beijing Daily). 2010a. "*Laodong Baochou Zhan GDP Bili Lianxu 22 Nian Xia-jiang, Yi Yingxiang Shehui Wending* (Labor Income Share of GDP Had Fallen for 22 Years, Threatening Social Stability)", May 12, 2010. Website: http://finance.eastmoney.com/ news/1346,2010051275119040.html.

European Capitalism: Varieties of Crisis

Ingo Schmidt

Abstract: The article rejects the notion that countries of the EU periphery, some of which were recently labelled as PIIGS, are prone to fiscal and sovereign debt crises because of spend-thrifty governments and their negative impact on private investments. As an alternative to such views, the article argues that the EU periphery is prone to crisis because its economies can't successfully compete with exports from core countries, especially Germany. It will also be argued that world market integration in a time of economic stagnation, combined with an explosion of debt, speculation and recurrent financial crisis, is no way to overcome a country's peripheral position. These arguments will be developed on the basis of some mini case studies on core and peripheral EU member states.

Keywords: European capitalism, centre-periphery relations, fiscal crisis, sovereign debt crisis

Introduction

In the midst of the 2008/9 crisis of the world economy (European Commission 2009), a new term crept into financial parlance: PIIGS, short for: Portugal, Ireland, Italy, Greece, Spain. At that time, the broader public was still trying to understand the meaning of CDOs (Collateralized Debt Obligations), CDSs (Credit Default Swaps), and other fancy financial products including their role in the financial crisis. Governments and central bankers were busy working to contain a sharp recession and save private profits with huge infusions of zero-interest credit, government spending and bank bailouts. As a result of these efforts, the crisis of private finance and capital more generally was transformed into a fiscal crisis of the state. Neoliberal economists and media pundits happily used their chance to point at rapidly rising levels of public deficits and debt but downplayed the share of bank-bailouts in rising deficits. At the same time, they constructed the PIIGS to show how spend-thrifty governments run the risks of capital flight and state bankruptcy.

The old familiar message: States, not markets, are the problem. Since states can't be totally abolished—after all, they serve capital interests quite well as protectors of private property and spenders of last resort—one has to carefully distinguish between good and bad. Good states turn the fiscal tap off as soon as big money asks them to do so. Bad states are either unwilling or too weak to turn to austerity once big money sees that as a necessity. Bad states need to be punished by disinvestment that will deplete their finances and drive them into the arms of financial parole officers like the IMF who offer urgently needed credit at high interest rates and unwanted policy advice. Retired government officials from around the world, from then socialist Eastern Europe through the Global South to the Asian Tigers and post-Soviet Russia can tell of their experiences with fiscal and sovereign debt crisis and IMF-intervention. Yet, the Wall Street crash and its aftermath offered an ironic turn of capitalist history.

When the Dow Jones was plunging and investment banks were defaulting, a number of European governments used the chance to advocate their variety of regulated capitalism as superior to the American model of free market capitalism. Then German finance minister Steinbrück, a Third Way social democrat and usually a good Atlanticist, went so far as to proclaim the end of Dollar-supremacy. But then the PIIGS destroyed the European dream of a multilateral world in which American great power politics would be replaced by European multilateralism. Rising levels of public and foreign debt, the neoliberal argument went, put the PIIGS at risk of state bankruptcy.

In the spring 2010, Greece, apparently the weakest member of this group, came close to bankruptcy, indeed. However, the reason was neither an uncontrollable explosion of debt, nor runaway inflation that neoliberal theory presents as an inevitable by-product of government debt. The risk of the Greek state defaulting was produced by international financiers who, fired up by the neoliberal PIIGS-story, denied credit to the Greeks at a rate of interest that would have allowed continuing circulation of capital within the country and beyond its borders. A €110bn credit from the EU, which the IMF co-sponsored and enriched by a structural adjustment program, solved this acute fiscal and sovereign debt crises, momentarily at least. This intervention, which essentially represents another case of throwing public money at private finance, certainly satisfies the short-term interests of international financiers. Whether it helps to avoid recurrent crises in the future is another question though. In this article, it will be argued that the reasons for the Greek crisis (Moschovis, Servera 2009) were not the ones presented in the PIIGS-story.

This story neglects three factors that are crucial for an understanding of the Greek crisis. First, it does not recognize that the current account deficits of one country are matched by respective surpluses of other countries. Second, poor countries are not the only ones who produce deficits (European Commission 2010). Current accounts and public households in the US and Britain, to name just the most two outstanding examples, are as deep in the red as those of the average PIIGS-state. Third, governments and central banks can't freely choose to either run deficits or surpluses; they may try either way but the ultimate outcome of their efforts will be determined by the competition for world market share. This competition has considerably stiffened during the neoliberal era. During that era, some states, like Britain and the US, found out that they can afford to run deficits and actually make them part of their accumulation strategy while Greece and countless other peripheral countries, were pushed into deficits by stronger competitors and then found structural adjustment policies imposed onto them.

Presenting experiences from a number of EU countries, this article will look at centre – periphery relations, macroeconomic imbalances and the design of the EMU as key factors that can explain why speculative attacks against an economically small country like Greece, contributing about 2.5% to the EU's total GDP, translated into a severe crisis of European capitalism (European Central Bank 2010). These case studies will show how neoliberal capitalism could successfully be established in the West, in some cases against left strategies of socialist transformation, and invade Eastern Europe after the collapse of the Soviet empire. They will also show that the crisis of neoliberal capitalism in Europe takes on a variety of different forms, which depend on a countries' position in the hierarchy of states and world markets.

Case Studies on the Crisis of European Capitalism

The country sample under consideration here connects the core countries France, Germany, and the UK, to the peripheral country Greece, Ireland, and Hungary. Italy is included in this sample because its position as part of the EU core was recently challenged by its inclusion into the PIIGS-group.

In this sample, Germany is the bullying powerhouse that puts weaker economies under competitive pressure through the export-orientation of many of its companies and the hardcore neoliberalism its political class managed to inscribe into EU-institutions. German export success is often presented as the result of high savings, hard work, and long-term perspectives as opposed to the allegedly wasteful way of short-term speculation in the Anglo-Saxon world. However, while it is true that the financial markets in the US play a key role in neoliberal capitalism, and the City of London can certainly be seen as the European outpost of the Dollar-Wall-Street-Regime (Gowan 1999), it is also true that German capitalists happily funnel their money through the financial centres in London and New York. Thus, the picture of European capitalism would be incomplete without understanding how the UK, once the workshop of the world, developed into such a powerful centre of world finance.

The recurrent quests of France to complement the European Central Bank (ECB) and its political impact on accumulation with some sort of economic government on the EU level is often understood as a Keynesian alternative to the combined powers of Germany's export economy and British financial markets. Yet, it will be shown that French Keynesianism was defeated by the interplay of domestic and international forces in the early 1980s. Since then, French governments have embraced, not always as successfully as they were hoping, neoliberalism and seek to institute European economic policies in such a way that would compensate French capital for its competitive disadvantages vis-à-vis German export companies and British financial firms.

The Italian experience represents the significance of centre-periphery relations within the EU. On the one hand, Italian governments are constantly struggling to keep the country's place in the core group of EU powers, which didn't stop international finance from classifying Italy as part of the PIIGS. On the other hand, centre – periphery divisions within the country have posed a key problem of internal cohesion which has undermined Italy's position within the EU. The inability to overcome such divisions domestically contains some lessons for the future of the EU with its even deeper divisions between centres and peripheries.

Another variation of this theme is the Irish case. For a while, Ireland seemed to prove neoliberal claims according to which free trade within the EU would allow poor countries to catch-up to the rich countries. However, neither a temporary spurt in foreign direct investment nor a housing boom could prevent a US-style financial crisis in Ireland. Hopes to catch up with the rich were not only dashed in Ireland but in Hungary, too. Like other Eastern European countries after the collapse of the Soviet empire, Hungarians had to recognize that a place in the periphery was all the EU had for them.

The last of the mini case studies in this article looks at Greece, which is obvious because this was the first target among the PIIGS. Apart from that, Greece shows that even a country that could never aspire to escape its peripheral position can play key roles for the core countries. Greece's enormously big merchandise fleet and its strategic position as a NATO-outpost on the borders to the Muslim and Arabic worlds are indispensible for European capitalism and its American allies.

Germany: Export über alles

In the early 1990s, when the terms and conditions of European Monetary Union (EMU) were negotiated, the German export-model, which was established with US-support after WWII and maintained its dominant position in world markets even during the crisis-ridden 1970s and the growth slowdown of the 1980s, was under stress. Accession of formerly socialist East Germany to capitalist West Germany in 1990 had boosted domestic demand including government spending significantly and produced current account and public deficits that reminded the German bourgeoisie of the much despised Twin Deficits their American friends and mentors were running under Reagan and Bush senior. Germany's balance on current accounts deteriorated from a 4.2%-surplus 1986-90 to a -1.2%-deficit in 1991-95, public deficits increased from -1.4% to -2.8% over the same period.[1] In an attempt to reign in its deficits, regain current account surpluses and extend its mercantilist model of accumulation (Schmidt, 2007) to all prospective EMU members, the German government pushed for tight limits on public deficits and debts, 3% and 60% of GDP respectively, and a maximum inflation rate of 2% as a precondition of EMU membership. The institutionalization of austerity policies in the Maastricht Treaty, 1992, and the Stability and Growth Pact, 1997, helped Germany to re-start its export-oriented growth machine (see Tables 1&2) after recessions in 1993 and 2002/3. Constant pressures on government spending and wages kept inflation and unit labour costs low. Yet, the same means that spurred exports put a lid on domestic growth. As a result, current account surpluses were soaring, producing complementary deficits on the side of most of Germany's trading partners, and increasing the German economy's dependence on demand created elsewhere (Lapavitsas, 2010, ch. 2-4). This dependence on foreign markets notwithstanding, the German ruling class is clinging to its export-orientation and keeps on pointing at other countries' deficits as a source of financial instability, although they are largely a result of German export surpluses.

France: European integration as a means against German domination

French governments used European integration in the post-war period as a means to contain Germany's real or perceived appetites for dominance (Parsons, 2003). This was true for the 1950s European Steel and Coal Community that subordinated German heavy industries, the long-time economic backbone behind German imperialism, to multilateral control. French consent to the EMU, including Germany's austerity prescriptions, was also motivated by an attempt to tie post-unification Germany into multilateral institutions. German governments agreed to this kind of political containment by integration because they clearly understood that the US, the unchallenged though sometimes unloved leader of the Western bloc, supported Germany's transformation from a great political power into an economic export power.

---

[1]   All data in the text: European Commission.

Hosting the world's largest corporations and controlling the world's money, the US found it easier to cope with German export competition than the French. However, this does not mean that the French bourgeoisie was necessarily hostile to the monetarist principles that Germany used, even in the Keynesian era from the 1950s to the 1970s, to fuel its export machine. Faced with a socialist-communist coalition government that tried to stem the general tide from Keynesianism to Monetarism in the early 1980s, French capitalists were quite happy that the German Bundesbank's tight monetary policies put pressure on the French balance of payments. A perfect invitation to capital flight, which was then used to urge the socialists in the government to abandon their left-Keynesian program and offend their communist coalition partners (Lombard, 1995). The French bourgeoisie was as eager as their German, American and other counterparts to embrace neoliberalism. Thus, French quests for EU-wide coordination of macroeconomic policies are not inspired by attempts to pursue Keynesian policies but are a recognition of the superior competitiveness and market power of German export industries. Policy coordination, from this angle, is meant to contain current account deficits and its negative impact on domestic growth and employment. Considering how much the French balance on current account deteriorated since the introduction of the Euro in 1999, which eliminated the possibility to limit imports through currency devaluations (see Table 2), it is understandable that the current Euro-crisis was accompanied by French complaints about Germany's beggar-thy-neighbour policies and new quests for macroeconomic policy coordination within the EMU.

Britain: Euro-Dollars in the City rather than Euros all over Britain

While the post-war boom allowed Germany to emerge as an export powerhouse, British industries were struggling with underinvestment and permanent current account deficits. Unlike France, where similar deficits were caused by the late development of large corporations, compared to its main competitor Germany, British deficits were the result of relative industrial decline (Kitson, Michie, 1996). And whereas the French ruling class eventually decided to follow the German way of promoting national champions as core of their neoliberal model, the British bourgeoisie not only accepted but furthered industrial decline in favour of its financial sector (Radice, 1995). The shift from industrial production to financial industries was so successful that Britain—the City of London, to be more precise—could emerge as the European outpost of the Dollar Wall Street Regime (Gowan, 1999; Gowan, 2009). Obviously the City never enjoyed the close connections and support that the US Treasury offered, and still offers, to Wall Street. Yet, in one respect, the City was even more attractive to profit-hungry investors than Wall Street: its Euro-Dollar markets bypassed US regulations and thus offered the least political control over financial flows and holdings. Naturally, the British government was eager to maintain this competitive advantage and thus rejected EMU right from the start. Ironically, a number of multinational corporations that discovered Britain as a low cost and union free location in the 1990s advocated for British membership in the EMU in order to limit the costs and risks associated with exchange rate fluctuations. EMU membership would have helped to turn Britain into a major site of transplant production to serve EU markets. Yet, the City's successful resistance against such plans made Ireland a more attractive destination for foreign direct investments in the late 1990s and early 2000s.

Just as in the US, Britain's dominant position in international financial markets went hand in hand with a depletion of household savings, a surge in real estate prices and debt-financed consumption. Though the Tories had paved the way, the British bubble economy really took off under New Labour. Private Household savings declined from 4.7% of GDP in 1991-95 to 2.2% in 1996-2000 to -0.1% in 2001-5 (see also Table 3), while GDP growth went from 1.6% to 3.4% and 2.5% over the same period. Though not impressive, this is more than the German combination of exports and domestic austerity had accomplished (respective growth rates for Germany are: 2.2%, 2.0%, and 0.6%; see also Table 1). Because of Britain's leading position in international financial markets, the financial crisis hit the British economy earlier and harder than other countries. Crisis containment consequently needed much higher doses of fiscal stimulus, which brought the British deficit close to the levels reached by the financial superpower America and peripheral countries in Europe, such as Greece and Ireland (see Table 2).

Italy: Subordination to Euro-austerity to escape regional disparity

From its early days, Italian capitalism developed in a highly uneven way that led to a deep polarization between the industrial North and the rural South (Goldstein, 1998). In the 1960s, the Italian bourgeoisie thought about the use of the Keynesian state to overcome this North – South divide. Yet, because the bourgeoisie was fractured as the country was divided economically, no consensus towards such an industrial policy extension of Keynesian demand management could be reached. In the 1970s, the Italian communists picked up this project as a building bloc towards the historical compromise with the conservatives who had dominated Italian politics in the post-war period but were thrown into a crisis of legitimacy and strategic reorientation by the class struggles and economic crisis of the late 1960s and 1970s. Like in France and Britain, key organizations of the left sought to use industrial policies as a means of a gradual transformation from the Keynesian welfare state towards socialism. However, the Italian version of this strategy, Euro-communism, failed as much as the Common Program of the French Socialist and Communist Parties and the Alternative Economic Strategy of the British Labour Party.

The neoliberal turn in Italy abandoned attempts to overcome the North – South divide by political means and put praise for regional economies and industrial districts in its place (Piore, Sabel, 1984). However, while Northern Italy was integrated into emerging international supply chains, the Italian South remained as dependent on fiscal transfers from Rome as ever. Continuing divisions between the Northern core and its Southern periphery were a source for right-wing regionalism, political tensions, a clientele state and the concomitant accumulation of public debt. Eventually, export-oriented factions of the Italian bourgeoisie, in conjunction with the post-Keynesian socialist party, saw EMU as a chance to escape the negative impact that political instability, accumulation of debt and recurrent currency devaluations had on their strategy of integration into international supply-chains.

The outcomes of Italy's subordination to EMU's policy guidelines were mixed. Public deficits were reduced from -11.5% in 1986-90 to -9.0 in 1991-95 to -3.0 in 1996-2000, but growth also slowed from 3.1 to 1.3 and 1.9, respectively, over the same period. Unemployment went from 9.4 to 9.8 and 11.0, respectively. Slow growth since the introduction of the Euro helped to keep imports and thus current account deficits lower than in other countries that had higher growth rates. Thus, dependence on capital imports to finance such deficits is lower than in many of EU's peripheral member states, modest public deficits make the country a lesser target for speculative attacks like the one Greece experienced in the spring of 2010 (see Table 2). However, EMU membership was anything but a way to solve Italy's long-time problem of uneven development.

Ireland: Showcase of neoliberal development gone bust

Most, if not all, core and peripheral countries in Europe experienced a growth slowdown after the crisis-ridden 1970s. In this respect, they resemble core countries and peripheries in other parts of the world. However, at any point in time there were also countries that could escape the tendency to economic stagnation: Japan in the 1980s, the so-called Asian Tigers in the 1990s, and China from the 1980s until today. Ireland earned the title of Celtic Tiger because its growth accelerated from 3.8% in 1974-85 to 4.6% in 1986-90 to 4.7% in 1991-95 to a peak level of 9.6% in 1996-2000. Everything neoliberals ever said about free trade as a means to promote growth seemed to be true in Ireland. The European Single Market program, which was launched in the mid-1980s and completed in the 1990s, coincided with a surge of foreign direct investments (FDIs) and growth.

Neoliberal economists see enhanced possibilities to move capital across borders as a key to higher growth rates. Yet, if this would be true, Irish growth in the 1980s and 1990s should have been the European rule rather than its exception. Arguably, the Irish experience owes more to the accumulation strategies of US-corporations than to the growth-effects of free trade (O'Hearn, 2001). Parallel to Britain's transformation into the European outpost of the Dollar Wall Street Regime, Ireland became a prime location for low cost production within the European Single Market and, later, the EMU. Production in Ireland allowed US-corporations to bypass import restrictions that goods coming from outside the single market are still facing. Moreover, Irish membership in the EMU eliminated the risks associated with fluctuating exchange rates. Yet, the ensuing foreign investment boom led to increasing control of foreign corporations over Ireland's economic and social development and was also accompanied by increasing social polarization (Kirby, 2004). Even in purely economic terms, FDIs had questionable results. First, the high volatility of FDI-flows translates into an unstable process of capital formation (see Table 1). Second, a significant share of foreign and domestic capital fuelled a US-style housing and consumption boom that used up much of Ireland's private household savings (see Table 3). Third, though FDIs massively contributed to the build-up of export production capacities they also led to high levels of parts imports. Together with the import of consumer goods that were spurred by the combined booms in housing speculation and consumption, Ireland was barely able to run current account surpluses at the height of its boom in the late 1990s. In the early 2000s, its current account turned negative.

The boom in Ireland was dependent on FDI-inflows, soaring house prices and debt-financed consumption. The world economic crisis in 2008/9 led to net-outflows of FDIs and a collapse of the housing market that had been so vital in propping up consumption. The combined effect of FDI-outflows and a plunging housing market made the crisis in Ireland much more severe than in the US or Britain, two countries that were also confronted with housing bubbles going bust but weren't dependent on FDI-inflows like Ireland was (Kanda, 2010). As a result, unemployment doubled from 4.7% in 2007 to 11.9% in 2009. Fiscal stimulus and a collapse of tax revenue drove public deficits to levels higher than in Greece (see Table 2) and led to an explosion of public debt from 25% of GDP in 2007 to 64% in 2009. To contain the ensuing fiscal crisis and avoid outside intervention from the EU and/or IMF, the Irish government turned to pre-emptive austerity as early as late 2008 (IMF 2009). Most likely, these policies will trigger a period of stagnation, during which the government won't be able to successfully consolidate public finances because of insufficient tax revenues. No Western European country was flying as high as Ireland before the crisis, but no other country was affected as badly by the crisis either.

Hungary: Lost between the Soviet empire and the empire of capital

The implosion of the Soviet empire in the early 1990s led to a period of economic downturn and political instability across Eastern Europe. These were the
conditions under which new capitalist classes struggled to constitute and consolidate themselves. EU membership appeared as one of the ways to achieve this goal
(Green & Petrick, 1999). In this respect, Hungary is just one case in point (Andor,
2000). Like other Eastern European countries who found themselves on the periphery of world capitalism after the state socialist system was gone, the new Hungarian
ruling class thought of EU membership not just as a way to gain political stability
but also to attract foreign capital and promote economic growth (Barnes & Randerson, 2007). This strategy to 'import' stability and growth through EU, and possibly
EMU, membership is actually similar to Italian attempts of overcoming a domestic
deadlock of the political system through subordination to EMU policy guidelines
and Irish efforts to use the European Single Market as a springboard for FDI-led
growth. Such attempts failed in Hungary as they failed in Italy and Ireland.

In the early 2000s, Hungary did achieve growth rates of GDP and capital
formation that were significantly higher than the respective rates in core countries
of the EU (see Table 1). Thus, it seemed as if Hungary, along with some other
Eastern European countries, had taken the road towards European integration and
catch-up growth as successfully as Ireland had done two decades earlier. However,
the period of high growth was short and followed a sharp and prolonged downturn in the 1990s. Moreover, the integration of Hungary into the capitalist world
market went hand in hand with massive imports. Hungary's new rich were keen
on Western luxuries to demonstrate their new status, and capital formation on the
ruins of the former state socialist economy created a market for Western makers of
investment goods. As a result, Hungary's current account was deep in the red until 2008, when the combined effects of IMF-intervention (IMF 2010), which the
government called for in November 2008, and recession led to import reductions
that were significantly higher than the crisis-triggered decrease of exports (see Table
2). Another reason for the improvement of Hungary's current account position was
the return to currency devaluations. The Forint had massively depreciated against
the Euro and its predecessor-currencies during the 1990s and could be stabilized
in the early- and mid-2000s when Hungary's rulers were hoping to move from EU
membership, which they achieved along with nine other Eastern European countries in 2004, to the introduction to the Euro. The current crisis dashed such hopes.
At this point, the Hungarian government is busy enough to deal with IMF policies
and may actually be quite happy that it doesn't also have to deal with EMU policy
advice. Failure to join the EMU and catch up with the per-capita incomes of EU
core countries are not the only disappointments for Hungary's rulers and ordinary

citizens. Measures taken to achieve these goals have led to the country's domination by Western corporations and international organizations like the IMF and the EU. There was just a short moment of independence between the collapse of the Soviet empire and Hungary's integration into the Western empire of capital as a subordinate state and peripheral economy.

Greece: Weak economy in a strategic location

Greece didn't experience a phase of accelerated growth since the 1980s like some other countries of the European peripheries. Its growth pattern is more like that of core countries with a strong post-war boom, a growth slowdown in the 1970s and 1980s and a limited resurgence of growth in the 1990s and 2000s (Maniatis, 2005). Consumer spending that used up household savings drove this resurgence—the savings rate deteriorated from 3.9 in 1996/2000 to -5.8 in 2001/5 (see also Table 3)—and was increasingly dependent on credit financing. Because of a lack of domestic funding sources and production, consumption-driven growth was accompanied by increasing foreign debt and extraordinarily high current account deficits (see Table 2). Thus, Greece showed all symptoms of a peripheral country whose hopes for prosperity are long gone. Yet, this macroeconomic picture should not conceal Greek's strategic importance for European and other core countries of world capitalism. During the Cold War, Greece served as NATO-outpost on the Balkans and today it balances Turkish influence in the Middle East. Though the latter is also a NATO member because of its strategic location on the borders of the Soviet Union, now Georgia, and oil-rich Iran and Iraq, Western governments see Turkey with suspicion because of its mostly Muslim population. Greece's strategic role partly explains continuing public deficits and current account deficits: Relative to GDP, Greece spends more than double the amount of money on the military than the NATO average, which includes the chief-military spender US (Kollias & Rafailidis, 2003). Moreover, Greece shipping companies operate the largest merchandise fleet of any EU member by far (Unctad 2007). They own and control 40% of EU's and 15% of the world's carrying capacity and contribute around 8% to the Greek GDP. Control over merchandise trade has become increasingly important since world market integration and international supply chains became key ingredients of neoliberal capitalism.

The media campaign that accompanied speculation against Greece's sovereign debt in the spring of 2010, presented the country as one that is run by spend-thrifty and corrupt governments who faked deficit and debt figures to sneak into the EMU without actually matching its macroeconomic accession criteria. Corruption is certainly not a privilege of governments in Athens and the faking of economic data has been an integral part of high-flying stock markets in the centres of world capitalism before the crisis revealed the poor performance behind much fancy-fake data.

What media commentators fail to mention is that EU core countries were eager to get Greece on board the EMU to underscore the country's strategic position and get some level of control over its merchandise fleet. So important were these goals that even Germany's chief Monetarists didn't ask too many questions when they approved Greece's EMU membership. Of course, these days the Germans happily use the chance to use speculative attacks against Greece as a pretext to reinvent austerity as the sole means to overcome economic crisis.

Conclusions

Some conclusions can be drawn from the 'mini case studies' above. The first one is that macroeconomic imbalances within the EMU, and the EU more generally, are largely caused by Germany's efforts to spur exports and growth through wage restraint and other anti-inflationary policies. The downside of these export-boosting measures is that they limit domestic demand so that export-growth didn't translate into growth of overall-GDP but into increasing current account surpluses. This was only possible because demand growth in other countries was high enough to absorb German export surpluses without their governments turning towards protectionist measures to reign in their current account deficits. This group of foreign deficit countries includes not only peripheral countries like Greece, Hungary and Ireland but also the EU core countries Britain and France. The difference between core and periphery is not that the former are, with regards to their current accounts, surplus countries and the latter are deficit countries; the difference is that, in times of economic crisis, core countries have the power to intervene politically, either directly or through international organizations like the EU or the IMF, in the periphery. This is the reason why crisis-management in high-deficit countries like Britain and the US is left to the respective ruling and political classes of these countries, whereas peripheral countries with similar or even lower deficits are either faced with direct EU- or IMF-intervention, for example Greece and Hungary, or are threatened with such interventions if their governments shy away from pre-emptive austerity policies like the ones adopted by Ireland during the 2008/9 crisis.

The second conclusion is that the integration of peripheral countries into international supply chains and world markets did not allow them to gain the same strength that Germany could acquire through the making of its export economy during the post-war prosperity. The build-up of additional capacities for export production can contribute, in a world economy that is already plagued with overcapacities, to short-lived investment booms like the ones Ireland and Hungary experienced. But this neither helped their economies to gain any significant share in world markets nor their states to climb up in the international hierarchy of states.

The significant share of construction in Ireland's investment boom—one of the reasons why the Irish boom lasted longer than the one in Hungary—leads to the third conclusion that can be drawn from the case studies above. Ever larger overcapacities can only be avoided if consumer demand keeps up with increasing production capacities. Housing construction, concomitant surges of house prices and the expansion of consumer credit based on rising property values have been key for the growth of consumer demand over the last two decades. The US, though most prominent for its housing bubble and subprime crisis, was not the only country witnessing such housing-speculation and debt-driven increases in consumer demand. The same is true for Britain, Ireland, Spain and Japan. To be sure, the financial instruments used to prop up house prices and consumer-demand are largely 'Made on Wall Street'. The City of London was crucial in making them available to European countries including those of the Euro-zone. Far from representing an alternative to the unregulated and speculative world of the Dollar Wall Street Regime (Schmidt 2009a), EMU is well integrated into the US-dominated system of world finance. Without the bubble economies in the US, Britain and a number of peripheral economies, German export success would have been impossible. Monetarist economists are right, and surprisingly close to many of their Keynesian counterparts, when they point at the instability that such bubbles produce. Yet, this was the way neoliberal capitalism solved the problem of insufficient demand after a decade of crises in the 1970s—until another 'great crisis' hit the world in 2008 (Schmidt 2009b).

References

Andor, L. (2000). *Hungary on the Road to the European Union: Transition in Blue.* Westport: Praeger.

Barnes, I; Randerson, C. (2007): EU Expansion and the Political Economy of Former Communist States' Accession: The Case of Hungary's 'Convergence'. *Capital and Class*, Vol. 93, 179-197.

Bonacich, E.; Wilson, J. (2008): *Getting the Goods – Ports, Labor, and the Logistics Revolution.* Ithaca, London: Cornell University Press.

European Central Bank (2010): *Monthly Bulletin*, June 2010, Frankfurt.

European Commission (2009): Economic Crisis in Europe: Causes. Consequences and Responses. *European Economy* 7/2009, Brussels.

European Commission (2010): Intra-Euro-Area Competitiveness and Imbalances. *European Economy* 1/2010, Brussels.

Goldstein, A. (1998): Recent Works on Italian Capitalism: A Review Essay. *Journal of Modern Italian Studies*, Vol. 3, 175-184.

Gowan, P. (1999): *The Global Gamble – Washington's Faustian Bid for World Dominance*. London, New York: Verso.

Gowam, P. (2009): Crisis in the Heartland – Consequences of the New Wall Street System. *New Left Review*, Jan-Feb 2009, 5-29.

Green, D.; Petrick, K. (1999): The Eastward Expansion of the European Union and the Transformation of the Financial System. *Review of Radical Political Economics*, Vol. 31, 78-90.

International Monetary Fund (2009): Ireland: 2009 Article IV Consultation, *IMF Country Report No. 09/195*, Washington.

International Monetary Fund (2010): Hungary: Fifth Review Under the Stand-By Arrangement, *IMF Country Report No. 10/80*, Washington.

Kanda, D. (2010): Asset Booms and Structural Fiscal Positions: The Case of Ireland. *IMF Working Paper*, Washington.

Kirby, P. (2004): Development Theory and the Celctic Tiger. *European Journal of Development Research*, Vol. 16, 301-328.

Kitson, M.; Michie, J. (1996): Britain's Industrial Performance Since 1960: Underinvestment and Relative Decline. *Economic Journal*, Vol. 106, 196-212.

Kollias, C.; Rafailidis, A. (2003): A Survey of the Greek Defence Industry. *Defence and Peace Economics*, Vol. 14, 311-324.

Lapavitsas, C. et al. (2010): Eurozone Crisis: Beggar Thyself and Thy Neighbour, *Research on Money and Finance, Occasional Report*, March 2010, London.

Lombard, M. (1995). A Re-examination of the Reasons for the Failure of Keynesian Expansionary Policies in France, 1981-1983. *Cambridge Journal of Economics*, Vol. 19, 359-372.

Maniatis, T. (2005): Marxian Macroeconomic Categories in the Greek Economy. *Review of Radical Political Economics*, Vol. 37, 494-516.

Moschovis, G.; Servera, M. (2009): External Imbalances of the Greek Economy: The Role of Fiscal and Structural Policies. *ECFIN Country Focus*, Vol. VI, Issue 6.

O'Hearn, D. (2001): *The Atlantic Economy: Britain, the US, and Ireland*. Manchester: Manchester University Press.

Parsons, Craig (2003). *A Certain Kind of Europe*. Ithaca, London: Cornell University Press.

Piore, M. J.; Sabel. C. F. (1984): *The Second Industrial Divide: Possibilities for Prosperity*. New York: Basic Books.

Radice, H. K. (1995). Britain in the World Economy: National Decline, Capital Success? In: David Coates and John Hillard (eds.): *UK Economic Decline*. Englewood Cliffs: Prentice Hall, 233-249.

Schmidt, I. (2007): Atlantic Capitalism – One World or More? *State of Nature – Online Journal on Radical Ideas*, Autumn 2007, http://www.stateofnature.org/atlanticCapitalism.html.

Schmidt, I. (2009a): New Institutions, Old Ideas: The Passing Moment of the European Social Model. *Studies in Political Economy*, Vol. 84, 7-28.

Schmidt, I. (2009b): Große Krisen seit den 1930er Jahren. *Prokla – Zeitschrift für kritische Sozialwissenschaft*, Vol. 157, 523-540.

United Nations Conference on Trade and Development (2007): *Review of Maritime Transport 2007*, Geneva.

Cutting Government Deficits: Economic Science or Class War?

Hugo Radice[1]

Abstract: The financial crisis of 2008 was widely blamed on reckless and predatory behavior by the banks, and public debate therefore centred on supporting employment and reforming the financial system. But during 2010, the focus of attention has shifted to the deficits and debts of governments, which are widely believed to be excessive and unsustainable. It is argued here that cutting government deficits is not an economic necessity, but a strategy for justifying attacks on the living standards of workers and heading off reforms that might threaten the power of the dominant business and financial elites.

Keywords: Public finances; Keynesianism; neoliberalism; class rule

Introduction

Shortly before the British General Election of 6 May 2010 an independent London economic policy think-tank, the Institute for Fiscal Studies (IFS), called for the major parties to 'come clean' about their strategies for reducing the public sector debt, if elected to office (Chote 2010). The IFS report resonated strongly with the overall public attitude towards the main political parties in the campaign: fuelled by the parliamentary expenses scandal that dominated British politics for much of 2009, many people had come to regard all politicians as devious and untrustworthy. The media response pandered to this attitude by unthinkingly echoing the IFS position. The centre-left *Guardian* asserted that the IFS was "the leading economics think-tank" in the country, clearly implying that its views must be accepted without question. In this particular case that meant accepting not only that

---

[1]   Life Fellow, School of Politics and International Studies, University of Leeds, Leeds, U.K.; correspondence to h.k.radice@leeds.ac.uk. This paper develops arguments originally presented in an article published in *The Bullet* on 4 May 2010: see http://www.socialistproject.ca/bullet/350.php.

the political parties had to be transparent, but also that the public sector debt had to be reduced.

To any critical social scientist, such claims require substantiation. Leaving aside the less contentious first claim, that political parties should be open about their intentions, the purpose of this paper is to examine the second claim. Is cutting the public debt really an objective economic necessity, or is it actually a deeply political stance, reflecting the interests of business and financial élites?

In the next section, I look at the historical reconfiguration of public finances over the last forty years, focusing on the shift during that period from post-war Keynesian state interventionism to the neoliberal hegemony that characterizes the current economic policy landscape across the world. The following section then examines the contemporary debates over public sector deficits and sovereign debt, arguing that because of the global savings glut that has persisted right through the crisis that began in 2007, it is not 'economically necessary' to give immediate priority to cutting public deficits and debts.

In the final section, I suggest that the real reason for the cuts is twofold. On the one hand, the business, financial and political élites—in short, the ruling classes—were obliged in 2008 to summon the interventionist state back onto the stage to avoid a total collapse of global finance, and now want to banish it once more to a merely supportive role. On the other hand, the cuts in state spending and increases in taxes are being structured in such a way as to transfer income and wealth from working people to the rich and powerful: ironically, this has now been authoritatively confirmed in a detailed study by the self-same IFS (Browne, 2010). This combined attack, at once economic, political and ideological, requires a response that breaks decisively both with the easy compromises of social democracy, as well as with the unpalatable elitism of vanguard communism.

The political economy of state spending in historical perspective

Over the last forty years, the theory and practice of economic policy has shifted markedly from mainstream post-war Keynesianism to the unchallenged hegemony of free-market neoliberalism. Although there have been many elements in this overall shift—notably privatization of state enterprises, deregulation of financial markets, the globalization of finance and attacks on trade union rights—public finances have consistently played a central role.

Continuing a long historical tradition, Britain was a pioneer in this shift to neoliberalism. There were two key campaigns in particular that affected the UK: the first during the 'stagflation' crisis of the mid-1970s, and the second during the sharp recession of the early 1990s.

The 1970s and the rise of Thatcherism

Through the 1950s and 1960s, economic growth in Britain had been slower than in continental Europe, let alone Japan. In the 1970s, slow growth came to be accompanied by both high inflation and the return of mass unemployment, a combination that was completely at odds with conventional Keynesian thinking at the time. A long decline of industrial employment in Britain also accelerated in the 1970s. This 'deindustrialization' was blamed variously on poor business management, a national culture hostile to scientific and technical education, the continuing cost of empire, excessive investment abroad, or the obstructiveness of highly-organized trade unions.

Attempts by successive governments to address these problems of decline started under the 1964-70 Wilson administrations, and continued through the Heath years to the return of Labour in 1974. In the decade from 1964, restricting public spending might have been necessitated when sterling was under pressure, but it was not seen as the key to macroeconomic stability. Instead, the predominantly Keynesian policy mainstream favoured state initiatives in the form of income policies and indicative planning, aiming to reconcile the conflicting interests of employers and unions through the good offices of the state. However, by 1976 these efforts appeared to have failed, as inflation reached a record level of 26% even though unemployment remained stubbornly high—an unprecedented combination that came to be called 'stagflation'.

Although Keynesians tried to argue that the inflation was largely the result of international developments such as the breakdown of the dollar-gold link in 1971 and the oil shock of 1973, their policies were clearly in disarray. This led to the emergence of two policy platforms standing to left and right of the mainstream. On the left, Labour and the unions flirted with an Alternative Economic Strategy which centred on a radical extension of state intervention in the modernization of British industry (London CSE Group, 1980). On the right, the monetarist followers of Milton Friedman offered an equally radical diagnosis, blaming stagflation on the fiscal and monetary indiscipline of the government (Laidler, 1982). While Friedman's followers argued that inflation was always due to excessive expansion of the money supply by the central bank, in Britain Bacon and Eltis (1980) argued that alongside this, successive governments had 'crowded out' private economic activity through the excessive growth of the public sector.

Following a sudden dip in Britain's trade balance in 1976, a run on the pound forced Chancellor Healey to turn to the International Monetary Fund (IMF) for help. The public spending cuts that followed signalled an early victory for the monetarist right, and the end of the road for both mainstream Keynesianism and the leftist Alternative Economic Strategy. Thatcher's election success in 1979, followed by Reagan's in the USA, signalled the return of pre-Keynesian economic and social conservatism. In Britain, the fierce monetary and fiscal squeeze that ensued put manufacturing to the sword, while the abolition of exchange controls allowed the burgeoning wealth from North Sea oil to be invested largely abroad. Trade union rights were severely restricted through a series of legislative measures. The breaking of the print unions by Rupert Murdoch and the defeat of the year-long miners' strike of 1984-5 signalled an end to the power of organized labour. The second half of the 1980s saw an eventual revival in economic growth, which was widely seen as a triumph for Thatcherism (Coates and Hillard, 1987). Politically, that triumph was very well summed up by Gamble (1988) as combining the free economy and the strong state: in order to liberate capital from the suffocating embrace of the state, it was necessary for the state itself to act decisively to restrict its own sphere of action.

Internationally there were soon clear parallels to the rise of Thatcherism in Britain. The Bretton Woods international monetary order, set up in 1944 and broadly inspired by Keynes, had tied most currencies to the US dollar, which in turn had been tied to gold. The availability of temporary loans from the IMF in principle gave governments the leeway to work out their own solutions to deficits in their balance of payments. This system had been abandoned in 1971-2, when the US no longer had the gold reserves to support it, and thereafter currencies were mostly allowed to float, meaning that their values were determined by international market forces. The revival of private international finance accelerated as a result of the massive 1973 rise in oil prices, when oil producers' revenues were recycled as loans to oil-consuming countries. In 1979, President Carter's Federal Reserve chairman Paul Volcker attacked US inflation through a dramatic monetary squeeze, raising interest rates sharply and plunging the US into recession.

This not only signalled a shift to monetarist economic policies in the US, but also directly contributed to the Third World debt crisis of the 1980s. Hit by falling export revenues and a rising cost of debt service from higher interest rates, many developing countries were forced to seek help from the IMF and the World Bank precisely when those bodies were themselves adopting the revived economic ideology of free markets and sound money. Loans were only made available on condition of cuts in public spending and the liberalization of trade and finance, the new development policy that became known as the Washington Consensus (Williamson, 1993).

The triumph of neoliberalism – and globalization

While the Third World was devastated by the debt crisis of the 1980s (Haggard & Kaufman, 1992), the UK and US financial sectors pressed forward with deregulation at home and expansion abroad, laying the basis for their joint domination of global financial markets. However, by the end of the decade, the US recovery under the Reagan administrations ended in a major financial crisis centred on the savings and loan companies that traditionally provided residential mortgage loans. Recovery in the UK centred on financial services, retail and property, generating a boom that led to renewed inflation and an unsustainable expansion of credit. Meanwhile in Japan too, a frenetic stock market and property boom led to a spectacular crash in 1987.

When these developments culminated in a global financial bust in 1990-91, coinciding with the fall of Communist regimes across the Soviet bloc, the free-market right once again blamed lax monetary policy and excessive public spending. Within the European Union, this resulted in the strictures of the Maastricht Treaty, first negotiated in 1991 and finally enacted, after some resistance, in 1993. In relation to public finance, from now on all EU member states were enjoined to limit their fiscal deficits to 3% of GDP, and their aggregate public debts to 60% of GDP. The free-market reforms that the Washington Consensus had imposed on the Third World were now also imposed upon the post-Communist 'transition' countries of Eastern Europe and the former Soviet Union.

As a result, economic policy regimes across the world began rapidly converging on a single model, that of neoliberalism. Within each country, this took the form of monetary and fiscal policies that prioritized open markets and low inflation, rather than full employment or the eradication of poverty. In the monetary field, the overriding purpose was to achieve a target rate of inflation. Because banking and finance were both deregulated and internationally integrated, the money supply became almost impossible to measure, let alone control, and selective state intervention in credit markets was now ruled out. As a result, the rate of interest became the key policy instrument; if inflation exceeded its target, the central bank would raise the rate of interest charged to banks, and if it fell below, they would reduce it. Meanwhile, the limits on public expenditure and government deficits not only brought to a halt the expansion of welfare states, but also accelerated the privatization of state-owned industries everywhere, most extensively in the ex-communist countries.

The wider political economy of neoliberalism centred on two significant processes through the 1990s. The first of these was *financialization* (Epstein, 2005), in which capital accumulation shifts to the financial services sector from the production of other goods and services. While financial firms certainly took full advantage of the sector's deregulation, the growth in financial markets and the development of new financial products was enthusiastically welcomed by businesses and households alike. For big business in particular, the 1990s saw a boom in mergers, buy-outs and restructuring, and the embedding of financial imperatives within the firm aimed at maximizing profits. This signalled an abrupt end to the more benign 'managerial revolution' of the post-war period, in which professional management and organized labour supposedly worked together in pursuit of growth, innovation and good working conditions. Households, suffering from stagnation in earnings as a result of fierce competition in labour markets, began to pile up debt as they sought to maintain the growth in living standards to which they had become accustomed. Unwittingly, they were being transformed from wage-earning workers into universal financial subjects, viewing the world in terms of investment opportunities and capital gains (Radice, 2010b).

The second important process of change was *globalization*, which became a dominant subject of study across the social sciences and in political and cultural discourse. After two decades of relative stagnation, the 1990s saw dramatic growth in trade and foreign direct investment (FDI) across all sectors of the economy and in all parts of the world. Within the Washington Consensus, FDI was to replace publicly-funded aid programmes as the primary means of modernization and development, enabling 'emerging economies' to take advantage of trade liberalization by expanding their exports to the consumer markets of the rich countries. FDI was also central to the remarkable acceleration of economic growth in Asia, especially the rise of China, and in Latin America. By the end of the decade, the conventional perception on the left of a Third World entirely and inevitably mired in poverty and stagnation had become seriously out of date.

These twin processes strongly reinforced the transformation in economic policy regimes everywhere. Globalization and financialization ensured that the state's fiscal and monetary discipline was backed up by the mighty power of global credit markets. The capacity to withdraw funds from states backsliding on their commitment to neoliberalism was exemplified in the dramatic crises that hit Mexico in 1994, many East Asian countries in 1997, and Russia in 1998. With active monetary and fiscal policies to pursue national economic goals now outlawed, the standard policy model became that of the 'competition state' (Cerny 1997), seeking to attract inward investment flows to boost employment and exports, and to provide the 'supply-side' infrastructure for domestic businesses.

Although the turn of the millennium was accompanied by further outbreaks of financial crisis—for instance, the 'dot.com' stock-market bust and Argentina in 2001—a new wave of global economic growth accompanied by low inflation appeared to justify the self-satisfied claim that 'the 'Great Moderation' had arrived (Bernanke, 2004). Until 2007, the hegemony of neoliberalism seemed assured.

The course of the crisis: government deficits and the bond markets

The origins and course of the crisis that began in that year have by now generated a large literature (for a fuller account see Radice, 2010b). The combination of a long period of growth with exceptionally low interest rates had led to the over-selling of 'sub-prime' mortgages to poorer households in the USA, who were persuaded that ever-increasing house prices could provide economic security. Like other forms of household loan, these mortgages were funded through securitization, issuing bonds whose value was based on the stream of expected mortgage payments. For the purchasers of such bonds, the risk appeared minimal, since each was based on a diversified bundle of mortgages, so that if some were to go into default, the rest would carry on generating income. In any case, the risk could also be laid off through a new form of insurance eagerly supplied by global investors—the credit default swap. Through 2005-7, mortgage defaults climbed as interest rates rose, while both house prices and employment stalled, and it slowly became clear that the risk to the value of mortgage-backed securities had been drastically underestimated. As defaults increased, thousands of banks, insurance companies and other investors such as hedge funds found themselves facing potentially catastrophic losses. With the markets unable to arrive at any clear idea of the real value of trillions of dollars worth of financial assets, day-to-day lending transactions between banks ground to a halt, not just in the USA but around the world. During 2008, the entire global financial sector slid inexorably towards total breakdown.

After the bankruptcy of Lehman Brothers in September 2008, governments began a hectic programme of concerted actions. These were aimed first at supporting the banks so that they could continue to manage the world's monetary flows, and then, as a world recession rapidly set in, at sustaining aggregate demand. Interest rates fell to near-zero and central banks pumped money into their economies. For the worst-hit countries, the IMF organised rescues using the methods established in the 1980s Third World debt crisis. The traditional G8 summits were hastily supplemented by larger G20 meetings, bringing China, India and Brazil among others into the mix. Global governance agencies, such as the Bank for International Settlements and the Organization for Economic Cooperation and Development, provided coordination and advice, and began the process of crafting regulatory reforms for the banking sector aimed at avoiding any repetition of the crisis.

Despite the obvious echoes of the global crisis of the 1930s, however, there has been no repetition, at least in the major capitalist nations, of the catastrophic rises in unemployment and falls in international trade that characterized that decade. This is surely partly due to the dense web of global governance institutions, which scarcely existed eighty years ago. The cooperative response has also reflected the dramatically greater extent of cross-border economic interdependence. However, the proximate reason is undoubtedly the adoption of massive fiscal stimulus packages, most notably in the USA and in China, but also in many other countries. The fiscal stringency of the Maastricht Treaty and the Washington Consensus was quickly abandoned from late 2008, with current budget deficits rising rapidly to levels ranging from 5% to 15% of GDP or more.

However, through the second half of 2009 the tide of support for public intervention began to turn. Precisely because the giant investment banks make their money from market-making and transactions, rather than loans and investments, their fortunes quickly recovered from the 2008 debacle, the supreme irony being the vast commissions they got for marketing the flood of new sovereign borrowing, and restructuring and refinancing busted large corporations like General Motors. As credit markets began to function again, even the derided ratings agencies like Moody's, which had happily taken fat fees for doling out AAA ratings on sub-prime mortgage-backed securities, recovered their nerve and began to pronounce upon the sustainability of the much higher—and still rising—post-crisis levels of government debt. As the Eurozone powers bickered over how to address Greece's fiscal crisis in late 2009, governments recently freed from the shackles of fiscal restraint found themselves once more on the defensive.

How and why has this happened? It is striking that at no point in the past forty years of debate on public finances did the monetarist economists—or their neoliberal successors—explain why any particular limit to public deficits and debt was *economically necessary*. Instead we have been offered, then as now, an entirely circular argument. We are told by supposed economic experts that deficit cuts are necessary because international bond markets require them. So why do the investors in international bond markets require cuts? Because the economic experts say they are necessary!

Now it is certainly the case that any single government which accumulates debts that are very high compared to those of other governments will find itself subject to special scrutiny by the bond markets, as the Greeks now know only too well, and as many Third World governments found out already back in the 1980s. We should of course also make allowance for the pernicious effects of speculators: for instance, the role of George Soros in Britain's 1992 crisis that forced it out of the European Union's Exchange Rate Mechanism, or the flight of 'hot money' from East Asia in 1997. But a reasonable case can still be made that governments should, in normal times, avoid excessive reliance on borrowing, especially to fund current expenditure as opposed to capital investments.

However, from the standpoint of macroeconomic stability, and especially that of maintaining full or near-full employment, our overriding concern today should remain that of Keynes: the need for governments to sustain economic activity at a time when savings in the private sector greatly exceed investments. This need is met by absorbing excess savings through the sale of government securities, the proceeds of which are then spent so as to sustain aggregate output and employment.

There are however big differences in the nature of capitalism today, compared to the 1930s when Keynes first made the case for counter-cyclical public spending. In 1933, after the failure of yet another international conference aimed at coordinating responses to the crisis, Keynes reluctantly made the case for a national solution led by the state. As a lifelong liberal, he rejected both the Soviet experiment of central planning, and the emerging Nazi model of extreme economic nationalism under the joint dictatorship of capital and the state. From then on, he consistently argued that international capital movements should be tightly restricted, so that governments could fully exercise the control over national financial markets that they acquired through the sheer scale of their borrowing and their control of the money supply (Radice, 1988).

But precisely as a result of the combined processes of deregulation, financialization and globalization discussed earlier, governments no longer have this degree of structural power over finance. In addition, for decades now, massive imbalances in international trade between countries have been sustained, with the huge trade surpluses of Japan, Germany, and now China being matched by the huge deficits of the USA and Britain. These trade imbalances are by definition offset by capital flows from surplus to deficit countries, and these flows—as well as the financing of expanded trade—have been a major feature of financial globalization. As a result the Keynesian premise, of the state's structural power over finance, can only be fully applied collectively at the global level. State power over finance could only be re-established within a single country by a radical disengagement from the world economy, but given the economic and political resources invested in building the global economy and its neoliberal order, the cost of doing so would be immense.

Adopting this approach, we can see that the continued growth and prosperity of countries with chronic trade surpluses, like Germany and China, depend, in conditions of global recession, on the willingness of other countries like the USA and Britain to continue to run trade deficits. As a corollary—and this is *really* an economic fact—there will be continuing matching outflows of capital from the former countries, and inflows into the latter. Given the current reluctance of businesses and households in the trade-deficit countries to borrow and spend, it is their *government* borrowing that keeps the world economy going. And the very fact that so many governments have been able to borrow so much since 2008 shows that, despite the global recession, there remains a *global savings glut*. This savings glut has arisen because of the massive shift from wages to profits, and from the closely-related subordination of hundreds of millions of peasants and independent producers to wage labour in those 'emerging' economies. As states have abandoned their earlier commitment to the fiscal mitigation of inequality, the wealthy have increased their grip on global savings.

As long as those savings continue to exceed global private sector investments, governments must continue to absorb that excess. Otherwise, the world economy will slip back into the famous 'double-dip' recession, a prospect that has become increasingly likely through the summer of 2010. Indeed, as and when the global recovery has reached the point where private sector investment has substantially recovered and cyclical unemployment has disappeared, why should 'the markets' require a reduction of government deficits to 'normal' levels? There is, after all, no economic law that dictates a 3% cap on the government deficit, and 60% on debt, or indeed any other numerical values. The level of aggregate economic activity is entirely unaffected by the proportion of demand that flows through the public rather than the private sector. As real interest rates swing back to being moderately positive, the power of compound interest is surely enough to sustain the economic advantage of the rich, as well as the pensions of the middle classes.

Resolving the crisis: restoring class rule

In the end, now as in the 1970s, the real reason for the attacks on state borrowing and state expenditure lies not in economics, but in politics, or more specifically in class warfare. For it is primarily through the politics of democracy—even our highly restricted form of it—that the privileged position of private wealth has historically come under threat. After 1945 the propertyless in most parts of the world, West, East and South, made remarkable gains in their well-being and in the strength of their political voice. By the mid-1970s, the propertied classes—whether capitalists, usurers, merchants or landlords, or indeed the Soviet-bloc bureaucratic élite—found themselves on the defensive on many fronts.

Many radical nationalist governments in the Third World continued to press for reforms in the governance of the world economy, challenging the new forms of economic colonialism that followed independence (Biel, 2000, ch.6). In the Soviet bloc, the 1968 Prague Spring and the first stirrings of the Polish workers' movement in 1970 threatened the bureaucrats' highly centralised power (Harman, 1974). And in the West, not only had new social movements challenged the elites on issues of gender, race and the environment, but workers were also advancing new claims to workplace democracy and economic security that seriously threatened the power of big business and high finance (e.g. Rowbotham, Segal and Wainwright, 1979; Gorz, 1985).

The previous two sections charted the rise of neoliberalism with a particular focus on public finances. With the benefit of hindsight, the historical logic of that rise seems all too apparent. But the political articulation of an effective response by the ruling classes to the combined challenges of the 1970s was by no means clear at the time. For more than thirty years, the ideologues of neoliberalism, with economists at the fore, worked assiduously to construct a new common-sense about the economy based on the old liberal mantra: property rights, individualism and the residual state. Yet they were constantly faced with resistance, not only from the diverse forces of the left, seeking to at least defend the post-war gains of workers, but also from political strands of the right: nationalism, religious authoritarianism, and even, in parts of the global South, the traditional paternalism that remained from the rule of precapitalist landed interests (Barrington Moore, 1966). Karl Polányi (1944) had argued that the nineteenth-century liberal utopia of a market society had historically foundered on the social consequences of subordinating not only produced commodities, but also land, labour and money, to the market—in Marx's terms, to the rule of capital. The result was a historical 'double movement': first towards the market society, and then towards social protection.

By the turn of the millennium, the restructuring of the state, the redistribution of income and wealth to the rich, and the removal of workers' collective rights had seemingly turned the tide once more towards the market society. Yet in 2007-9, the crisis immediately led to widespread public challenges to the neoliberal order, and the ruling classes were obliged to tear up the neoliberal rulebook in favour of vigorous state intervention. Perhaps this heralded the second phase of a new Polányian double movement, as Hettne (1997) had argued a decade earlier (for a sceptical view see Wade, 2010). But as we have seen, within about six months the neoliberals regrouped. In Britain, as the debate over Labour's 2009 Budget already showed, their ownership of the economic common sense allowed them to steadily shift the focus of debate from exacting retribution and repayment from the banks, to blaming governments for assuming the vast fiscal deficits that have kept capitalism afloat. Meanwhile, those who spoke up for real alternatives—for Green New Deals, for radical reform of the banks, for a new international financial architecture—have been pushed to the margins of public attention.

The immediate need, at this juncture, is for the left to continue to make the case for maintaining public expenditure, supporting the efforts of Keynesian economists such as Paul Krugman, Robert Reich and Joseph Stiglitz in the US, or David Blanchflower and Robert Skidelsky in Britain. Across the EU, the progressive economists of the EuroMemorandum Group (2009) have argued this case, and even the International Monetary Fund has argued that "growth prospects in advanced economies could suffer if an overly severe or poorly planned fiscal consolidation stifles still-weak domestic demand" (IMF, 2010, p. 7).

However, it is becoming increasingly clear that this is by no means enough, because it takes the easy course of looking back at how the world was before neoliberalism—and often doing so through rose-tinted glasses. James Ferguson (2010) argues, in relation to the global South, that returning to the alternative of the developmental state is not enough because the building-blocks of politics—workers, markets, nation-states—have been so fundamentally reconfigured by neoliberal restructuring. In the context of a realistic appreciation of these changes, we can see that the assault on public spending goes far beyond the simple matter of the macroeconomic management of effective demand. In this respect, Britain is leading the way, as has so often been the case historically. Following the election on 6 May 2010, a coalition government was unexpectedly formed between the Conservative Party under David Cameron, which had won the largest number of seats but not an overall majority, and the much smaller Liberal Democrats under Nick Clegg, which had widely been assumed to favour a centre-left coalition with Labour.

On 22 June, the Coalition announced an Emergency Budget, setting out savage cuts in public spending of up to 25% in all areas except health and overseas aid" (for details see Radice, 2010a). However, as government ministers began to detail their substantive plans for the years ahead, it quickly became clear that the immediate macroeconomic consequences were only one issue for the government's critics. In the key areas of health, education and welfare, the Coalition intends a far more radical assault on the nature of the state and its relation to society. This assault is not only aimed at deepening the neoliberal restructuring of institutions, but also at banishing the very idea that societal goals can be advanced through the collective state provision of public goods. The message is relentlessly driven home, that the Coalition wants to 'restore power to the people', linking service provision directly to clients and engaging the public actively in the substantive shaping of that provision. In historical terms, this is taking Britain back not merely to the era before the post-1945 welfare state, but to before the Liberal reforms of the early 20[th]cent ury.

However, in every respect the Coalition is cleverly building upon initiatives and perceptions already established not only by the Tory administrations from 1979 to1997, but also under New Labour from 1997 to 2010. New Labour dropped the Tory experiment under which family doctors commissioned specialist medical services; but in opting for an indirect commissioning model via local bureaucracies under central state control, they ensured that the NHS would still be driven by financial motives and managed along private-sector lines. In education, New Labour persistently undermined democratic local control through central initiatives and through the creation of specialist academies at the secondary level. And in welfare, despite some successful initiatives aimed at tackling child poverty, they pursued 'modernization' and 'value for money' programmes that did nothing to break the weary cycles of poverty and welfare dependency in which so many millions were trapped.

However, at a deeper level the neoliberal project is also about reshaping the very nature of citizenship, the way in which individuals imagine and live their relations with each other and with social institutions. In the post-war period, it was generally taken for granted that these relations were shaped by institutions structured around class interests: trade unions, professional associations, and political parties whose ideologies reflected the interests of capital or labour. Today, any such concept of class as a mediating force has been expunged from public discourse. On the left, the retreat from statism (social-democratic or communist) led in the 1990s to the famous 'third way' of Giddens (1999), and the search for progressive elements in 'civil society' and 'social movements'. On the right, the currently-fashionable British 'red Tory' thinker Philip Blond (2010) argues that the modern citizen can be mindful of social needs and active in ensuring their provision, while still responding to market signals in the more narrowly economic sphere.

The consequence is to deprive anyone seeking to pursue traditional progressive goals of equality, solidarity and sustainable livelihoods of the potential for a *collective* response to neoliberalism. So can the concept of class be resuscitated? In Marx's work in particular, class is a relational concept centred on the way in which society's material reproduction is ensured. Under capitalism, the predominant but by no means exclusive form of this is capitalist production, based on the separation of the majority from direct appropriation of the means of production. This separation divides society into workers and capitalists, with the many and varied strata of society comprehensible only in terms of their standing in relation to that fundamental division.

Neoliberalism has developed a double denial of the significance of class division in this sense, building upon the dominant theoretical traditions of mainstream sociology. First, class is redefined empirically in terms of the detailed differentiation of income levels and occupations in society, whose multiple groups are then aggregated into 'working class' and 'middle class'. Many Marxists have been drawn into this position, accepting the divide between the two, and arguing only that elements of this middle class could still challenge the rule of capital, either in conjunction with or in place of the industrial working class (Walker, 1979; for a general review of 'new class' theories see King & Szelényi, 2004). But as long as the main axes of differentiation are rooted in the production of goods and services as commodities, the common subordination to the dynamics of capitalist accumulation ensures common experiences that potentially unite these supposedly separate 'classes', however elusive this unity may have become (Meiksins, 1986).

The second denial addresses this problem directly, by positing other systematic determinants of the relation between individual and society, firmly based *outside* the realm of production. This has also been a perennial feature of mainstream sociology, but in recent decades it has been fuelled by the universal rejection of most varieties of Marxism for their 'economic determinism'. Twentieth-century Marxism, from Gramsci to Poulantzas and on, had in many respects accepted the criticism, downplaying the analysis of 'economic' production relations in favour of an approach in which 'the political' is constituted as 'relatively autonomous'. But equally, since the 1970s much of the left has rejected 'class politics'—interpreted narrowly as the sectional interests of the traditional male industrial working class—in favour of the 'rainbow politics' of social movements, rooted in the different, supposedly more authentic needs of particular social groups.

It seems clear that the rejection of class politics goes hand in hand with the view that economic activity *really is* constituted separately from other aspects of life in capitalist societies, including politics. However, such a view is at the very core of liberalism as a political ideology. For if the economic is really separated from the political, then its regulation can and should lie outside the realm of political action. In other words, the institution of private property cannot be politically challenged, and property rights cannot be subordinated to human or civil rights in forms such as 'the right to livelihood'.

It is precisely in order to develop a substantive underpinning for this proposition that neoliberalism now seeks to redefine the individual in effect *as a capitalist*, an economic subject whose engagement with others is mediated by the market, and structured by the accumulation of private capital. Since it is self-evident that the great majority of individuals are not 'capitalists' in Marx's sense—possessing a sufficient mass of money-capital that can generate at least a subsistence income— they are, instead, seen as capable of accumulating 'human' or 'social' capital (Fine, 2010), the possession of which enables them in principle to *acquire* money capital. Yet they can only do that through the sale of their labour-power—in other words, through wage labour, as members of the working class.

In order to escape from the trap that neoliberalism is now springing the left needs to reassert the class nature of capitalism in these terms, albeit without in any sense denying the political significance of other forms of oppression. In a letter to Marx, Engels (1858) famously quipped that "the English proletariat is actually becoming more and more bourgeois, so that the ultimate aim of this most bourgeois of all nations would appear to be the possession, *alongside* the bourgeoisie, of a bourgeois aristocracy and a bourgeois proletariat". The reality is that Britain is *the most proletarian* of nations, in terms of the proportion of its population who rely on wage-labour for their subsistence: there are no peasants left, and small-business capitalism has always been feebler than in other capitalist countries. By recognizing such foundations in present-day economic reality, it may yet prove possible to build a movement of universal appeal that can challenge the class rule of capital.

References

Bacon, R. and Eltis, W. (1980). *Britain's Economic Problem: Too Few Producers*. London: Macmillan.

Barrington Moore, J. R. (1966). *Social Origins of Dictatorship and Democracy: Lord and Peasant in the Making of the Modern World*. Boston: Beacon Press.

Bernanke, B. (2004). 'The Great Moderation'. Speech to the Eastern Economic Association, 20 February 2004. See http://www.federalreserve.gov/Boarddocs/Speeches/2004/20040220/default.htm.

Biel, R. (2000). *The New Imperialism: Crisis and Contradictions in North/South Relations*. London: Zed Press.

Blond, P. (2010). *Red Tory: How Left and Right Have Broken Britain and How We Can Fix It*. London: Faber.

Browne, J. *et al.* (2010). 'The distributional effects of tax and benefit reforms between June 2010 and April 2014: a revised assessment'. Institute for Fiscal Studies Briefing Note BN108, 25 August, available at www.ifs.org.uk/publications/5246.

Cerny, P. (1997). 'Paradoxes of the competition state: the dynamics of political globalization'. *Government and Opposition 32*(1), 251-74.

Chote, R. *et al.* (2010). 'Filling the hole: how do the three main UK parties plan to repair the public finances?'. Institute for Fiscal Studies 2010 Election Briefing Note no.12, 27 April, available at www.ifs.org.uk/publications/4848.

Coates, D. and Hillard, J. (eds) (1987). *The Economic Revival of Modern Britain: the Debate Between Left and Right*. Aldershot: Edward Elgar.

Engels, F. (1858). Letter to Marx of 7 October 1858, in Marx-Engels *Collected Works 40*, 343.

Epstein, G. (ed) (2005). *Financialization and the World Economy*. Cheltenham: Edward Elgar.

EuroMemorandum Group (2009). *Europe in Crisis: a Critique of the EU's Failure to Respond*. At http://www.lwbooks.co.uk/ebooks/EUROMEMORANDUM%202009-2010.pdf.

Ferguson, J. (2010). 'The uses of neoliberalism'. *Antipode 41*(S1), 166-84.

Fine, B. (2010). *Theories of Social Capital: Researchers Behaving Badly*. London: Pluto Press.

Gamble, A. (1988). *The Free Economy and the Strong State: the Politics of Thatcherism*. London: Macmillan.

Giddens, A. (1999). *The Third Way: the Renewal of Social Democracy*. Cambridge: Polity Press.

Gorz, A. (1985). *Paths to Paradise: on the Liberation from Work*. Boston: South End Press.

Harman, C. (1974). *Bureaucracy and Revolution in Eastern Europe*. London: Pluto Press.

Haggard, S. and Kaufman, R. (eds) (1992). *The Politics of Economic Adjustment*. Princeton: Princeton UP.

Hettne, B. (1997). 'Development, security and world order: a regionalist approach'. *European Journal of Development Research 9*(1), 83-106.

International Monetary Fund (2010). *World Economic Outlook Update*. 7 July, at http://www.imf.org/external/pubs/ft/weo/2010/update/02/pdf/0710.pdf.

King, L.P. and Szelényi, I. (2004). *Theories of the New Class: Intellectuals and Power*. Minneapolis: University of Minnesota Press.

Laidler, D. (1982). *Monetarist Perspectives*. Oxford: Philip Allan.

London CSE Group (1980). *The Alternative Economic Strategy: a Response by the Labour Movement to the Economic Crisis*. London: CSE Books.

Meiksins, P. (1986). 'Beyond the boundary question'. *New Left Review 157*, 101-20.

Polányi, K. (1944). *The Great Transformation: the Political and Economic Origins of Our Times*. Beacon Hill: Beacon Press.

Radice, H. (1988). 'Keynes and the policy of practical protectionism', in J. V. Hillard (ed), *J. M. Keynes in Retrospect*. Aldershot: Edward Elgar, 153-71.

Radice, H. (2010a). 'Britain's austerity budget: a class act', *The Bullet 385*. At http://www.socialistproject.ca/bullet/385.php.

Radice, H. (2010b). 'Confronting the crisis: a class analysis'. *Socialist Register* 2011, forthcoming.

Rowbotham, S., Segal, L. and Wainwright, H. (1979). *Beyond the Fragments: Feminism and the Making of Socialism*. London: Merlin Books.

Wade, R. (2010). 'Is the globalization consensus dead?'. *Antipode 41*(S1), 142-65.

Walker, P. (ed.) (1979). *Between Labour and Capital*. Brighton: Harvester Press.

Williamson, J. (1993). 'Democracy and the "Washington Consensus"'. *World Development 21*(8), 1329-36.

The Keynesian Revival: a Marxian Critique

Richard D. Wolff[1]

Abstract: The global economic crisis, unfolding since late 2007, has begun to undermine the hegemony of neoclassical economics and neo-liberalism generally, thereby provoking a widespread resurgence of Keynesian economics in various forms. The historical adequacy of Keynesian economics to modify, reverse or prevent capitalist crisis is criticized systematically. Capitalism is shown to have exhibited re-peated oscillations between private and state-interventionist forms for centuries, since neither proved capable of preventing recurring crises. An alternative to both neoclassical and Keynesian responses to crises—a new kind of Marxian response—is developed. It stresses micro-level transformations, adding them to balance the one-sided macro-focus of the traditional interpretations of Marxism, socialism, and communism.

Keywords: economic crisis, Keynesian economics, Marxian economics, Marxian critique

A Critique of the Revival of Keynesian Counter-Recessionary Policies

In the modern history of capitalism, Keynesian counter-recessionary policies (broadly defined) have failed in two major ways. First, those policies have not *consistently* succeeded as means to end capitalism's cyclical downturns. They failed, for example, to extract the US from the Great Depression of the 1930s. As this is written, their effectiveness in today's global capitalist crisis is questionable. Second, the promise that has almost always accompanied each application of Keynesian policies

---

[1]   Richard D. Wolff is Professor of Economics Emeritus at the University of Massachusetts, Amherst and currently Visiting Professor in the Graduate Program in International Affairs of the New School University in New York City. Wolff has authored many articles and books, often together with Stephen A. Resnick; their latest book is **New Departures in Marxian Theory** (2006). Wolff has written widely on the current economic crisis, produced a DVD and book, each entitled "Capitalism Hits the Fan", and made much of his work freely available at **www.rdwolff.com**.

everywhere—that it would also *prevent future economic downturns*—has never yet been kept.

The Keynesian policies have included varying mixtures of monetary (easing) and fiscal (expansionary) policies and market regulations (especially in finance). They have sometimes included controls on capital flows as well as subsidies, bailouts, and outright nationalizations of private enterprises. Different combinations of these components characterize Keynesian policies in different countries and at different historical moments.

The chief means that actually ended capitalism's downturns have been *declines* in the following: productive laborers' real wages, finished product inventories, means of production prices, and the associated costs of securing profits (managers and other non-productive workers' wages and operating budgets, taxes, access to credit, rents, etc.). Once those declines sufficed to reach certain thresholds, capitalists could see profit possibilities and so resumed productive investment. That generated more or less "recovery" via multiplier and accelerator effects particular to each place and time. In short, capitalism is a systematically unstable economic system whose cycles are basic features of its normal functioning. Keynesian policies have never basically altered that systemic instability.

Keynesian policies, I propose to argue, have largely provided quite *secondary* supports to the normal functioning of capitalist cycles. They marginally moderate the cycles' amplitude and duration. They temporarily impose both costs and constraints on the profit-seeking activities of corporate boards of directors. In these ways, Keynesian policies successfully buy both political space and time for the capitalist cycle to run through its usual downward phase. In the current global capitalist crisis, massive Keynesian deficit spending, as well as credit-market bailouts have generated huge increases in many capitalist countries' national debts. Lenders eventually balk at further loans to the most over-indebted nations, demanding that they raise taxes and/or cut spending to qualify for more loans. If and when that proves politically impossible for lenders to impose on borrowing nations, multilateral agencies offer less onerous terms for loan assistance but with the same demand for austerity conditions. Those conditions—conveniently imposed by others and not the national government—all serve to drive down wages and other costs of business and so once again set the stage for the usual capitalist cycle.

Besides their secondary role, Keynesian policies also serve an important diversionary function. Governments appear to be working mightily to "overcome the economic crisis" by implementing those policies with great fanfare. They thereby distract publics from yet another repetition of the normal capitalist's cyclical downturn. Exploding national debts, like other Keynesian policy programs constitute an elaborate diversionary political theater.

As capitalist crises deepen and last, politicians of most persuasions increasingly express concern, compassion, and/or anger about mass unemployment, home foreclosures, bankruptcies, poverty, etc. They engage in heavily publicized debates and legislative contests over the appropriate monetary, fiscal, regulatory, subsidy, bailout, capital control, and private-enterprise- take-over policies to be executed by the state. These theatrics usually absorb the political energies of many left and right forces that might otherwise, separately or together, make the capitalist system itself the object of opposition, struggle, and transformation. Left-tilting inflections of Keynesian policies often include, for example, direct state subsidies to or hiring's of un/underemployed workers, controls over private investment flows, and enterprise nationalizations. Right-tilting inflections often include, for example, restrictions on immigration, reduced taxes on small businesses, and spending on business-friendly infrastructure construction.

In the context of this argument, Figure 1 below supports the basic irrelevance of Keynesian policies to the basic contours of capitalist exploitation measured roughly by the relation between labor productivity and real wages.[2] First, it covers a long period of US economic history: before, during, and after Keynesian interventions occurred in their classic form in the 1930s. Figure 1 reveals trends for manufacturing, in both labor productivity and real wages *that show no systematic sensitivity to either the imposition or the negation of Keynesian policies over the last century.* The complex over-determinations of real wage and productivity movements were not much influenced by the rise and fall of Keynesian policy regimes nor by whether neo-liberal/neo-classical economics or Keynesian macro-economics prevailed in academic and policy-making circles.

---

[2] Graphically juxtaposing productivity and real wage trend lines is suggested by but not the exact equivalent to the Marxian notion of surplus value (s/v or the ratio of value added less productive workers' value of labor power – numerator - to productive workers' value of labor power – denominator). First, what contemporary statistical practice counts as manufacturing workers' wages conflates both productive and unproductive laborers in manufacturing; Marxian theory keeps these separate. Second, the relevant variable for Marxian theory–value of productive laborer's labor power—is not equivalent to real wages, but is rather real wages adjusted for changes in the productivity of producing real wage goods. Because of the difficulties in translating available statistics into their Marxian analogues, I use here the available manufacturing productivity and real wage trends which allow me to substantiate the argument offered in the text.

Figure 1: Productivity and the Hourly wage
(U.S. Ecnomomy, 1890-2009)

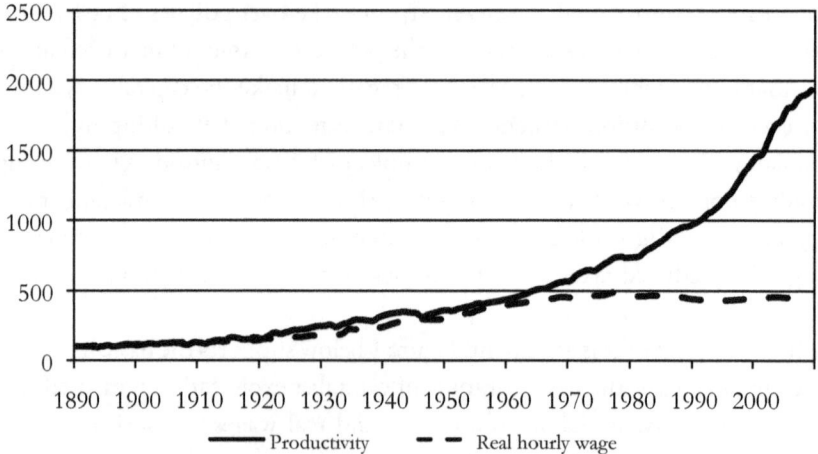

(Index: 1890 = 100; Sources and details for Figure 1: see Appendix)

Indeed, the relatively laissez-faire period before the 1930s saw productivity and real wages rise more or less together, whereas productivity rose somewhat faster than real wages during the 1930s when Keynesian policies were imposed. However, in the second half of the 1960s into the 1970s, during a second spurt of Keynesian policies (Johnson's "Great Society", etc.), productivity rose much faster than real wages. Then, driving home the irrelevance of Keynesian policies to the productivity-real wage relation, the extreme laissez-faire, neoliberal undoing of Keynesian policies after 1980 then saw the last century's most unequal of productivity to real wage ratios.

The end of World War I marks the beginning of a near century of capitalist growth in the US (notwithstanding the Great Depression's impact) that saw a self-reinforcing divergence between what workers produced for their employers (productivity) and what they were paid by their employers for doing so (real wages). Capitalist cycles punctuated but did not basically alter that growth pattern.[3] Keynesian policies punctuated but did not basically alter the cycles, let alone the growth pattern.

---

[3]   This point parallels an argument about capitalist growth globally presented by David Ruccio (1991).

For the working classes, the alternation between laissez-faire and Keynesian policy regimes made little discernible difference in the long-run relationship between labour productivity and real wages. Put otherwise, both regimes could and did facilitate growing gaps between productivity and wages over the last half century, much as earlier both regimes facilitated minimal gaps between them.

In rough terms, the productivity of labor exceeded the real wage in 1890, the base year used to compute Figure 1 above. That is, in Marxian terms, workers produced a surplus for their employers already then. Thereafter, that surplus grew both absolutely and relative to real wages. Measured in value terms, the Marxian metric, the rate of exploitation rose as US capitalism prospered across its cycles. Alternations between Keynesian and laissez-faire policy regimes, like the accompanying oscillations of theoretical hegemony between neoclassical and Keynesian economics, were secondary side shows to the main event of rising exploitation.

If workers in the US hoped that supporting the Keynesian policies of Roosevelt, Truman, Kennedy, Johnson, Nixon and others would alter their basic positions inside US capitalism, they were disappointed. Notwithstanding their rising real wages from the 1940s to the 1970s and all sorts of political and cultural obfuscations (about everyone being "middle class" or the US being a "people's capitalism"), the workers lived in the growing gap between their real incomes and the wealth of those who took the lions' share of the surpluses they delivered to employers. Their accumulating disappointment helps to explain some periodic disaffection of workers from the Democrats. After real wages stopped rising in the late 1970s, workers increasingly defected even to clearly pro-business Republicans (Greenberg, 1996).

A Critique of Keynesian Theory's Revival

The laissez-faire (neo-liberalist) phase of capitalism that dominated the world economy over the last 30 years has crashed. That, in turn, has now challenged the hegemony of neo-classical economics as the theoretical rationale for celebrating private enterprise and free markets, privatizing public enterprises, and deregulating markets. Keynesian economics is reviving (Skidelsky, 2008). As states everywhere again intervene in the "private" economy—more massively than ever this time—Keynesian economics provides many of the prescriptions and rationales for state economic interventions.

With revival come renewed contestations among different interpretations of Keynes. The differences reflect especially long-standing pressures upon Keynesians from both the left (those who criticize them for "saving" capitalism) and the right (those who attack them for "threatening" capitalism). The most widespread Keynesianism is what prevails in the treatments by most economics textbooks and among advisors to most governments now intervening in their economies to contain and reverse the damages from the current capitalist crisis. This interpretation of Keynes-ian theory rationalizes state interventions (especially expansionary monetary and fiscal policies and financial market regulations) in an otherwise *private* capitalism. It represents the predictable first (and quite moderate) phase of a Keynesianism just emerging after 30 years of neoclassical theory's near total hegemony. This Keynesian theory's goal is quite clearly to save capitalism from what it understands to be the dangerous consequences of laissez-faire (neo-liberal) policy regimes.

Most partisans of another interpretation, the relatively new variant sometimes called Green Keynesianism, want traditional monetary, fiscal, and regulatory poli-cies redesigned to stress ecological goals (Jones, 2008). They seem, at least implicitly, to offer an alliance, a political deal to the dominant Keynesians. Green Keynesians will basically support the goal of saving capitalism in exchange for a Keynesian pol-icy package that makes capitalism significantly greener. Thus, for example, Green Keynesians want expansionary deficit government spending to favor energy-saving mass transportation, installation of solar energy facilities, etc., while tax cuts should favor those who undertake pollution reduction.

Left Keynesians typically want larger, more extensive, and more intrusive state intervention into the private economy. They seek state seizures of private enterprises when their demise threatens broad economic collapse (sometimes referred to as corporations "too big to fail"). They particularly favor state controls over invest-ment and other capital flows, domestically and internationally, to limit and prevent those flows' otherwise destabilizing effects. Many left Keynesians share the Green Keynesians' goals and thus offer them an alternative political deal. Instead of allying with the socially prevalent, rather moderate Keynesians, the Green Keynesians are invited to see better chances of realizing their environmental goals with left Keynes-ian policies in command. Left-right divisions among Green Keynesians are now shaping who among them allies with whom.

The furthest left Keynesians advocate the most intrusive state interventions. Many of them refer to such interventions as key parts of a transition to what they sometimes call socialism. Allied with other kinds of socialists, including some Marxists, the far left Keynesians seek to expand state intervention to include of-ficials *permanently* replacing share-holder elected corporate boards of directors and officials *permanently* controlling or even replacing markets (with more or less cen-tral planning of the distribution of resources and products). For them, those two permanent replacements define socialism.[4]

---

[4]   For a systematic critique of definitions of socialism in terms of state ownership and state planning, see Resnick & Wolff, 2002. We show there why and how capitalism has oscillated between private and state forms that are both as old as capitalism itself.

Whether and to what extent *any* interpretation of Keynesian economics can now displace the last 30 years' hegemony of neoclassical economics will depend on all the economic, political and cultural processes shaping the contesting protagonists of both paradigms. Those processes will simultaneously over-determine the outcome of disputes among alternative interpretations of Keynesian economics.[5] Meanwhile and contrary to notions that neoclassical versus Keynesian economics encompasses the total range of possible economic theory, the Marxian alternatives offer something different from both of them.

One particular Marxian approach does not ally with any variant of Keynesian economics; it stresses its differences from all of them. I want to develop that approach briefly here by noting first that it rejects the Keynesians' nearly exclusive focus on the macro-level of the economy. This Marxian theory goes well beyond state regulation, controls, and ownership of capitalist enterprises (versus their private counterparts) and likewise beyond planning (versus markets). The hallmark of this Marxian theory is an explicit micro-focus drawn from Marx's critique of the class structure of production.

A Marxian Theoretical Alternative

This Marxian theory begins from the historical observations summarized in this paper's first paragraph.[6] Keynesian policies have not overcome the capitalist system's inherent instabilities. Nor have Keynesian economists seriously measured, let alone found ways to eliminate, the vast and long-lasting social costs of that instability. As we now live through the second great crisis of capitalism in 75 years, we do know that its global social costs are again immense. Between the end of the Great Depression and the onset of today's crisis, the National Bureau of Economic Research (NBER) counts an additional eleven "business cycle downturns" that also generated large social costs (NBER, 2008). So many large and small crises underscore Marxian theory's advocacy of changing the economic system as a solution for such crises, rather than repeated oscillations between neoclassical (private) and Keynesian (state or state-interventionist) forms of capitalism. Modern society can do better than capitalism.

From the standpoint of this Marxian theory, the failures of Keynesian policies—and the Keynesian economics that rationalize them—flow from their neglect of the micro-dimensions of capitalism. In short, the unattended contributor to capitalist instability is the relationship *inside* enterprises between the workers who

---

5   Limited space and the main foci of this paper prevent a discussion here of the alternative, contesting variants of neoclassical economics. Those constraints have also minimized attention to the different interpretations of Marxian economics; such attention is available in Resnick & Wolff, 2006.

6   For the basic propositions of this Marxist theory and its differences from alternatives, see Resnick & Wolff 1987; 2006.

produce the surpluses and the employers (e.g. corporate boards of directors) who appropriate and distribute those surpluses.[7] Because Keynesian policies impose costs and constraints on employers in their exploitative relations with workers and in their competitive struggles within and across industries, those employers have great incentives to evade, weaken or end those Keynesian policies. Because employers appropriate the surpluses (and hence the profits) of enterprise, they dispose of the resources needed to respond positively to those incentives.

That is what happened to Roosevelt's 1930s New Deal and what has more recently been happening to much of western European social democracy (Clayton & Ponstusson, 1998). In both cases, the employers used the surpluses appropriated from their employees to move their societies back toward a laissez-faire policy regime as soon as they secured the political conditions enabling them to do so.[8] Macro-level efforts to control and constrain capitalism's instability failed because of the capitalists' continued appropriation and politically effective distributions of the surpluses produced inside enterprises.

Marxian theory emphasizes how employers' decisions about distributing the surpluses are significantly influenced by the struggles between producers and appropriators of surpluses inside capitalist enterprises as well as by the competitive struggles among them. Hence Marxian theory suggests the internal transformation of enterprise structures. Instead of their typical capitalist structures that split employers from employees, a post-capitalist structure would position workers as, collectively, their enterprise's own board of directors—i.e. Marx's "associated workers." The era of capitalist employers (e.g., corporate boards selected by and responsible to major private shareholders) would then have come to an historic end. The capitalist class structure of production would have been superseded by such a collectivization of surplus appropriation inside enterprises (Wolff, 2010).

For example, consider enterprises newly structured such that the workers produce outputs in the usual way Mondays through Thursdays, but on Fridays, assembled in both plenaries and subgroups, they make decisions previously taken by boards of directors selected by (major) shareholders. That is, the workers democratically decide what, where, and how to produce and how to distribute their realized surpluses. They decide when and how to expand and contract. But they do not do that alone. They enter into co-respective power-sharing agreements with the local and regional communities where their physical production facilities are located.

---

[7]   A full exposition of how capitalist enterprises organize the production, appropriation, and distribution of surpluses can be found in Resnick & Wolff, 1987 (Chapter 3).

[8]   An alternative mode of articulating this argument—one that uses the terms "private capitalism" and "state capitalism" to differentiate laissez-faire from CRS policy regimes—is developed in Resnick & Wolff, 2002. There we extend the analysis to include the state capitalisms of the USSR and other "actually existing socialisms" which have demonstrated the same vulnerability to reversals back to laissez-faire or private capitalism as have CRS policy regimes and for parallel reasons.

The workers participate in the residential communities' decision-making processes and vice-versa.[9]

Such a micro-based level of socialism becomes the *necessary new complement* to the classic macro-level socialisms that stressed socialization of means of production and planning over markets. Indeed, the micro- and macro-levels of socialism would then support and, just as importantly, constrain one another. Macro-level property socialization and economic planning would emerge from and be accountable to the micro-level collectives appropriating the enterprise-level surpluses they would use to enforce that accountability. At the same time, the micro-level enterprise collectives would have their production and distribution decisions constrained by the macro-level (social) needs, priorities, and planning mechanisms (possibly co-existing with market mechanisms).

This micro-level socialism supports genuine democracy inside each enterprise. It also creates the parallel economic partner for democratic political institutions in residential communities. Democratic collectivities inside enterprises and their residential community counterparts would henceforth together reach their interdependent decisions. Likewise, they would share their interdependence with macro-level institutions, both economic and political.

Today's reviving Keynesianism once again largely ignores the micro-level issues raised in and by the Marxian criticism and alternative briefly sketched above. Most Keynesian programs now aimed to end the economic crisis, if they actually re-stabilized contemporary capitalism, would thereby initiate their own demise. That is, they would then repeat the historical pattern of oscillating back to a laissez-faire capitalism. The Marxian alternative program that included the micro-level transformation of production sketched above would break, finally, from the repeated oscillations between private and state-interventionist capitalisms and the unnecessary social costs of capitalism's instability.

---

[9]   A rich literature explores experiments in and analyses of such enterprises (producer co-operatives modeled on the Mondragon enterprises in Spain, Yugoslavia's worker-run enterprises, etc.) in which workers more or less appropriate and distribute the surpluses they produce; see Gibson-Graham (2006) for a theoretically sophisticated entrée into that literature.

Appendix: Sources for Figure 1
[Compiled by Jason Ricciuti-Borenstein]

1. For wage series for manufacturing workers, 1890-2007
A. Historical Statistics of the United States (HSUS), Series D 765-778, "Average Hours and Average Earnings in Manufacturing", 1890 to 1926
B. HSUS, Series D 845-876, "Average Days in Operation Per Year, Average Daily Hours, and Annual and Hourly Earnings, in Manufacturing", 1889 to 1914
C. HSUS, Series D 830-844, "Earnings and Hours of Production Workers in 25 Manufacturing Industries", 1914 to 1948
D. HSUS, Series D 802-810, "Earnings and Hours of Production Workers in Manufacturing", 1909 to 1970
E. U.S. Bureau of Labor Statistics, Current Employment Statistics, "Average Hourly Earnings of Production and Non-supervisory Workers in Manufacturing", 1939 to 2007, http://www.bls.gov/ces/.

2. For consumer price index:
F. HSUS, Series D 735-738, "Average Annual and Daily Earnings of Nonfarm Employees", 1860 to 1900
G. HSUS, Series D 722-727, "Average Annual Earnings of Employees", 1900 to 1970
H. U.S. Bureau of Labor Statistics, http://www.bls.gov/cpi/.

Notes: The series was constructed first by converting the various hourly wage series into real values of 2007. Second, in years for which multiple entries of the hourly wage existed, an average was taken such that:

       1890-1914, average of sources A and B
       1914-1919, B was the only source
       1920-1938, average of sources C and D
       1939-1948, average of sources C, D and E
       1949-1970, average of sources D and E
       1970-2007, E was the only source

Next, this hourly real wage series was converted into an index, in which 100 was set equal to the real hourly wage for 1890.

3. For productivity series for manufacturing output per hour

A. Historical Statistics of the United States, Series D 683-688, "Indexes of Employee Output", 1869 to 1969

B. U.S. Bureau of Labor Statistics, http://www.bls.gov/lpc/ "Industry analytical ratios for the manufacturing, all persons," http://www.google.com/search?ie=UTF-8&oe=UTF-8&sourceid=navclient&gfns=1&q=Superseded+historical+SIC+measures+for+manufacturing%2C+durable+manufacturing%2C+and+nondurable+manufacturing+sectors%2C+1949-2003++ftp%3A%2F%2Fftp.bls.gov%2Fpub%2Fspecial.requests%2Fopt%2Flpr%2Fhistmfgsic.zip

C. U.S. Bureau of Labor Statistics, http://www.bls.gov/lpc/, Series Id: PRS30006092, 1987 to 2007

Notes: The above data sources provide the annual percentage change in the quantity of output per hour for the manufacturing sector. The index was constructed as follows:

>   1890 to 1949, from source A
>   1949 to 1987, from source B
>   1987 to 2007, from source C
>   Year 1890 was set equal to 100.

References

Cayton, R., & Pontusson, J. (1998). Welfare State Retrenchment Revisited: Entitlemet Cuts, Public Sector Retrenchment, and Inegalitarian Trends in Advanced Capitalist Societies, *World Politics*, 51(1), 67-98.

Gibson-Graham, J.K. (1996). *A Post-Capitalist Politics*. Minneapolis: University of Minnesota Press.

Greenberg, S. B. (1996). *Middle Class Dreams: The Politics and Power of the New American Majority*. New Haven and London: Yale University Press.

Jones, V. (2008). *The Green Collar Economy*. New York: Harper Collins.

National Bureau of Economic Research. (2008). *US Business Cycle Expansion and Contradiction*. Retrieved August 21 2010, from   http://www.nber.org/cycles/cyclesmain.html

Resnick, S., & Wolff, R. D. (1987). *Knowledge and Class: A Marxian Critique of Political Economy*. Chicago: University of Chicago Press.

Resnick, S., & Wolff, R. D. (2002). *Class Theory and History: Captalism and Communism in the USSR*. New York and London: Routledge Publishers.

Resnick, S., & Wolff, R. D. (2006). *New Departures in Marxian Theory*. New York and London: Routledge Publishers

Ruccio, D. F. (1991). When Failure Becomes Success: Class and the Debate over Stabilization and Adjustment, *World Development*, 19, 1315-34.

Skidelsky, R. (2008, December 12). The Remedist. *The New York Times Magazine* [online]. Retrieved December 12, 2008, from http://www.nytimes.com/2008/12/14/magazine/14wwln-lede-t.html.

Wolff, R.D. (2010). Taking Over the Enterprise: A New Strategy for Labor and the Left. *New Labor Forum*, 19(1), 8-12.

Free Transit and Social Movement Infrastructure: Assessing the Political Potential of Toronto's Nascent Free Transit Campaign

Rebecca Schein

Abstract: This article examines the movement-building potential of a campaign for free and accessible public transit in the city of Toronto. The campaign, launched by the newly formed "Greater Toronto Workers' Assembly," calls for the de-commodification of Toronto's transit system, arguing that mass transportation is a public good that should be paid for by fair taxation. The demand for free transit represents a positive, concrete anti-capitalist vision for the future of the city, which could open a space for a broader public dialogue about public goods and public control over resource allocation. The process of developing and organizing a free transit campaign will present a productive set of challenges to the newly formed Assembly, pushing it to develop the relationships, skills, and internal processes necessary for nurturing a broad-based anti-capitalist movement.

Keywords: G20; transit; public sector; social movements; "right to the city"

The demonstrations surrounding the G20 summit in Toronto unfolded more or less as scripted. The state spent obscene amounts of public money to install security cameras in Toronto's streets, build an enormous fence, and augment the capacities of the local, provincial, and national police forces, both logistically and legally. Demonstrators marched peacefully along a designated route through deserted downtown streets. A few people broke windows and set fire to abandoned police cars. Police made full use of their brand new riot gear and special legal powers. Steve Paiken of TVO was shocked, *shocked*, to see police aggression directed at journalists and, as he put it, "middle class people" peacefully assembling. A thousand arrests.

Denunciations of police lawlessness and brutality. Calls for a public inquiry. Denunciations of vandalism. Calls for solidarity. And of course, the perennial lament that the voices and messages of labour and civil society were lost in the clamor.

To say the events were scripted is not to say that the violence and rights violations were not serious, or that people's anger, shock, and frustration are not real, righteous, and deeply felt. The problem with this script is that our side loses. We get bogged down in the postmortem, denouncing each other, and then denouncing the denouncers. We pour scarce resources of time and money into mobilizing for legal defense: we are literally put on the defensive. We react with renewed outrage to the predictable "over-reaction" of the state and continue to mourn the movements we should be working to build.

The aftermath of the G20 summit will be an important test for a newly formed activist organization called the Greater Toronto Workers Assembly (www.workersassembly.ca). Formally convened in January 2010, the Assembly is comprised of individual members from a diverse array of unions, leftist political groups, and grassroots community organizations[1]. The Assembly's organizational culture is still very much a work in progress, and it has not yet proven its capacity to sustain over the long haul the diligent, principled non-sectarianism that it has begun to cultivate over the past year. But coming out of the G20 summit, the analysis and political ambitions that have driven the Assembly's formation seem all the more urgent and necessary.

The impetus behind the Assembly, as I see it, is the idea that "changing the script" will require a new form of organization, one deliberately geared to gain traction against the contours of contemporary capitalism. At a time when unions have largely stopped acting like organs of a labour movement, and when workers increasingly identify their own fate with the fate of capital (and not without reason, given the financialization of many pensions), we need an organization capable of confronting the specific ways in which neoliberalism divides, demobilizes, and demoralizes its potential opponents. Since joining the Workers Assembly, I have often been asked about the use of the word "worker" in the organization's name. My answer has been that the work of the Assembly is to rebuild the meaning of "working class." That meaning will not be realized by fiat, and no organizational vision statement, however comprehensive or inclusive, will generate the cultural meanings that give shape and power to political identities. To rebuild the meaning and political potency of working class identities, we need an organization that will foster sustained relationships and sustained political dialogue—not as a precursor to movement-building, but as an intrinsic feature of the movement itself.

---

[1]   For a list of members' organizational affiliations see http://www.workersassembly.ca/links

In the weeks since the G20 summit, I have had many conversations debating the need for various organizations to weigh in on the question of property destruction, "diversity of tactics," and the meaning of solidarity in the face of state repression. Although I was dismayed that broken windows played their part in the G20 drama, it was hard for me to feel that a movement had been discredited, or that the messages of "legitimate protestors" had been undermined. In the absence of a movement with clear ambitions, an ostensibly tactical debate quickly becomes unmoored from strategy and devolves into a discussion of principles—principles of non-violence, solidarity, opposition to police violence, etc. As long as we are neither harnessed by the practicalities of building a mass movement nor oriented towards a vision we really believe we can win, these debates are unlikely to generate productive disagreement and dialogue on the broader left.

The Greater Toronto Workers' Assembly, however, has embarked on a project that has real potential to develop into the kind of movement in which impassioned debates over tactics will be inspiring and energizing, rather than defeatist and moralizing. At its general meeting in April, 2010, the Assembly voted to dedicate significant energy to a campaign for free, fully accessible public transit in the city of Toronto. Many of our members have been inspired by recent efforts to elaborate the "right to the city" as a rubric organizing demands for public services and city infrastructure (Harvey, 2008; World Charter on the Right to the City, 2004). In Toronto, recent fare-hikes, strikes, provincial funding cuts, cancelled or delayed construction projects, insufficient service, piecemeal and inadequate accessibility infrastructure, and public relations debacles have made our transit system the target of considerable public anger, much of which has been channeled into generalized anti-union resentment and calls for privatization. The Assembly began to see a role for itself here—not only to respond to rhetoric pitting transit riders and transit workers against each other, but to popularize an analysis of public goods and an argument for democratic control over city resources.

Mass transit is an essential pillar of Toronto's public infrastructure, yet its transit system is among the least "public" public systems in the world. Estimated at between 70 and 80 percent, Toronto's "fare-box recovery ratio"—the percentage of the system's operating budget paid for by individual riders at the fare-box—is among the highest in the North America and more than doubles that of some other large cities around the world (Toronto Environmental Alliance, 2009; Toronto Board of Trade, 2010). Many other transit systems in comparable cities "recoup" less than half of their operating budgets from fares, relying more heavily on subsidies from multiple levels of government. According to the Toronto Board of Trade (2010), "essentially no North American or European transit systems operate in [the] manner [of Toronto]" with respect to transit funding.

Riders rarely think about rising "fare-box recovery ratios," but few have failed to notice that fares have increased from $1.10 in 1991 to $3.00 in 2010—the last fare-hike in January 2010 arriving in the context of high unemployment and rising demand for emergency food and shelter services in the city. The fare-box recovery ratio represents a rough quantification of the efficiency with which neoliberal governments have divested from the public sphere and downloaded costs to the most vulnerable individuals. The failure to invest seriously in mass transit in recent decades has meant, moreover, that many Toronto residents outside the downtown core pay high fares for service that is inconvenient and inefficient. While the operating subsidies that support other transit systems reflect an understanding of mass transit as a public good, yielding benefits to entire communities and ecosystems, Toronto's system increasingly treats transit as a commodity, consumed and paid for by individual riders. The funding structure of Toronto's transit system is effectively a form of regressive taxation: although all of Toronto's residents benefit from transit infrastructure—including the car-owners who never ride a bus—our "public" system is funded disproportionately out of the pockets of the low- and middle-income people who rely on mass transportation in their daily lives.

The demand for free and accessible public transit has the potential not only to develop into a broad-based movement, but also to drive the development of the new kind of organization that the Assembly aspires to become. The Assembly is committed to its call for the outright abolition of transit fares, not merely a fare-freeze or fare-reduction. What is exciting to me about the free transit campaign is that the expression of a radical anti-capitalist principle—the outright de-commodification of public goods and services—actually serves in this instance to invite rather than foreclose genuine political dialogue about values, tactics, and strategies. While still in its early stages, the free transit campaign is already pushing us to elaborate both analytical and strategic links between commodification, environmental justice, the limits and capacities of public sector unions, and the interlocking forms of exclusion faced by people marginalized by poverty, racism, immigration status, or disability. Free transit could represent a site of convergence between many distinct activist circles in the city and foster greater integration and collaboration between environmental advocacy, anti-poverty work, and diverse human rights organizations. If the free transit campaign does succeed in bringing diverse and distinct activist cultures into conversation with each other, it will force the Assembly to grapple with strategic questions about its relationship to less radical organizations in the city. Given the marginalization and isolation that have long plagued leftist groups in Toronto and elsewhere, this should be a welcome challenge, particularly if the Assembly hopes to become an effective left pole in a broad alliance.

Among the strengths of the free transit campaign is the concreteness of vision. Within the left, efforts to elaborate a broad anti-capitalist vision too often run aground at the level of abstractions, generalities, and platitudes. Most Toronto residents would draw a blank if asked to "imagine a world without capitalism," but what Torontonian who has ever waited for a bus can't begin to imagine an alternate future for the city, built on the backbone of a fully public mass transit system? The invitation to imagine free transit is an invitation for transit riders to imagine themselves not simply as consumers of a commodity, but as members of a public entitled to participate in conversations about the kind of city they want to live in. Without devolving into abstract and alienating debates over the meaning of, say, socialism, the call for free transit invokes the things we value: vibrant neighbourhoods; clean air and water; participatory politics; equitable distribution of resources; public space where we are free to speak, gather, play, create, and organize. Even the most skeptical response to the idea of free transit—"how will you fund it?"—is the opening of a productive conversation about taxation and control over public resources. The call for free transit can effectively open a space for an unscripted political dialogue about the meaning of fair taxation, public goods, collective priorities, and public accountability for resource allocation.

But perhaps more fundamentally, the free transit campaign is a rare example of a political project on the left that is not reactive, defensive, nostalgic, or alarmist, but hopeful, proactive, and forward-looking. "Crisis talk" is pervasive in much of contemporary culture, but in left circles, it has become difficult to imagine a mode of organizing that is not oriented around predicting or responding to punctuated calamities of various kinds—whether a financial meltdown, an un/natural disaster, the latest wave of layoffs and service cuts, or the systematic violation of basic civil liberties on a weekend in downtown Toronto. In the case of free transit, however, we are free to move ahead with the campaign on our own timeline, to seek out and develop the kinds of relationships and democratic spaces that are necessary to sustain grassroots movements over the long term. For the Assembly, this will mean having the space and time to realistically assess its own capacities and to organically develop its own strategies and priorities.

The Assembly does not have modest ambitions: it hopes to nurture a broad-based anti-capitalist movement and to vitalize a new working class politics (Rosenfeld & Fanelli, 2010; Dealy, 2010). Its members are, I think, tired of listening to militant rhetoric unanchored to any genuine hope of winning. The push for an excellent, fully public and accessible transit system is a radical demand with immense popular appeal, an ambitious, long-range goal for which clear, achievable interim political victories are possible along the way. Free transit is not a crazy idea. Arguments in favour of free transit have surfaced sporadically in Toronto over the years, whether in an editorial by CAW economist Jim Stanford in *The Globe and Mail* or in a CBC interview with Deborah Cowen, a professor of geography at the University of Toronto (Stanford, 2005; Cowen, 2010). Some cities already have free transit systems, and many have partially free systems—in the downtown core, during holiday seasons or off-peak hours, or on "spare the air" days when smog levels are high. But in Toronto there has not yet been an initiative focused on building a broad-based movement dedicated to the eventual abolition of transit fares in the name of social, economic, and environmental justice.

Without abandoning or compromising its radicalism, the Assembly can push for concrete steps in the direction of de-commodified transit and build productive relationships with individuals and organizations who do not necessarily identify themselves as anti-capitalist. It will be in the process of pushing for interim reforms along the way to a de-commodified transit system that the Assembly will most need to articulate its political principles and its analysis of the spatialization of race and class in Toronto. Free transit in the downtown core may, for instance, be good for Toronto's tourism industry, but will it benefit the immigrant and working class communities in transit-poor areas of the inner suburbs, who spend proportionately more of their income to access poorer quality services than those available downtown? Proposals to pay for free transit through suburban road tolls will similarly hit hardest those working class communities whose neighbourhoods are so underserved by transit that they have no choice but to drive into the city for work. The process of developing interim priorities will not, in other words, postpone the challenge of articulating and popularizing a class-based and anti-racist argument for public infrastructure. Instead, the Assembly will be forced to pursue its most radical aspirations by cultivating a sustained dialogue about the interim remedies and strategies that will both address real needs in our communities and help build a broad-based movement over the long term.

It will be through this process of dialogue, I hope, that a new articulation of a politicized working class identity might emerge. Our earliest discussions of the free transit campaign are already pushing us to think about the social complexities that will need to be navigated if we are to build an effective free transit movement. Success will depend on our capacity to carve out and sustain a space for dialogue and negotiation among transit workers and riders, within unions, and across neighbourhoods and communities that have been unevenly affected by fare hikes and inadequate services. Questions of tactics and strategy cannot be divorced from the process of identifying, developing, and strengthening the complex connections between the people who need and use public goods and services and the workers who provide them. We will need to recognize the different ways in which our various constituencies are powerful and vulnerable and learn how to defend and protect each other. The free transit campaign lends itself to the kind of intensely local organizing through which honest dialogue, trust, and long-term relationships can be developed and nurtured—within and across neighbourhoods and among transit riders and workers. And of course, without these things, the campaign will go nowhere.

Among the strengths of the free transit campaign is its potential to foreground and develop an analysis of our collective stake in the protection of public goods. It is not difficult to talk about public goods in the context of mass transportation infrastructure. The shared benefits of public transportation are difficult to deny, particularly in a city as large and as sprawling as Toronto. Even setting aside the obvious ecological imperatives that should be driving public investment in greener infrastructure, there are powerful economic reasons to support a massive re-investment in Ontario's transportation sector. A serious effort to expand the reach and accessibility of the public transit system would serve not only to ease the burden of Toronto's most vulnerable residents and reduce the economic and health costs associated with air pollution and traffic congestion: such an investment could re-direct the wasted skills and resources embodied in Ontario's laid-off auto-workers and silent auto-plants, which could be converted to the production of high efficiency mass transit vehicles. As Sam Gindin and Leo Panitch (2010) argued recently in the *Toronto Star*, public borrowing to finance such investments represents not a wasteful burden on future generations, but a commitment to securing them a future. The real squandering of our collective resources lies not in public borrowing or benefits packages for public employees, but in our failure to direct existing skills, knowledge, and material capacities into a coherent strategy for building sustainable communities.

The idea of a free transit movement immediately foregrounds a number of thorny strategic questions for the left in Toronto: how to build trust, dialogue, and support for a free transit movement within the transit union; how to address and re-focus the widespread anger, mistrust, and resentment directed at the public sector in the current climate; how to sustain and advance anti-capitalist principles while building productive relationships within broader progressive milieux. Navigating these questions will be challenging, and the Assembly is still a long way from a coherent and systematic approach to answering them. But the fact that these questions surface so quickly and urgently is a positive sign of the ambition and seriousness with which the Assembly is approaching the organization of a free transit movement. The free transit campaign will push the Assembly to develop further its internal organizational and decision-making capacities, but it will also demand an outward-looking, inclusive process, in which the Assembly's role is to open space for debate, dialogue, and collective strategizing.

In fact, the transit system itself can provide the venue for us to stage public discussions about our collective resources and to share alternative visions for our city: the transit system is a readymade classroom, theatre, and art gallery, attended every day by people who could come to recognize their stake in the de-commodification of public goods of many kinds. My hope is that Toronto's buses, streetcars, and subway platforms could be places for experimentation, places to develop the new tactics, organizing skills, and relationships that might permit us to really depart from the prevailing script.

References

Dealy W. (2010). The Greater Toronto Workers' Assembly: Building a Space of Solidarity, Resistance, Change. *Relay*, 30, 27-28.

Gindin S, and L. Panitch. Public Sector Austerity Unreasonable and Irrational. *Toronto Star*. Retrieved on August 25, 2010 from, http://www.thestar.com/opinion/editorialopinion/article/837616--public-sector-austerity-unreasonable-and-irrational.

Greater Toronto Workers Assembly. Retrieved on September 9, 2010 from, www.workersassembly.ca

Harvey D. (2008). The Right to the City. *New Left Review*. 53, 23-40.

Rosenfeld H, and C. Fanelli. (2010). A New Type of Political Organization? The Greater Toronto Workers Assembly. *MR Zine: A Project of the Monthly Review Foundation*. Retrieved on August 23, 2010 from, http://mrzine.monthlyreview.org/2010/rf050810.html.

Stanford J. (2005). Free Public Transit on the Dirty Brown Horizon? *The Globe and Mail*. Retrieved on August 12, 2010 from, http://freepublictransit.org/Jim_Stanford.php.

Toronto Board of Trade. (2010). *The Move Ahead: Funding 'The Big Move'*. Retrieved on September 12, 2010from, http://www.bot.com/AM/Template.cfm?Section=Growing_the_Economy&Template=/CM/ContentDisplay.cfm&ContentID=4702.

Toronto Environmental Alliance. (2009). *Transit Commission Briefing Note TTC Operating Budget 2010: Fare Increase*. Retrieved on September 8, 2010 from, http://www.torontoenvironment.org/campaigns/transit/fareincrease2010.

Transit Funding Challenges for Toronto's Communities -- Interview with Deb Cowen. *Metro Morning*. Canada: Canadian Broadcasting Corporation March 29, 2010: runtime 8:03; http://www.cbc.ca/metromorning/2010/03/transit-funding-challenges-for-torontos-communities-runs-803.html

World Charter on the Right to the City. (2004). Social Forum of the Americas, Quito, Ecuador. Retrieved on September 12, 2010 from, http://v1.dpi.org/lang-en/events/details.php?page=124.

Peripheralization of the Centre: W(h)ither Canada?
- *Revisited* -

Dave Broad[1]

It has been over two decades since my article on the peripheralization of the centre was written, and a long time since I had taken a look at it.[2] When I was asked by the editors of *Alternate Routes* to revisit the article, my first thought was that it might simply be a curious exercise in nostalgia. A lot has happened since 1988, but it was interesting to discover that much of the analysis of the article still holds. With continuing global economic restructuring, or globalization as it came to be called in the 1990s, and the neoliberal politics of deregulation, privatization and free trade, the world economy has become ever more integrated under the control of transnational corporations and their respective states. The negative impact on work and welfare has been considerable. Though unanticipated, the original *Alternate Routes* article provided the basis for my continuing exploration of these trends.[3]

Peripheralization of the Centre

In the *Alternate Routes* article I had succinctly defined peripherlization as "the transformation of high-wage, liberal-democratic societies into low-wage, authoritarian societies" (Broad, 1988: 5). Let me comment on the main thesis of the article, and then I will turn to its relevance for current trends. The thesis of peripheralization of the centre, as put forward by a number of authors cited in my original article, is drawn from world systems analysis. World systems and dependency theo-

---

[1] Dave Broad is a Sociologist and Professor of Social Policy in the Faculty of Social Work at the University of Regina, Saskatchewan, Canada. His publications include Dave Broad, Hollow Work, Hollow Society? Globalization and the Casual Labour Problem, and Dave Broad and Wayne Antony (eds.), Capitalism Rebooted? Work, Welfare and the New Economy (both Fernwood Publishing).

[2] To give credit where credit is due, my original *Alternate Routes* article began life as a doctoral paper for a graduate seminar led by Professor Dennis Olsen. While absolving him of any blame for the final product, I wish to thank Dennis for providing a stimulating educational environment, and will put in a plug for his excellent book *The State Elite* (Olsen, 1980), which needs to be ranked along with books by John Porter (1965) and Wallace Clement (1975; 1977) as one of the seminal publications from the Carleton School of Sociology.

[3] See Broad, 1991; 1995a; 1995b, 1995c; 1997; 2000a; 2000b; and Broad & Antony, 2006.

ries posit that the capitalist world economy is a product of colonialism and imperialism, which has divided the world into an interlinked system of centre-periphery relations of unequal exchange, with centre (First World) domination of peripheral states and regions (the Third World).[4] Initially, the classical international division of labour (CIDL) of colonialism caste peripheral regions was as suppliers of labour power and raw materials for industrialization of the centre. Imperial centres went so far as to destroy budding industries, such as British destruction of the textile trade in India, or central Canadian erosion of 19th Century industries in Maritime Canada after Confederation (Acheson et al., 1985; Brym amd Sacouman, 1979).[5] The CIDL lasted through the eras of mercantile and industrial capitalism into the 20th century, but changed in the 1960s and 1970s with the advent of a new international division of labour (NIDL) (Frobel et al., 1980), which saw increasing industrialization of the periphery. There had, of course, been industrialization of some peripheral states, such as Argentina, in the mid-20th [6]century, while the major imperial powers were embroiled in World War II on their home fronts. This is referred to as import-substitution industrialization (ISI) by Third World scholars (Klaren and Bossert, 1986).

Imperial domination of the globe resumed after WWII under US tutelage, and with it the re-peripheralization of the Third World.[7] But by the 1960s, growing labour strength and expanding welfare-state legislation and state welfare services in the First World were contributing to a decline in profit rates (Kotz, 2003). This prompted transnational capital to promote the NIDL as a way to cut production costs and escape organized labour and First World regulatory regimes. In the Third World this brought industrialization based on superexploitation of labour (Frank, 1980; 1981). The flipside was a combined deindustrialization and reindustrialization of the First World, which included increasing unemployment and underemployment, restructuring of work, assaults on organized labour and the welfare state. This involved the shift from Fordism to flexible production regimes much discussed in the sociology of work. It is these processes of neoliberal globalization that led to

---

[4]   The post-World War II era of the Cold War resulted in the terminology of First World to describe the developed capitalist countries, generally found in the Northern hemisphere, Second World to describe the nominally socialist countries of the so-called Eastern Bloc, and Third World to describe the underdeveloped countries, found mostly in the Southern hemisphere. Hence the terms North and South are sometimes applied to the First World and Third World. Dependency theorists have also used the term sub-imperialism to describe the larger countries of the Third World, such as Brazil and South Africa. World-systems theorists have used the term semi-periphery to describe these countries, which lie between the centre and periphery in economic and political power. Some authors (e.g., Amin, 2004) now refer to certain countries in Africa, which have been largely marginalized from the world economy, as the Fourth World. This term has also been applied to the situation of many of the world's indigenous populations.

[5]   Dependency theorists writing in Canada and elsewhere have applied the concept of centre-periphery relations to political-economic relations within as well as between countries.

[6]   In my article I had quoted Frobel et al. (1980: 45) as saying that the NIDL "should be understood as an ongoing process, and not a final result."

[7]   With the breakup of the Soviet Union in 1989, we witnessed the same process with the re-peripheralization of countries in Eastern Europe by the West (see, e.g., Rosenberg, 1991).

erosion of living and working conditions and the trend referred to as the peripherlization of the centre.

When I was discussing the peripheralization process at a conference of Cuban, Latin American and North American social scientists and philosophers in Havana in 1997, one North American participant challenged the peripheralization thesis by saying that there is still a significant degree of difference between First World and Third World working and living conditions. My response was to agree, though noting the plight of many indigenous populations, immigrants and peoples of colour in First World countries, and to point out that we are talking about a trend, not a fait accompli.[8] Indeed, authors like Samir Amin contend that the First World domination of the Third World persists despite industrialization of peripheral zones. Amin (1994:17) asks: "Is third world industrialization the start of a geographical spread of capitalism that will gradually obliterate the center-periphery polarization? Or will the polarization be replicated in new forms? If so, what forms?" His answer is that "The most dynamic central capitalist powers benefit from all kinds of monopolies on a world scale" (Amin 1994: 208). Of particular note are financial and technological monopolies, and the military monopoly that the United States in particular holds.

Disposable Labour

Despite observable differences between the First and Third Worlds, there has clearly been an erosion of living and working conditions in centre countries like Canada. We have seen high levels of unemployment and underemployment, with increasing labour market insecurity and stagnation in real wages since the 1970s. Writing in the mid 1990s, I referred to six processes affecting work: (1) the degradation of labour; (2) the feminization of labour; (3) the housewifization of labour; (4) the informalization of labour; (5) the casualization of labour; and (6) the peripherlization of labour (Broad, 1995c). The first two processes will be familiar to most readers, degradation of labour having been discussed by Braverman (1974) and numerous labour process writers, and feminization of labour being a common theme in feminist writings on work. The notion of housewifization of labour was developed by a group of German sociologists to describe the ways that both the workforce and work itself were taking on the characteristics of housewifery (Mies, Bennholdt-Thomsen and von Werlhof, 1988).[9] Increasingly, work was becoming low status, low paid and ostensibly low skilled, but with employers expecting the ingenuity and output typical of housework.

---

[8]   In my article I had quoted Frobel et al. (1980: 45) as saying that the NIDL "should be understood as an ongoing process, and not a final result."

[9]   See page 12 of my *Alternate Routes* article (Broad, 1988).

Related to the housewifization of labour is the informalization of labour, a major concern for the International Labour Organization (ILO), which has been noting the prevalence and increase of informal economic activity across the globe. The ILO's concern is that this unregulated work is incredibly low status and low paid, with no job security. While the ILO focuses mainly on the Third World, some authors have been noting that informalization is a process that has advanced in the First World as well (Portes et al., 1989; Tabak and Crichlow, 2000). We see this especially where there are concentrations of immigrant and migrant labour in the centre, particularly in what are called global cities (Sassen, 1994). The ILO has a "decent work agenda" which includes, among other things, the need to improve working conditions in the informal sector. To do so, the ILO advocates formalization of the informal sector, but this misses the point that capital has always relied upon and continuously cultivates the informal sector for reproduction of labour power and access to cheap labour that can easily be disposed of (Broad, 2000b). Such labour can include home-based production, and production in informal workshops that is integrated into worldwide commodity chains. This has been commonly noted in production of textile and electronics goods, but can also be found in service work such as data processing and telemarketing.

Regarding the casualization of labour, British researchers began to note in the 1980s that more and more workers were being employed in part-time, temporary and contract positions (e.g., Allan and Wolkowitz, 1987), sometimes referred to as non-standard work because it does not have the security and working conditions of the full-time jobs of the post-WWII Fordist era (Broad, 1997; 2000a). Casualization is a structural trend and not simply the result of recessionary cycles, though there has generally been an increase in casualization during recessions, but with absolute increases in non-standard labour not disappearing in subsequent recoveries (Broad, 2000a; Pupo and Thomas, 2009).

Overall, these trends affecting the economy and work have continued to lead to deterioration of working conditions and welfare for many workers, as forecast by the now defunct Economic Council of Canada in its studies on good jobs and bad jobs in the service economy (ECC, 1990; 1991). But this prognosis did not stop a blossoming of studies in the later 1990s on a so-called New Economy of the information age that predicted an expansion of good jobs based on new information and communication technologies (ICTs), following earlier post-industrial society themes of writers like Daniel Bell (1973). The prognosis was that Canada, along with other First World countries, would witness a boom in New Economy jobs, and there was, in fact, an emergence of good jobs in ICT areas, but there was also a growth of many more drone jobs in this New Economy as well, not to mention the continuing loss of jobs that new technologies often brings (Broad and Antony, 2006). Some authors questioned the actual significance of the New Economy, and pronounced it dead with the dot-com crash of 2000-2001 (Henwood, 2003). The introduction of ICTs did, however, contribute to a trend of employment polarization and a declining of middle incomes and jobs, which also became a research theme in the 1990s. And while some workers benefited from the ICT boom for a time, Ross (2004), for example, provides case studies of the fallout for the favoured high tech workers when New Economy industries crashed, followed by the subsequent casualization of many of these jobs (Ross, 2009). Much high tech work like computer programming is now outsourced to Eastern Europe, the Third World, where workers are paid wage much lower than in centre states of the world economy.

Neoliberal Politics

In 1988, when I was writing the original article for *Alternate Routes,* the political trends of the time were being referred to as neoconservative, based on a so-called new conservatism epitomized by the regimes of Margaret Thatcher in the United Kingdom and Ronald Reagan in the United States. But because the political economics of this movement showed more affinity for classical liberalism than classical conservatism, neoliberalism soon became the term globally applied to the restructuring programs, which drew heavily on classical liberal thinkers like Adam Smith (1776).

There has been much discussion in the era of neoliberal globalization about the changing role of the capitalist state (McBride, 2005; Teeple, 2000). What we might call the *neocon con* was that the state would be shrunk. However, we have seen that, under neoliberalism, the state has not been downsized, but rather has assumed different emphases. In my article I had discussed the shift from liberal democracy to authoritarianism, from the Keynesian welfare state to free market policies. At the time (1988), Canada had signed a major free-trade agreement with the United States, which was followed by the North American Free Trade Agreement (NAFTA), formally incorporating Mexico in 1994. Clearly the rule of free enterprise was to be fully unleashed, with privatization, deregulation and cuts to social services being the order of the day, many governments announcing that they were "open for business". General Pinochet's Chile served as a model for Grant Devine's Tory government in Saskatchewan in the 1980s, based on Milton Freedman's Chicago school of economics. And despite obvious failures of liberalism and neoliberalism around the world (Wallerstein, 1995), the belief in neoliberalism persists. In the wake of the 2007 financial crisis we saw state bailouts of the failing finance sector, along with some other industries such as automobile manufacturing. But as state deficits have predictably mounted, we now see neoliberal politicians, economists and businesspeople calling for cutbacks to state spending on public programs. So once again, market economics are being used as an excuse to attack programs for the working class, while the wealthy have literally laughed all the way to the banks.

With regards to work, we have seen a shift from welfare to workfare policies in Western states (Peck, 1996; Vosko, 2000; Broad and Hunter, 2009). Social assistance programs have been cut back, made more difficult to access, and restructured to emphasize promotion of labour market attachment, sometimes even for those mentally or physically unable to participate in the labour market. Unemployment insurance programs have also been restructured and made more difficult to access, and treated more like social assistance programs than social insurance programs, with the Canadian system being euphemistically renamed "Employment Insurance".

As for the shift to a more authoritarian state discussed in my original article, we still have the trappings of democracy in Canada, though it is too often observed in the breach. Political commentators have noted for some time now that Western governments have moved to more executive decision-making, bypassing parliamentary procedures, and Canada is no exception. An example was the negotiations for the Multilateral Agreement on Investments (MAI) through the Organization for Economic Co-operation and Development (OECD) in 1995-1998, which bypassed parliamentary processes in Canada and other countries. This move to executive rule has become especially obvious under the reign of Steven Harper, who assumes the persona of an emperor. *The Globe and Mail* even ran a political cartoon on its editorial page after Harper's first 100 days in office likening him to Napoleon. Harper's successive minority governments have taken Canada further down the path to a military state, the case of Canada's participation in Afghanistan being a prime example. Prior to the Afghan engagement, Canada had a formal reputation as a peacekeeper, serving mainly under United Nations auspices. But under Harper, Canada has become more clearly a puppet of US foreign policy.

Within Canada, the state has continued a generally anti-labour stance previously identified by writers like Panitch and Swartz (1985).[10] This stance is sometimes obscured if we view only the federal level, because Canada's provinces have jurisdiction over much labour policy. Looking at the provincial level, we have seen numerous neoliberal programs of deregulation, privatization and anti-labour legislation since the 1980s. Most recently, in my home province of Saskatchewan the government of Brad Wall has passed Bill 80, allowing more non-union hiring in the building trades, and since taking office has persistently taken an anti-labour approach of attacking trade union rights and deeming many jobs to be "essential services," therefore not allowing strike action. Federal, provincial and municipal

---

[10]   Panitch and Swartz' book *From Consent To Coercion: The Assault On Trade Union Freedoms* was updated and expanded twice, most recently as Panitch and Swartz, 1993.

governments have also shown their teeth with strong police presences at recent events such a protests against the Winter Olympics in Vancouver and the G20 meetings in Toronto.

The essence of parties and governments like that of Harper is anti-democratic, despite frequent self-proclamations to be saviours of the people from the state. There is a libertarian populous streak to these governments, but very much tempered by right-wing ideology, and a strong "law and order" streak. Ideology clearly trumps democracy, as we have seen with the recent debate over the Canadian Census, with the Harper government wanting to shorten and gut the Census. Ostensibly this is because the mandatory long-form Census is a state intrusion on citizens' lives. But critics have argued that the stance taken really reveals the Harper government wanting to dispense with a data source that provides information that can be used to counter the Tories' very ideological positions taken on political and social issues like crime and poverty. Fortunately, significant numbers of Canadians have come out in opposition to the Harper government on this issue.

Overall, working and living conditions have continued to deteriorate for many people since the 1980s (Jackson, 2009). In the labour market we see continuing high levels of unemployment and underemployment, with the latter often masking the former. The numbers of unemployed and underemployed youth are especially high, and many aboriginal people and immigrants are either marginalized or superexploited in the formal and informal economies. In western Canada we see frequent reporting of deplorable conditions for migrant workers in the meat-packing industry which, for example, led to an important union drive in Brooks, Alberta.

Women in Canada have made some gains, but continue to be found in inferior positions in the labour market, and subject to the double day of formal and domestic work. One area that is still sadly neglected in Canada is child day care, despite the significant research that shows both the need for, and benefits of child care for families, women workers and for children's development.[11] Despite a 1989 all-party vote in the Canadian Parliament to eradicate child poverty by the year 2000, the fact that one in five Canadian children live in poverty is an international disgrace.[12] The situation of Aboriginal children in Canada is especially disgraceful, and certainly warrants Third World comparisons. And the Harper government has further embarrassed Canadians by being one of only four governments in the world to vote against the United Nations Declaration on the Rights of Indigenous Peoples.[13]

---

[11] The Child Care Resource and Research Unit at the University of Toronto is a good source for materials on child day care. See www.childcarecanada.org.

[12] The Canadian Centre for Policy Alternatives provides useful studies on employment, poverty and other social issues in Canada. See www.policyalternatives.ca.

[13] The four governments were Canada, the United States, Australia, and New Zealand, but with the subsequent election of a labour government Australia ratified the Declaration.

Global Resistance

In my original article, I would have to say I was a bit too sanguine regarding the probable success of opposition struggles. But there have been successes, not least of which is the ability of the labour movement in Canada to maintain a fairly high union density. While US labour is now only 12 percent unionized, a third of Canada's workers are still unionized. Activists were successful in thwarting the undemocratic behind-closed-doors negotiations of the Multilateral Agreement on Investments, and were also successful in fights against plans to expand private-public partnerships (PPPs) in Canada (Loxley and Loxley, 2010). The Council of Canadians and others have persistently fought the privatization of Canadian water. Anti-poverty and social activists have shown a strong presence in opposition to authoritarian and inegalitarian thrusts of G8 and G20 meetings in Quebec City and Toronto, and the Winter Olympics in Vancouver. In these struggles we have seen the state trying to implement anti-insurgency tactics that have been the norm in the Third World, including the struggle for "hearts and minds" through ideological means. There has not been the same level of oppression here, but the Canadian government has certainly been guilty of complicity in extreme repression in its participation in conflicts such as that in Afghanistan, promoting warfare, not welfare. Fortunately, Canadian activists have also been involved in global rights struggles, including participation in the World Social Forum, the global movement of movements. Trade unionists have been active in making linkages with Third World workers with, for example, the United Steelworkers, which represents 850,000 workers in Canada, the Caribbean and the United States, recently announcing plans to form an international union with the National Union of Miners and Metal Workers, which represents 180,000 workers in Mexico (La Botz, 2010).

I noted in my original article that the biggest obstacle in the fight to improve living and working conditions globally is the ideology of liberal individualism, and this is still the case. The neoliberals have been quite successful at appealing to people as individuals, using ideological and practical attacks on the welfare state, trade unions and so-called special interest groups, meaning any group that opposes their right-wing views. But despite right-wing efforts in Canada, and despite the disarray of formal opposition parties and informal opposition political groups, the Harper government has not managed to win a majority government in Canada after three elections. This in itself is a good sign for those of us interested in promoting social justice, and bodes well for continuing struggles against both the peripheralization of the centre and for global rights generally.

References

Allen, Sheila and Carol Wolkowitz. 1987. *Homeworking: Myths and Realities.* London: Macmillan Education.

Amin, Samir. 1994. *Re-Reading The Postwar Period.* New York: Monthly Review Press.

Amin, Samir. 2004. *The Liberal Virus: Permanent War and the Americanization of the World.* New York: Monthly Review Press.

Braverman, Harry. 1974. *Labor and Monopoly Capital: The Degradation of Work in the Twentieth Century.* New York: Monthly Review Press.

Broad, Dave. 1988. "Peripheralization of the Centre: W(h)ither Canada?" *Alternate Routes,* Vol. 8, pp. 1-41.

Broad, Dave. 1991. "Global Economic Restructuring and the (Re)Casualization of Work in the Centre: With Canadian Illustrations," *Review,* Vol. 14, No. 4 (Fall), pp. 555-94.

Broad, Dave. 1995a. "Globalization, Free Trade and Canadian Labour," *Critical Sociology,* Vol. 21, No. 2, pp. 19-41.

Broad, Dave. 1995b. "Globalization and the Casual Labour Problem: History and Prospects," *Social Justice,* Vol. 22, No. 3 (Fall), pp. 67-91.

Broad, Dave. 1995c. "Globalization Versus Labour," *Canadian Review of Social Policy,* No. 36 (Winter), pp. 75-85; *Monthly Review,* Vol. 47, No. 7 (December), 20-31.

Culture

Political Poetry

Lyle Daggett[1]

"Political" poetry. All human activity is political because it takes place in a context — the context of history. Sending someone a recipe for crab meat salad is one thing if you work food prep in a restaurant kitchen. It means something else if you're Nancy Reagan.

Poets have been political, in some sense of the word, from the earliest beginnings to the present. Enheduanna, Sumerian poet, priestess of the moon goddess Inanna, the earliest poet whose name is known. The Chinese government compiled collections of popular folk songs — for example, the *Shih Ching*, the Book of Songs — as a way of learning something about what the people were thinking. (Did Nixon listen to Bob Dylan or Joan Baez or Pete Seeger? Does George Bush listen to Billy Bragg or Tracy Chapman or rap music?)

Homer was political. (George Bush on the walls of Troy.) The *Bhagavad Gita* (which J. Robert Oppenheimer quoted as he watched the first atomic bomb explode in the New Mexico desert) was and is political. The plays of Aeschylus and Sophocles and Euripedes were defining forces in Greek society. Dante and Shakespeare were all political. (If Dante were writing today, who would he consign to the ninth circle of Hell?) The great flowering of art and culture in medieval Spain grew originally from the founding of a new Umayyad dynasty in exile by survivors of the conquest of Damascus by the Abbasids. The trouveres and troubadours of medieval France lived in a time of constant upheaval and displacement and continuously shifting political alliances, in which most if not all of them were intimately involved. (Many died during the wholesale slaughter that took place during the Albigensian crusades, following which troubadour poetry essentially came to a halt.)

---

[1]   This work was first published by Pemmican Press.

Chaucer was political, Tu Fu (or Du Fu) was political, Murasaki Shikibu was political. Andrew Marvell, William Blake, Shelley, Keats, Byron, Whitman, Rubén Darío, José Martí, Yosano Akiko. Political, in at least some sense of the word.

What we're talking about here is something more specific. We're talking about poetry that expresses or reflects — either explicitly or at least by suggestion — politics that are left-wing, working-class, populist, or of a similar character.

How to combine politics with creative work remains an unsettled question on the political Left. This is not simply a question of Socialist or Communist Realism versus whatever else.

The widespread stereotype of Socialist Realism emphasizes the huge public portraits and statues of Lenin, Stalin, Mao, etc., and maybe allows for some murals and poster art of muscle-bound workers in factories and rosy-cheeked starry-eyed young men and women gazing off at the bright horizon of the future. This, again, is the stereotype.

But it should be patently obvious that public portraits and monument sculpture, poster art, and so on, comprise only a portion of (and not necessarily the best) of a culture's art. We cannot judge the effectiveness of Socialst Realism (or any other artistic movement or tendency of the political Left) based only on the more mediocre or homogenized examples.

Should we judge the art of capitalist societies based only on Norman Rockwell and Mount Rushmore? Should we judge American literature based on *McGuffey's Reader*? Are these the basis for the prevailing critical standards advocated by the literature and art departments at leading universities?

For every Norman Rockwell there's a Diego Rivera, a David Siqueiros, a Walter Crane, a Sue Coe; for every Edgar Guest and Joyce Kilmer there's a Thomas McGrath, a Muriel Rukeyser, a Hugh MacDiarmid.

Some people argue that there is much badly written political poetry — that much of it reads like a political pamphlet chopped into line breaks, or sing-song rhyming doggerel — and that this proves that political subject matter is not suited to poetry.

But there is also much badly written love poetry, badly written poetry about religion, nature, and every other subject. Do we then conclude that love, religion, nature, etc., are also unsuitable subjects for poetry? Do Hallmark greeting cards invalidate the work of Dante and Shakespeare and Shelley and Wordsworth?

Journalism reports facts; poetry tells the truth. In our time much political discourse in English — including discourse on the political Left — is weighted with high-sounding rhetoric, with the Greco-Roman vocabulary of philosophy, psychology, and the other social sciences. One of our tasks, when writing about political subject matter (or any other subjects) is to make decisions about the vocabulary we use.

There is nothing wrong with using, in a poem, words such as "capitalism," "working class," "imperialism," "revolution," etc. The challenge is to ground such language in the concrete physical texture and detail of the world we live in from day to day, to reclaim it from the bourgeois abuse and alienation it has suffered, to give it the life and meaning it can actually have.

We are not talking about merely taking a political speech or pamphlet, or a set of theoretical statements, and simplistically grafting them onto the skeleton of a poem — as if writing a poem were an act of taxidermy. It's difficult to write a love poem if you've never been in love, or to write a poem about nature if you've never touched a tree.

Similarly, it can be difficult to write a good political poem if you've never marched in an anti-war demonstration, or faced a platoon of police in riot gear preparing to charge, or tried to pay rent or medicals when you've been unemployed for six months. The best examples of good left-wing political poetry are written out of an organic understanding of the politics, and out of a passionate involvement in the political movements of the time and place in which the poet lives.

Poetry of the political Left from the twentieth century has developed along several currents or tendencies. My intention here is not to define rigid categories but to give examples of some of the possibilities poets have explored. Though one or two of the poets I've named below might not strictly be considered politically Left, all have at least shown a general outlook in their work that is populist, working-class, anti-fascist, radically democratic, or of a similar character.

1. Poetry rich in metaphor and imagery, poetry that works mainly be evoking feeling and sensory experience (rather than by elaborating intellectual argument or rhetorical appeal). Example poets might be Pablo Neruda (usually), Paul Éluard, Lorca, Yosano Akiko, Mahmoud Darwish, Dale Jacobson, René Depestre. Sometimes verging on surrealism, as with Éluard and Lorca and Depestre.

2. Poetry that is agitational in tone, spare in imagery and metaphor, working by the kinetic energy of public speech. Examples are Bertolt Brecht, Mayakovsky, Sol Funaroff, Langston Hughes, César Vallejo in *Spain, Take This Cup from Me.*

3. Poetry similar to the second type above but with a quieter voice, more personal, direct face-to-face speech rather than public oratory. Examples are Nazim Hikmet, Otto René Castillo, Roque Dalton, Claribel Alegría, Maria Aliger, Anna Swir, Joy Harjo sometimes, Carl Sandburg, Luis J. Rodríguez often, Faiz Ahmed Faiz.

4. Poetry that derives from or consciously imitates folk song. Examples include Brecht (sometimes), Thomas McGrath (sometimes), José Martí, Hugh Mac-Diarmid occasionally, Langston Hughes, Naomi Replansky at times.

5. Poetry that is essentially traditional or classical lyric in tone (whether or not employing the external forms — sonnets, quatrains, etc.). Examples are Thomas

McGrath (most characteristically), Louis Aragon, Miguel Hernández, Rafael Alberti, Mao Tse-Tung [or Mao Zedong], William Blake (in the shorter lyric poems), Rubén Darío, Yannis Ritsos, Nancy Morejón, Don Gordon, Olga Cabral, Nelly Sachs.

6. Poetry that communicates by its rhetorical strength, poetry of ecstatic utterance. Similar to type 2 above but with more elevated language. Examples are William Blake (in the "prophetic" poems), Léopold Senghor, Walt Whitman, Kenneth Fearing, Yannis Ritsos in some of his longer poems, Anuradha Mahapatra, Joy Harjo sometimes, Dennis Brutus, Janice Mirikitani, Muriel Rukeyser.

7. Poetry that communicates mainly by intellectual argument or statement. Examples are W. H. Auden, Edwin Rolfe, Jack Beeching.

8. Poetry that is documentary or journalistic in tone and method. Examples are Agostinho Neto, Javier Heraud, Leonel Rugama, Zöe Anglesey (often), Yannis Ritsos (sometimes), Anna Swir (sometimes), Nazim Hikmet especially in his book-length poem *Human Landscapes from My Country*.

9. Poetry that works by humor or satire, or by an overall humorous or satirical tone. Examples include Kenneth Patchen (often), Thomas McGrath now and then, Kenneth Fearing from time to time, Mayakovsky often.

Obviously none of the poets named above wrote purely in the manners or styles outlined here. All have written poetry that fluidly combines the various approaches described above, and are certainly not limited to the possibilities given here. The above list is, again, intended to suggest some of the existing possibilities, not to limit or define rigidly.

Let us state here for the record that political correctness, understood properly, is a good thing. The expression "politically correct" originally meant "politically (and/or ethically/morally) the right thing to do." It became a little confusing, sometimes, to talk about what was "politically right" because it sounded a little bit like "*the* political right" (who are, of course, politically wrong). So people got into the habit of saying "politically correct" instead, which sounded a little pompous sometimes but tended to be less confusing. To write poetry with political content that is left-wing, working-class, populist, or of a similar nature, is the right thing to do.

The examples above make it clear that it is thoroughly possible to write poetry that has progressive political content and that is well-written. The fact is that left-wing political poetry, taken as a whole, is *better poetry* than poetry in which the poet has tried to leave politics out of it, or in which the poet has deliberately written from a right-wing perspective (I suppose a few examples of the latter do exist).

We should have no hesitation about saying this — not, obviously, as absolute decrees from Olympus, but as acts of affirmative belief: Carl Sandburg wrote better poetry than Ezra Pound. Muriel Rukeyser wrote better poetry than T. S. Eliot. Thomas McGrath wrote better poetry than Robert Lowell. Langston Hughes wrote better poetry than Wallace Stevens. Gwendolyn Brooks wrote better poetry than Marianne Moore. Mayakovsky wrote better poetry than Akhmatova or Mandelstam. Brecht wrote better poetry than Rilke. Otto René Castillo and Leonel Rugama wrote better poetry than Octavio Paz. Etheridge Knight wrote better poetry than John Berryman. Sharon Doubiago and Joy Harjo and Dale Jacobson and Luis Rodríguez and Nellie Wong write better poetry than Jorie Graham or Marvin Bell or C. K. Williams or Billy Collins or Sharon Olds.

We don't need the ruling class (or its representatives in arts and letters) to tell us whether or not we're good poets. The record of our poetry, and the history from which it arises, speaks for itself. We reject "literary" standards that preclude politics as acceptable or essential subject matter. We belong in the real world of the living — breathing, changing, revolutionary — and the real world (and the poetry that grows from it) is the only answer we need to give.

Play Review

Multinational [G]rape Corporation written and directed by Ozgur Cinar, performed by Ozgur Cinar and Chara Berk. 2010.

Reviewed by: Aaron Henry[1]

"Welcome to the market time. Everything has turned into a market today ergo it is not that surprising to see urinals exhibited in museums". Enter Multinational [G]rape Corporations (MGC), the play that took this year's Ottawa Fringe Theatre and Arts festival by storm, winning the outstanding original work award. Yet reviews of this play, for the most part, have entirely missed what is truly outstanding about it. While several reviews have praised the actors, who were indeed electrifying, or marveled over the irreverence and the spectacle of the play, none of them have discussed the meaning of this play. The meaning has been largely shoved aside, one reviewer even went so far as to suggest that "it defies explanation" (Marr, 2010). This is disappointing because it is in the structure of the play where Cinar's brilliance, the play's originality and its message lie. It is, then, the architecture of the play that needs to be given attention, if MGC is going to be reviewed for not just its spectacle but for its internal content. However, the two are necessarily interdependent.

The set of the play is austere. It features a table and two chairs upstage, a suitcase full of different props and two squares on the floor formed by red-tape labeled security. The play opens with a man and a women vomiting through a slit in the closed curtain while eating and drinking behind it, a married couple who are the key subjects of the play. The play scrolls through many different locales in capitalist society, ranging from the interior of an immigration office where the man is made to pay over and over again to gain permanent residency; a doctor's office where tapeworms are removed from the woman—played indomitably by Chara Berk—

---

[1] Aaron Henry is a MA student at Carleton University in the Department of Political Economy. He can be reached at ahenry2@connect.carleton.ca

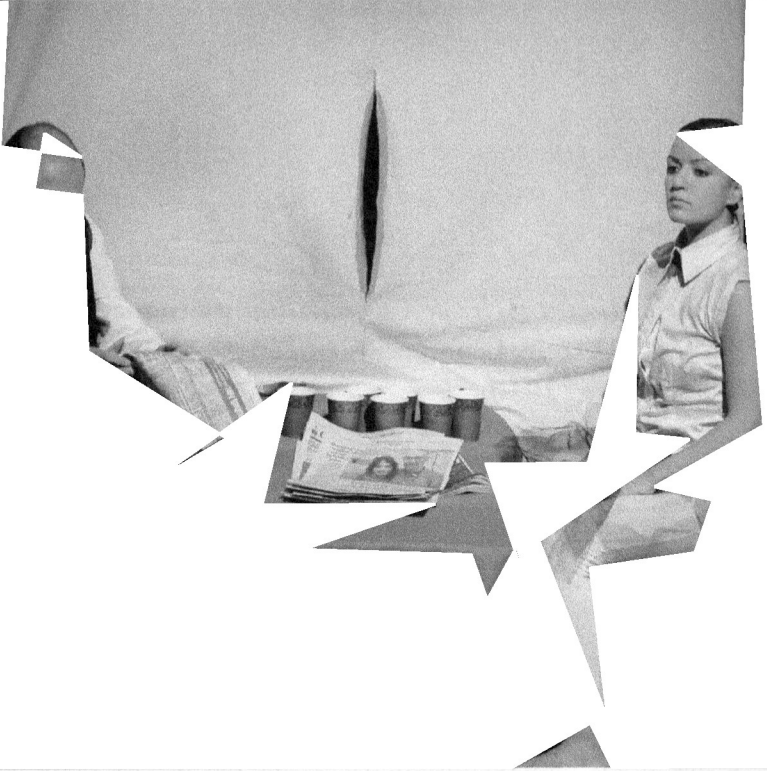

where, as a consequence, the doctor informs her of not eating organic food; the first date between the married couple, to a scene of protest against exploitation. Each of these scenes closes with the couple's retreat to the table. The next scene begins with the transformation of the woman, following a sound cue that imitates defecation, into an advertisement for different products and services ranging from fair-trade coffee, CDs or for a holiday vacation. Following this metamorphosis of the woman into a commodity, the couple retreats into their respective security boxes where the man, played by Cinar, attempts to commit suicide over and over again to no avail.

This structure has a number of important effects that taken together form Cinar's critique of capitalist society—a critique that goes far beyond being merely anti-consumerist and anti-security, as other reviewers have commented on. Foremost, the play is presented as a number of instances between subjects. The thread of unity that binds these instances is not that of unified characters with a linear narrative but the existence of the market within these relations. This is perhaps epitomized by the scene where the man applies for a study permit and then a permanent residency card to integrate into Canada. This scene unfolds as primarily a monetary relationship between the man and the Canadian immigration officer who remains alienated from the man and treats him from a distance established by both the cash relationship and the sterile rationality of the bureaucracy. Similarly, on the couple's first date the romantic evening is disrupted as the woman laments that she must "take a dump" but that they can't afford access to a toilet. The scene sublimates the tender moment of the couple back into the market. The love between them cannot exist without the commodification of the most basic and biological human needs.

MGC produces its scenes around subjects that are produced by market relations. This forecloses on the unified character one would find in the classic plays of Shakespeare, Jonson, Wilde, Synge, etc. and substitutes this character for a fragmented subject that develops and disappears in line with the market relations that Cinar exposes. The play progresses not as a linear narrative but as a process of interaction between fragmented subjects as the man and woman transform before the audience, into police officers, immigration officials, doctors, waiters and lovers. The subjects are then formed in context to the power relations that develop within capitalist society and, as such, they develop and disappear discontinuously and through this disclose the totality of these relations. This structure conveys the message that the market has fully crept into social life, to the degree where one is at once an advertisement and a person. Living under these conditions produces a number of contradictions that constitute the insanity and hypocrisy of living in capitalist society.

Market society then, produces not only fragmented subjects but the complete fragmentation of social life. This fragmentation allows the brutality of capitalism to colonize the human condition. As Cinar laments, we get urinals next to the wonders of human history, cosmetics next to the death tolls in Afghanistan and Iraq, the marketing of vacations alongside brutal exploitation and dictatorship. Cinar reveals the societal response to this through the couples retreat to their own private security boxes, provided to them by the market. In this sense, the complete commodification of social life finds its terminal point of expression in the partitioning of our own social beings from these processes and our own feeble attempts to secure ourselves from them. The consequences MGC aptly shows is the reinforcement of our own alienation from ourselves and from each other, precisely because we all form part of capitalist society. The man, in particular, is a paragon of this reality as he attempts suicide in his own private security box to end his imprisonment from the market only to be distracted by the very processes he revolts against in disgust. His repeated failure to commit suicide is caused by his inability to see that he himself constitutes part of this market society. Cinar in fact lays this theme out quite clearly and succinctly in the opening lines when the woman declares "We are the flowers of the commercial world. We are the vomit of the commercial world". They, like all of us, are at once both of these things, nurtured and cared for as consumers, the subjects of society and at once the objects of it - the refuse, the labourers who are exploited to constitute its existence. The tragedy and insanity is that the couple cannot recognize themselves as the subjects that constitute the processes that transform them into these wretched objects.

This is one of the central messages of MGC. The structure of the play conforms to that of capitalist society insofar as capitalist society cannot be understood through a single narrative. Instead it can only be understood under the fragmentary conditions its relations of exploitation and alienation produce. Superficially this reality appears disjointed, chaotic, and beyond explanation. However, with greater focus we see ourselves as the subjects of capitalist society that constitute these relations. Our imprisonment to the market stems from the fact that we ourselves play a part, much like the man and woman, in the exploitation and alienation that constitute capitalist society. In the end we cannot understand this reality; we have after-all "only applied for cleaner, dish-washer or waiter positions". We don't understand that in these positions we ourselves are both the subject and object of these processes. Cinar's play is a scream to see outlining this insanity. As such, Cinar's play constitutes an important critique of capitalism in Canadian society and warrants engagement by all.

References

Marr, Den. Fully Fringed, June 28th, 2010. www.fullyfringed.ca
Photos by A. Erdem Ozcan.

Movie Review

Eyes Wide Shut, **Director: Stanley Kubrick; Scenario: Stanley Kubrick, Frederic Raphael; Starring: Nicole Kidman (Alice Harford), Tom Cruise (Dr. William 'Bill' Harford), Madison Eginton (Helena Harford), Sydney Pollack (Victor Ziegler), 1999/USA, 159 min., adaptation from Traumnovella by Arthur Schnitzler.**

Reviewed by: Bora Erdagi[1]

Eleven years after its release, it is worth remembering Stanley Kubrick's last film *Eyes Wide Shut* for its critique of dehumanized (bourgeois) lifestyles of our times. Kubrick worked on the screenplay for quite a long time and could finish shooting only months before his death. The inspiration was the novel *Traumnovella* by Arthur Schnitzler who was a close friend of Sigmund Freud. The film is an attempt to question the notions of love, trust, and sexuality in order to unfold the taken-for-granted relations between these notions. It also reveals the role these notions play in constructing and reconstructing social bodies in a certain way. It tells the story of an upper-middle class New York couple (Bill Harford performed by Tom Cruise and Alice Harford performed by Nicole Kidman) who lose their way upon having a few existential crises in three consecutive days. The diverse routes Alice and Bill take to deal with their own traumas opens up the possibility to observe the conditions of different levels of (un)consciousness. Alice, as opposed to Bill, is neither attached in an unbounded way to the dream she was thrown into nor is she too heavily involved in the circumstances surrounding her way of life. Bill, on the other hand, is capable of easily justifying the conditions of his life through his instrumental rationality; nevertheless, he easily falls apart within the first crisis. This review attempts to unfold the ways in which the characters try to overcome

---

[1] Dr. Bora Erdagi is a research assistant in the Department of Philosophy at Kocaeli University, Izmit, Turkey. He can be reached at berdagi@gmail.com.

these crises with respect to their class positions. In so doing, it also undertakes a broader search to speculate about the reified nature of current social relations. In other words, while the film reflects the psychoanalytic exploration of the characters, this review aims at a socio-political analysis of the characters.

Bill is a medical doctor working for upper-class people, and his wife Alice works as an art director. In the opening scene we see them in an extremely fancy Christmas ball where they find themselves separated and try to find each other for the rest of the evening. The next night, during a moment of drunkenness before having sex, Alice and Bill start talking about the previous night. Alice suddenly starts asking Bill questions about their relationship. Bill has a hard time answering Alice's simple questions such as "why do you love me?" As he tries to get out of the situation he is trapped in, he is faced with a confession from Alice. Alice tells him that she cannot avoid thinking about another man. More strikingly, she confesses that she was once ready to leave everything behind for the man she was thinking about. This confession shatters Bill's preconceived beliefs about his marriage as well as his own being. He is thus forced to open his eyes. However, he is not totally woken yet since opening one's eyes does not necessarily imply they have abandoned the dream. Bill, nevertheless, is now left scared and vulnerable, far from the stability of his security zone.

Upon receiving a phone call from a patient's family, Bill leaves home. But this trip will turn into a nightmare as he is now entirely defenseless. This nightmare will go on until Alice wakes him up. When he arrives at the patient's house, he is informed that his patient has died. Afterwards, the deceased patient's daughter confesses her love for Bill in the funeral room to which he does not respond and leaves the house. Walking on the street he encounters a prostitute, chats with her for a bit and goes to her place, something he would not have done before. These experiences greatly complicate things for Bill, especially after losing his footing on the taken-for-granted ground upon which he formally stood. The light of the real world now dazzles his eyes and yet he does not stop there. For him, the night turns into a search for a story through which he may obtain a counter-position to his wife's story so that he can reconstruct his lost self-esteem and strengthen his ego.

The audience is then brought to a pivotal moment in the story when Bill meets a friend in a pub. His friend mentions a private sex party for upper class New Yorkers. Bill obtains the secret password from his friend and attends by infiltrating the party house with a rented mask and costume. However, Bill's identity is revealed and a prostitute sacrifices herself in an effort to rescue him. After having to leave the party, he gets back home and finds Alice talking in her sleep. He wakes her up. Alice tells Bill that, in her dream, he and she were naked in a deserted place. She says that when he left her to find their clothes, she felt better. Then, the man she had been constantly thinking about appeared and they began having sex in front of a crowd. Alice's dream brings forth an absolute possibility for Bill to be woken up from his own dream that is his reality. However, Bill denies that possibility and retains his calm position. The next day, he returns the rented costume and witnesses the store owner selling his teenage daughter to others for sex. In light of these, and other shocking events in two consecutive nights, he realizes that he has to face his own reality. That same night Bill, who finally has something of his own to confess, starts explaining to Alice what he had experienced over the last three days. This, for both of them, may denote the end of the sleep, but still not the dream. Their sleep ends and eyes are now wide open! With the first sunlight falling on the ground, the Harford family is metamorphosed.

While Christmas shopping the next day, we hear a short dialogue between our "exhausted warriors":

Bill: *What do you think we should do?*

Alice: *What do I think? I don't know. Maybe I think (...) we should be grateful that we've managed to survive through all of our adventures (...) whether they were real or only a dream.*

Bill: *A dream is never just a dream.*

Alice: *The important thing is we're awake now.*

Alice's open, questioning and repentant attitude throughout the film proves to be healing for their relationship. She helps, despite all the hardship, the lived experience arise to the level of consciousness rather than suppressing it. Throughout the film, Bill appears on the screen much more than Alice does. Alice however, appears only in critical moments, mimicking the relationship between the conscious and unconscious.

Bill, on the other hand, acts 'rationally' under almost all circumstances. But his rationality lacks content; it is completely instrumental, and he observes reality from a paradigmatically representational perspective. Questioning is rarely a feature of his rationality. He fears falling apart as he experiences something new and shocking. However, falling apart in Bill's case does not spring from the 'shock of experience', which Walter Benjamin defines in his miscellaneous writings as a norm of nineteenth-century intellectuals. According to Benjamin, shock disintegrates people's emotional world, but it also restructures their intellectual world. In Bill's case, it is hard to observe this restructuring of his reason because he does not utilize the shocking experiences to transform his reality. It is more as if Bill has had an accident and keeps chasing whatever has crashed into him rather than trying to understand what had happened. It is, therefore, obvious that Bill is not a typical inheritor of the nineteenth-century shock experience. In this sense, he indeed behaves in the exact opposite way to which Benjamin describes. Bill represents the instrumental reason

that Theodor W. Adorno radically criticizes. Moreover, Bill resembles a typical rec-
onciliatory bourgeois of twentieth-century Keynesianism who declares himself as
participative in social and political life, while completely ignoring the ongoing class
struggles and yet wanting his 'heroism' to be acknowledged by others. His dreams
and fantasies about the world—and about his heroic position in it—replace his real
life experiences, and therefore it is difficult for him to be woken from his dreams
(his constructed reality).

Alice, on the other hand, positions herself at the complete opposite pole. She
thinks that it is foolish to hide behind masks, especially after the masks are uncov-
ered. Thus, unlike Bill, she chooses to deal with reality, not through fantasy but
through language. In that, she also tries to emancipate language from its given
constraints. Emancipating language from its chains allows for slippages and enables
consciousness to set itself free from tensions. This opens up room for spontaneity.
Her use of story-telling, her first story occurring while her and Bill were smoking
marijuana and the second after just waking up, represents this process. Alice's peaceful reconciliation with reality is therefore much easier than Bill's, which moves Alice
to an advantageous position over Bill. However, it by no means puts her in a revolutionary position because Alice in a sense occupies the position of the bourgeoisie
in the totality of the capitalist system, as Georg Lukacs would put it. For Lukacs,
the bourgeoisie is aware of the reality of class struggles with respect to their position within the master-slave dialectic. However, for the sake of their very existence,
'the master' (the bourgeoisie) forces 'the slave' (the proletariat) to obey. What this
contradictory mechanism of subordination generates for the bourgeoisie is twofold:
the awareness of their dependence on the proletariat and possibility of manipulation. Yet this awareness does not put the bourgeoisie in a revolutionary position,
which would allow them to overcome this contradiction. Broadly speaking, as long
as the bourgeoisie can survive this contradiction, the system will continue to benefit
them. In this context, Alice, unlike Bill, is well aware of her and Bill's own class
position and behaves in the way this awareness requires. She knows that, as members of the upper-middle class, they are afforded the privilege of enjoying their life
through the denial and manipulation of the shocking contradictions their material
conditions may reinforce. It is this knowledge that makes her a healing agent in
their relationship even during times of crisis. This knowledge provides her with the
flexibility to easily adjust her reality to the changing circumstances and assume the
different stances necessary in defense of both herself and her husband.

The two portraits drawn above help us to unpack two different modes of
politics. The first, represented by Bill, depends entirely on traditional modalities;
the functioning of which is dependent less on awareness than it is on repression
techniques as a defense mechanism. As opposed to its rational outlook, it is never

reconciled with critical reasoning. This is a bourgeois politics. The second, represented by Alice, relies on awareness as well as manipulation; it also emanates from a bourgeois politics. Despite the differences, both modes of politics require masks to be performed. Because, as it is illustrated above for both Alice and Bill, family replaces free sex in their relationship, reality replaces fantasy, recognition by others replaces conflict, the conservation of lifestyle replaces alteration and finally, dream/masks replaces real life.

Then, it seems reasonable to claim the following: Waking up is not as difficult as imagined. It is however, more difficult to awaken from a dream that is thought to be limited by the sleep itself. Because dreaming is not something that consciousness can deal with easily, unpacking a dream is only possible through the denial of various masks. Abandoning the masks however, requires a realistic revolutionary position acknowledging the real life experiences and material conditions of today's world where dreaming is made tremendously charming through the fantasy, ideologies and ubiquitous reification that occupies almost every aspect of modern life.

In the last scene of the film, both Alice and Bill obtain awareness of their bourgeois lifestyles. In other words, both characters finally wake up from their sleep. Neither of them however, abandons their dreams because neither wants to lose their world of fetishized commodities. In this way, Lukacs's prophecy does not come true: totality is preserved for the sake of totality.

The Faces of Austerity

Kyle Hamilton

Philippines: A Culture of Impunity

Confronting AFP soldiers, Lanao del Sur, Autonomous Region of Muslim Mindanao, Philippines. Election day in the Philippines (May 10, 2010) a local Marano woman right, confronts an Armed Forces Philippines soldier looking for answers regarding a fight that took place inside a polling precinct only minutes before.

Couple in the Green Cart, Manila, Philippines. A young couple is found sleeping as the city comes to life for another day. The green cart is their home which serves as their bed and carries all their possessions. A common site throughout metro Manila, a city where poverty is the norm and many are forced to live in such circumstances.

Boy on makeshift raft – Manila, Philippines. Young boy wades through garbage on a river in hopes of recycling his way out of abject poverty.

Girl in her doorway - Smokey Mountain, Manila Philippines. Young girl stands in the doorway of her home, which is constructed out of discarded spring mattresses. Smokey Mountain is a landfill site in metro Manila where thousands scavenge for their livelihood.

Toronto: G8/G20 Summit

Flower Offering, Toronto, Canada. Peaceful Protesters on the front lines offer police flowers in exchange for dropping their heavy arms.

Protester Sitting on Yonge St. Toronto, Canada. A Protester peacefully confronts a wall of riot police in downtown Toronto as world leaders gather only steps away to commence the G20 summit.

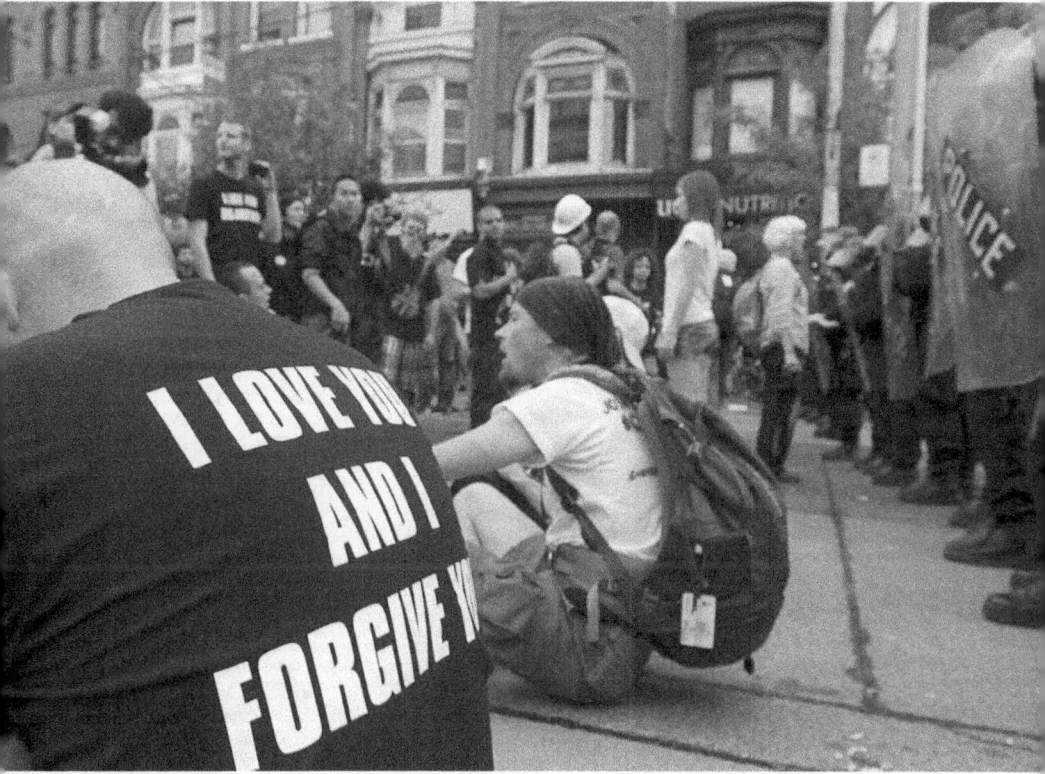

Sitting protestors, Toronto, Canada. Protestors join hands and sing to win the hearts of police and passers by. One man's shirt reads, "I LOVE YOU AND I FORGIVE YOU".

Peaceful Protesting, Toronto, Canada. As protestors marched down the streets of Toronto, multiple police blockades were set up at each intersection, preventing protestors from gaining access to the secure area where world leaders gathered for the G20 Summit.

Reviews

Book Review

About Canada: Animal Rights, by John Sorenson.
**Black Point, Nova Scotia and Winnipeg, Manitoba:
Fernwood Publishing Company Limited, 2010. $17.95
CAN, paper. ISBN: 978-1-55266-356-1. Pages: 1-192.**

Reviewed by Priscillia Lefebvre[1]

About Canada: Animal Rights is one in a series of books that critically examines
vital issues pertaining to social justice, healthcare, and public services in Canadian
society. John Sorenson delivers an extensive analysis of animal rights in Canada,
which is both extremely disturbing and informative. In his exploration of this important and controversial topic, Sorenson provides us with numerous examples of
the exploitation and abuse of animals within industry, as well as the sad shortcomings of Canadian legislation intended to regulate it. He explains the issue of animal
rights in a comprehensive and yet extremely accessible way. Because of its broad
nature, Sorenson does not delve into an exhaustive analysis of any one topic but
provides the reader with an excellent overview of the legal, historical, and social
issues surrounding animal rights in Canada as well as the arguments, misconcep-
tions, and industry propaganda embedded within it.

Sorenson begins with a discussion of animal rights within the broader social
justice movement by remarking that all too often animal rights are disregarded by
many otherwise progressive people as a legitimate concern. For many, he explains,
animal rights are considered inferior to the widely accepted notion of the hierarchi-
cal order of nature in which human beings dominate and take priority over concerns of other species. Labeled as pretentious or sentimental, animal rights issues are
placed at odds with other struggles instead of being considered central to many sites

---

[1] Priscillia Lefebvre is a Ph.D Candidate in the Department of Sociology & Anthropology with a concentration in Political
Economy. She can be reached at plefebvr@connect.carleton.ca

of oppression. Sorenson takes issue with this by stating that to view a compassion for the suffering of animals as somehow indicative of a disregard for the suffering of humans is nonsensical and creates a false dichotomy between the two, as if systemic violence towards animals and the environment does not also include an attack on human labour and health under patriarchal capitalism. Animal rights activists, to a great extent, are also accused of extremism and called terrorists, mainly pointing to groups such as the Animal Liberation Front, by those who would defend animal exploitation and cruelty under the present system. Sorenson likens this socially con-structed bifurcation to racism and sexism, ideologies which have been historically used to justify the oppression of marginalized others. Sorenson readies his audience for this discussion with the following passage (p.11):

> Capitalism involves exploitation of animals as well as humans and the profit-motive extends suffering to a broader scale: billions of animals are killed each year in the food, vivisection, fashion, hunting, and entertainment industries. Mistreatment of animals is shaped by systems of oppression that developed over time to maintain profit, privilege and power.

Sorenson's abolitionist perspective is based first and foremost on the premise, outlined by Gary Francione, that animals are to be recognized as having one basic right—the right not to be considered property. All animals are sentient beings who deserve respect and are not to be seen as at the disposal of humans, and for this he makes no apologies. Sorenson maintains that the commodification of animals enables their usage by humans to attain whatever ends deemed fit by the owner, be it for profit, labour, experimentation or otherwise. He details accounts of the grue-some activities taking place in industrial meat production, factory farming, and in the slaughter of cows, pigs, chickens as well as the production of more so-called upscale delicacies such as duck *foie gras*, marine animals, and exotic meats. He explores animals being tortured and abused for entertainment purposes and sport such as in hunting, rodeos, horse-racing, circuses, and zoos. Sorenson also speaks of the ugliness of the pet industry in his examples of puppy mills, as well as cases of extreme animal cruelty on the part of pet owners and individuals. He also refers to and provides examples of the redundancy and ineffectualness of animal research in Canada. Although reading numerous accounts of violence and excruciating pain being inflicted on animals does not make for an enjoyable read per se, it is an im-portant one for those willing to confront the truly horrible production methods of what we, as a society, consume on a daily basis.

Sorenson reestablishes the links between animal and human suffering through a survey of the detrimental role that animal exploitation and the killing of animals for profit plays in capitalist colonial expansion. He argues that animal rights issues must be integrated as part of the greater ecological and economic crisis by interrogating the animal industry's contribution to serious threats to human survival such as global warming and starvation. Corporate interests will never allow for animal rights as that would interfere with their profits. To combat this, corporations have invested millions of dollars, a significant portion of which comes from taxpayers awarded through government subsidies, in public relations propaganda. For example, Sorenson outlines the opportunistic use of Indigenous people by the fur industry as marketing tools to promote themselves as preserving Canada's rich cultural heritage and supporting traditional ways of living by paying Aboriginal fur-trappers next to nothing for the bloody work of killing animals. Many would say this relationship is far more representative of Canada's tradition of colonization and genocide of Indigenous people than it is of respecting or preserving Aboriginal culture.

Lending to the strength of his arguments, particularly when speaking of Canada's indefensible seal hunt, he also lays out the irrationality of much of the animal industry's practices not only in moral, but economic terms. In doing so, he calls into question the sustainability of such practices and explores who really profits from them. In most cases, such as the seal hunt, it is fur industry corporations who lobby the federal government's Department of Fisheries and Oceans to continue defending the mass killing of seals under the guise of job creation for off-season fishermen and animal population control, even in the face of embarrassing international public anger and costly boycotts. Ironically, this also follows the same Orwellian logic that conservation through culling initiatives propagate in that in order to preserve animals we must kill them. Sorenson also points out that, in reality, these brutal annual practices only account for a tiny fraction of income for labourers, while producing hazardous consequences for the ocean's ecosystem and costing governments several times more money to orchestrate than it generates. In fact, one gets the impression that it would be cheaper to cancel the hunt altogether and just give sealers the money they make during this mass killing outright. As the fur market declines, it would seem that the seal hunt, referred to by many as 'Canada's Shame,' is only lucrative for the commercial fur industry.

In the final chapter, Sorenson presents veganism as the only ethical choice when facing an industry bent on such cruelty and total disregard for the wellbeing of both animals and humans; an industry inflicting countless long-term harms on the environment in search of profit. However, his call for veganism as a (at least partial) solution fails in part due to the lack of addressing the shortcomings of following a vegan lifestyle without examining other forms of exploitation that, on its own, veganism does not address. Problems surrounding grain production and other foods under capitalist industrial agriculture that are not animal based, for example.

Where does veganism situate itself, in the resistance of not only animal exploitation but human exploitation as well, in the import of fruits and other foods from countries such as the Philippines and Costa Rica grown under extremely oppressive, dangerous, and environmentally harmful conditions, not to mention the use of migrant labour in Canada's own fruit and vegetable production? Sorenson's call for veganism would have been much stronger had he clarified this point. Nor does Sorenson problematize his call for eco-tourism as an alternative to safari-style vacationing as a colonial practice in itself which often requires the appropriation and 'clearing' of land already in use by indigenous people in order to prepare it for viewing as a pristine wilderness. In my opinion, these are vital topics for discussion if we are not to simply trade one oppression for another in an attempt to, as Sorenson himself would say, "salve our consciences." That said, *About Canada: Animal Rights* provides an excellent overview of this issue, as well as its far-reaching implications and vital place within the broader movement for social justice for all.

Book Review

Cops, Crime and Capitalism: The Law and Order Agenda in Canada by Todd Gordon. Halifax: Fernwood Publishing, 2006. $21.95 CAN, paper. ISBN 1-55266-185-7. Pages 1-171.

Reviewer: Gulden Ozcan[1]

Debates around the notions of security, police, the state and the dissent have accelerated in the aftermath of the G8/20 summit in Toronto. On the face of these debates, revisiting one of the ambitious contributions to the critical literature on police in Canada is important. Todd Gordon's *Cops, Crime and Capitalism: The Law and Order Agenda in Canada* provides two primary insights that can be utilized in current discussions. First, Gordon situates his analysis of the broader police project in the context of massive restructuring of social relations after each crisis of capitalism. Thus, the increasing adoption of the 'law-and-order policies' by the Canadian state since the 1990s is depicted in relation to the neoliberal restructuring of social relations after the downfall of Keynesian policies. Second, Gordon's focus on racialised and gendered aspects of policing in Canada opens up the possibility for new approaches to locate this long-delayed discussion at the very centre of the materialist analysis of state power, capital and labour relations. Gordon, by conducting a careful empirical study of legal regulations, demonstrates how police practices have served the systematic subordination of racialised and gendered populations in Canada.

The theoretical stance Gordon employs in the book is informed by Open Marxism and the concepts developed by Mark Neocleous, one of the leading figures in critical police/security studies. The Open Marxism approach provides him with theoretical tools in defining the state as the political form of the class antagonism between labour and capital. Even though the organization of social relations are

---

[1]   Gulden Ozcan is a PhD Student in the Department of Sociology & Anthropology at Carleton University. She can be reached at gozcan@connect.carleton.ca

operated by the state and its apparatuses, Gordon argues these operations originate from the struggles between labour and capital. Gordon draws on Neocleous's historical analysis of the broader police project in relation to the rise of capitalism as well as his conceptualizations of the "political administration" and the "fabrication of social order". Paralleling Neocleous, Gordon defines policing as a form of "political administration" that has historically played an important role in the "fabrication of social order" (pp. 38-50).

I shall also acknowledge a third theoretical stance Gordon uses, that is, his critical attitude towards "Marxist-oriented functionalism" and Foucauldian "panoptical theories". Although he mentions the former very briefly only in the introduction, he spends a great deal of the first chapter on the latter. It is, therefore, important to mention Gordon's critique of what he calls "panoptical theories", i.e., theories that take "governing at a distance" approach as their starting point. Gordon pinpoints a "gap between the reality of contemporary policing and its portrayal" in this literature (p. 7). He identifies three main assumptions of panoptic theories: (1) policing is done electronically at-a-distance; (2) electronic policing is exercised equally on everybody regardless of class, race and gender differences; (3) electronic policing reinforces the emergence of more local and autonomous forms of policing (pp. 7-8). Gordon's position toward these assumptions unfolds in the question of "at a distance or in your face?" (p. 13). He basically argues that the new tactics of policing does not change the historical objective of police forces, i.e., targeting working-class, racialised and gendered populations through ever-ascending centralized and intense state power (pp. 8-27).

Drawing attention to the problematic aspects of panoptic theories strengthens Gordon's approach to police as a state-centred strategy. Although his criticisms of the panoptical and at-a-distance approaches are persuasive, his equation of Foucault with Foucauldians is not. It is obvious that Foucault's work has generated a basis for both panoptical theories and governing at a distance approach. However, some aspects of these approaches contradict Foucault's own writings. Gordon does not distinguish Foucault from the Foucauldians and thus presents a reductionist attitude towards Foucault's contribution to the literature on police. His miscomprehension of Foucault's *oeuvre* results in a few literally wrong assumptions such as the naming of 'at a distance approach' after Foucault—which was originally suggested by P. Miller and N. Rose in 1992[2]—, the rejection of Foucault's meticulous attention to material social relations, the denial of Foucault's understanding of police as a state-centric initiative at its birth, and his attack of Foucault's notion of "docile bodies" on the basis of the absence of agency. Nevertheless, this confusion neither

---

2   Rose, N. and Miller, P. 1992 "Political Power Beyond the State: problematics of government", British Journal of Sociology 43(2): 173-205.

diminishes the strong basis of the arguments in the book, nor contributes anything to it.

Following the theoretical debate in the second chapter, Gordon draws on the history of police in the making of the capitalist social order from the nineteenth century onwards. Gordon defines this historical role of police as such:

> Police power has been mobilized [by the ruling classes] to crimi-
> nalize a series of street-based activities that either provide peo-
> ple with an opportunity to survive outside market relations or
> serve as distractions from waged work. In the process, policing
> has worked to constitute a class of labourers dependent on the
> wage for subsistence and thereby a bourgeois order rooted in the
> authority of private property and the subordination of working
> people to the imperatives of capital accumulation (p. 50).

In what follows, he compares and contrasts nineteenth-century police practices with more current police practices and thus illustrates the continuous dynamic that lies at the very *raison d'etre* of the police project, i.e., targeting labour power to build a more orderly, disciplined, regulated and supervised society in accord with the changing needs of capitalism.

The third chapter provides a brief history of the neoliberal transition from Keynesianism in advanced capitalist countries, with specific attention to Canada. In order to respond to the growing structural imbalances in the economy, Gordon explains that labour costs have been reduced significantly since the 1960s through increasing the number of non-standard, non-unionized, and unqualified types of labour as a state policy. This of course was not a pain-free process. Although the initial attempt of consecutive governments was to have policies of "austerity by consent", Gordon argues this did not work due to the disruptive power of labour at the time. As a result, the coercive power of the state has been increased and law-and-order policies increasingly adopted (pp. 54-57).

The fourth chapter portrays that new regulations introduced with the law-and-order policies that target not so much the poor, but the contemporary indigent that seek to live outside the labour market. In this sense, Gordon examines the Vagrancy Act of 1869 and shows that following the economic crisis of the 1970s, vagrancy status did not come back to the criminal code; however, substitutes have taken their place in an attempt to serve the same objective. This is evidenced, for example, in provincial legislation and municipal by-laws such as the Safe Streets Acts, panhandling by-laws, and the adoption of targeting and intelligence policing strategies (pp. 82-85). Accompanying this new work ethic has been a re-regulation of social assistance programs. Gordon reveals that people in need of social assistance due to unemployment are encouraged to gain and/or improve their "transferable skills" (p. 105). These skills are defined as self-discipline, getting to work on time, meeting the expectations of the employer and being motivated to work.

In the last chapter of the book Gordon problematizes how policing as "an administrative feature of state power" takes on a certain position when it comes to immigrant communities (p. 128). Unlike some Marxist approaches to immigration, Gordon does not limit his account to portraying immigrants only as a source of cheap foreign labour. Although the initial emphasis is put on the role of immigrant labour in filling the worst jobs Canada has to offer, Gordon does not ignore other circumstances surrounding immigrants. He especially takes issue with the conditions of women and non-white immigrants. For instance, he demonstrates how the points system used in immigration applications neglects the unpaid domestic labour of women and makes them rely on their husband in the application process (p. 115). Moreover, he establishes the link between the exploitative immigration policies of the federal government and the cheap labour requirements of capital by drawing attention to the Non-Immigrant Employment Authorization Program (NIEAP), Live-in Caregiver Program, as well as the government's blindness to non-status immigrants' participation in the labour process. Gordon also speaks to the fact that the criminalization of certain drugs are strongly related to Canada's immigration policies. He claims, for example, that the prohibition of opium in 1908 was a direct response to Chinese immigration. The ruling class was concerned that opium shows "signs of non-conformity with "Canadian" order, and that this vice of bodily pleasure might infiltrate the ranks of the white working class" (p. 130). The same applies to the prohibition of cocaine in 1911, cannabis in 1923 and khat in 1997, however this time as a response to Black, Mexican and Somalian immigrants, with the explicit aim being to produce public order on the streets (p. 135).

All in all, Gordon's book provides a significant overview of policing in Canada. It has much to contribute to the current debates on the role of police in the current reformation of the neoliberal order. Although Gordon's approach to police as a state-centred strategy leaves some questions unanswered such as the ever-increasing numbers of private police, he provides an accessible account to remind us that policing is a strategy driven by a moral discourse on the importance of employment and self-discipline, rather than a strategy to fight crime.

Book Review

The Ecological Revolution Making Peace with the Planet, by John Bellamy Foster. New York: Monthly Press Review, 2009. $17.95 US., paper. ISBN-13: 9781583671795. Pages: 1-328.

Reviewed by: Alda Kokallaj[1]

John Bellamy Foster's book is a critical treatise of the ecological crisis facing our planet and a scholarly contribution to the literature of political ecology. The book's primary aim is to provide "resources for a journey of hope" towards an eco-social revolution, while we stand at a crucial point regarding humanity's relation to the earth. The book is divided in three parts. Part one, entitled "The Planetary Crisis" begins by pointing out the ecological crisis that is looming upon the planet and briefly discusses the unsuccessful endeavors for addressing this crisis. Particular attention has been paid to efforts undertaken as part of the 1992 Rio Earth Summit and the Johannesburg Summit, which are seen as failed attempts to achieve a sustainable future. Foster argues that sustainable development is increasingly seen as an opportunity for business, thus environmental reform is to be achieved through market-driven models. This part of the book reads easily and is rich in information about the inconsistencies that have lead to questionable environmental policies and the failure to achieve environmental reform on a large scale.

In the second part entitled "Marx's Ecology", Foster sets the ground for theorizing the ecological revolution. While its theoretical richness cannot be addressed here in its entirety, it is crucial to focus on the concept of 'metabolic rift'. Foster explains that instead of seeing Marx's work as blind towards nature, his work needs to be seen as providing a powerful analysis for the ecological crisis of our time. Foster achieves this through an in-depth discussion of Marx's later work on political economy, especially by revealing his discussion of 'the Second Agricultural Revolu-

---

[1]   Alda Kokallaj is a Ph.D Candidate in the Department of Political Science with a concentration in political economy. She can be reached at akokalla@connect.carleton.ca

tion' and by unfolding Marx's inspiration with the work of German chemist Justus von Liebig (*Organic Chemistry in Its Application to Agriculture and Physiology, 1840; Animal Chemistry, 1842; Letters on Modern Agriculture, 1859*). For Foster, Marx employed the concept of 'metabolic rift' in order to "capture the material estrangement of human beings in capitalist society from the natural conditions of their existence" (p.180). Such discussion reveals that although Marx did not attempt to provide a treatment of all ecological problems, his work was not 'ecologically blind'. Indeed, Foster rightly maintains, that Marx's work "constitutes a possible starting point for a comprehensive sociology of the environment" (p.196). Foster establishes that Marx argued and wrote as if nature mattered, and that is the crux of his contribution to sociology as a field, as well as to the movements for an ecological revolution.

The third part entitled "Ecology and Revolution", presents an integration of theory with practice for establishing the argument that an ecological revolution needs to originate from 'the social' realm. Thus, it is through a social revolution that secures the provision of basic human needs that an ecological civilization can be achieved. In this way Foster maintains that the human relation to nature lies at the heart of the transition to socialism. This identification along with the discussion of the 'metabolic rift' found in Marx's work constitutes a significant contribution to socialist theory, which can serve as the starting point for the theorization of the transition from capitalism to socialism. This can also serve in understanding the struggles for sustainable society and human development that are taking place in the periphery of the capitalist system, which need to be seen as examples for fundamental change at the centre. In the last two chapters Foster broadly discusses examples from Cuba, Venezuela, Brazil and India as "islands of hope" for the establishment of the human metabolism with nature along with practices of human development, instead of solely economic development. Although these are important cases for illustrating the transitional steps from capitalism to an ecological society, the discussion is somewhat insufficient. While expecting the argument for the ecological revolution to acquire more depth towards the end of the book, the reader encounters a rather romanticized and superficial treatment of the struggles for sustainable human development that have taken place in the periphery of the capitalist world system.

One further problem with the book is that Foster spends a lot of time trying to tie together theory and practice while dealing with some complicated theoretical questions and not-so-easy to sort out practical issues. This has resulted in often repetitive and overburdened sections, rather than providing more straightforward treatment of the practical and theoretical issues. Better editing would have assisted the reader to get a clearer understanding of the dynamics of the socio-ecological revolution presented in the book. This, coupled with the fact that the book is a collection of articles turned into chapters, demonstrates its lack of focus and at times makes it a difficult read.

Despite these problems Foster's book does offer an excellent discussion of some key concepts of Marx's work regarding the metabolism of humanity with nature and relates them to the problematique of eco-social sustainability. Foster's main achievement is to draw together a difficult body of theory with urging political questions and convincingly argue that it is high time ecological crises were addressed via a socialist, as opposed to a capitalist, approach. The root of addressing environmental crises for Foster involves a "civilizational shift" that would be revolutionary for culture, economy and society. Foster compellingly reveals that questions surrounding the capacity of the capitalist mode of production to wrought environmental destruction have been treated in the classical works of critical political economy. In this way, Foster's book is an important addition to the scholarly works, which assert that the work of Marx, especially his later political economy, is characterized by an understanding that nature (non-human nature) matters. Hence, the genesis of the questionable sustainability of capitalism can be discerned via Marx's discussion of 'the Second Agricultural Revolution'. Another disciplinary contribution is for the field of sociology. Through his discussion of Marx, one of the classical thinkers of the field, and by unfolding the 'metabolic rift' as well as society – nature relation, Foster reveals that theorization, particularly in environmental sociology, can be done on a more theoretically solid ground. More generally, from Foster's argument it can be discerned that in the face of ecological crises we need to think and act beyond disciplinary boundaries. He asserts that a "sociology of the environment" must recognize and consider changes that take place in the social and natural realms, as well as their mutual interaction. Thus, social transformation cannot be understood without ecological transformation and vice versa.

Book Review

In and Out of Crisis: The Global Financial Meltdown and Left Alternatives, **by Greg Albo, Sam Gindin and Leo Panitch. Oakland, California: Spectre PM Press, 2010. $13.95 U.S., paper. ISBN: 978-1-60486-212-6. Pages: 1-140.**

Reviewed by Carlo Fanelli[1]

In and Out of Crisis is a thought provoking, accessible and politically engaging contribution to debates on the origin, severity and historical significance of the so-called "Great Recession". Furthermore, as the subtitle *The Global Financial Meltdown and Left Alternatives* suggests, Albo and authors provide an unapologetically socialist analysis of what to do about it. Albo, Gindin and Panitch remind the reader that the classical meaning of crisis is turning point, to which they ask: Has the crisis marked a turning point in the balance of class power and the organization of the state? Or can the political alliances and power structures that have dominated the last four decades be reconstituted in what so clearly has been a monumental crisis?

For the authors, the short answer to the first question is no and, for the second, yes. This book departs from the tendency of writers (both from the Left and Right) to view the current responses to crisis as somehow marking a return to Keynesianism, or in terms of states versus markets, finance versus industry. Instead, rather than lay emphasis on the economic determinations of the crisis, the authors (p.10) seek to politicize and get at the social roots of the problem by moving beyond limited technical or policy solutions to capitalist crises by instead placing democratic and social rights at the centre of their analysis. As they state (p.122): "The interpretation in this book is quite distinct".

---

[1]   Carlo Fanelli is a Ph.D Candidate in the Department of Sociology & Anthropology with a concentration in political economy. He can be reached at cfanelli@connect.carleton.ca

Fortunately, the authors have preemptively summarized the outline of the book (p.25):

> 'Chapter one explores whether or not we are currently witnessing the end of neoliberalism; chapter two engages in current debates regarding the nature of capitalist crises, and the relationship between the state, finance and production in a neoliberal era; chapter three traces the historical process through which, over a century punctuated by previous cries, the American State and finance developed in tandem, and came to play a new kind of imperial role at the centre of global capitalism; chapter four traces the development of the crisis that began in 2007 and explains the active role of the American state, both under Bush and Obama, in containing the crisis in ways that reproduced the structures of class inequality and power domestically and internationally; chapter five analyses how the relationship between industry and finance played itself out in the auto sector, bringing to the fore the full class dimensions of the crisis; chapter six reflects on the impasse of the North American labour movement and the implications for the North American Left; and Chapter seven tries to think creatively about alternatives, not least in terms of how advancing the case for democratic economic planning, including the nationalization of the banks and auto industry, must become integrated with demands for immediate reforms.'

If the reader does not have the time for chapters one through seven, chapter eight's *Ten Theses on the Crisis* succinctly summarizes the gist of their arguments. For the purpose of this review, however, I would like to provide a glimpse of what makes *In and Out of Crisis'* analysis distinct. Or, in other words, what are likely to be the major points of contention stemming from their investigation.

First, contrary to authors that claim that the New Deal was an attempt to impose greater 'regulation' or 'controls' upon capital, Albo et al argue that following the Great Depression of the 1930s, private banking institutions had been nurtured back to health in the post-war decades and then unleashed in the explosion of global innovations that have defined the neoliberal era. And that, despite the meltdown, (p.17) "[t]he conditions that kept neoliberal policies in play for so long have not been exhausted or undone by the crisis."

Second, taking aim at a broad spectrum of liberal, Keynesian, Minskian and orthodox Marxist views that posit the end of the American Imperium, a return to greater "regulation" or the stagnation tendencies of "mature" capitalist economies (such as Robert Brenner and the *Monthly Review* School for instance), Albo and authors argue that, if anything, the crisis has reconfirmed the world's dependence on the American state and financial system as capital everywhere ran to the safe haven of the US Treasury bond. As opposed to the end of American hegemony or the birth of a multi-polar world, the resolution of this international crisis has rested fundamentally on the actions of the US state in leading a more or less coordinated response, and in the process integrating the G20 members into the US's informal empire in what has been an extraordinarily dynamic period of capitalism.

Third, Albo, Gindin and Panitch provide a unique examination of the relationship between states and markets, industry and finance and, therein, the class relations that underpin them. Rater than viewing 'financialization' as narrowly superstructural, parasitic or speculative, or as a result of the tendency for the rate of profit to fall, they situate finance-led neoliberalism in historical terms in the sense that financial volatility actually becomes a developmental feature of neoliberalism that reinforces, rather than undermines the central position of financial interests in capitalist power structures. In their view, neoliberalism is understood as a (p.28) "particular form of class rule and state power that intensifies competitive imperatives for both firms and workers, increases dependence on the market in daily life and reinforces the dominant hierarchies of the world market, with the US at its apex."

Fourth, the authors claim (p.91) that a new historical project must be placed on the agenda. In order to do this, the Left must come to the bitter realization that the forms of protest, means of organizing and daily practices of activism, most visible in the anti-globalization movements and world social forums, just aren't working anymore. This means soberly reflecting on the impasse of the North American labour movement, in addition to the successful "disorganization" (on the part of capital) of old working class institutions (labour parties, cooperatives, benefit societies) that has been central to neoliberalism and which threatens to become a historic class defeat.

Throughout the book, Albo et al raise the question as to whether or not the Left can develop the confidence to think as big and radical as "they"—the ruling class—are doing in terms of both how workers see the future and what needs to be done to build the capacities to get there. "The way forward", they argue (p.114) however, "is not to take one step first and another more radical step later, but to find ways of integrating both the immediate demands and the goal of systemic change into the building of new political capacities." As they remind (p.128), 'democracy is not just a form of government but a kind of society', which unavoidably remains fractional and incomplete within capitalism.

A few questions, however, may beg further unpacking. In light of the shifting composition of the working class and the role of women's reproductive labour, how would the expansion of collective social services such as in health care and education, for instance, impact women's paid and unpaid life experiences given their position in the labour market as a whole and concentration in specific sectors? Given the legacy of defeats and setbacks over the period of neoliberalism, how may unions—many trapped in erstwhile social-democratic parties and the constraints of formal union structures—find some basis of unity that could help shape collective struggles in working-class communities and connect the linkages between the employed and unemployed, and those denied a chance to work? What kinds of fresh organizational structures and emergent forms of activism throughout North America and abroad carry potential?

On the whole, *In and Out of Crisis* is all but certain to have a broad appeal to researchers and academics, as well as students and lay persons alike. The era of neoliberalism—that is, capitalist militancy, is by no means over. In fact, it seems to be gaining new momentum the world over. Albo, Gindin and Panitch, in their short but no less provocative book, do much to not only shed light on what led to the enduring socio-economic and political uncertainty, but provide a much needed analysis on what may need to be done in order to avoid such relapses in the future.

Book Review

Canada's 1960s: The Ironies of Identity in a Rebellious Era
by Bryan D. Palmer. Toronto: University of Toronto Press,
2008. $35.00 US, paper. ISBN 978-08020-9954-9. Pages:
1-605.

Reviewed by Edward Hilchey[1]

Curious about 'what it is to be Canadian'? If so, you are not alone. Grounding
this question of identity in history, Bryan Palmer theorises that the turbulence of
the 1960s played a significant role in the destabilization of established notions of
Canadian identity. Re-evaluating the personalities and movements of the 1960s,
Palmer argues that the 60s push towards an equitable society acted as a catalyst
for questioning Canada's historic British identity. However, these movements did
not provide any long lasting certainty over what Canada's national identity should
entail.

Palmer's style of writing quietly and gently guides us into his perception of
Canada's experience of the 1960s. Layering his work topically, Palmer demonstrates
himself to be as much of a cultural as he is a labour historian. Well-supported
with 143 pages of notes, he adds a humanistic depth to this work through a series
of anecdotes from newspapers, poems, activist manifestos and other lesser known
works. Through the effective use of these resources with broader themes and debates, Palmer critically engages the developments of the 1960s. Palmer connects a
range of events which emerged in the 1960s through creative and concise language,
blending the transformation of this social and political climate.

The choice to examine Canada during the 1960s for Palmer lies precisely in its
overt activism. The 60s were marred with patterns of hostility demarcating regional,
political, cultural, and linguistic disparities. Through a Marxist definition of irony
(drawn from Terry Eagleton), Palmer comments that "capitalism is that of a system

---

[1]   Edward Hilchey is an M.A. candidate at Carleton University. He can be reached at ehilchey@connect.carleton.ca

frozen in its fixed modes of representation, yet mobilizing a desire to overturn all representation; which gives birth to a great carnival of difference... which constantly conjures material inequality out of abstract equality; which is in need of an authority it continually flouts" (p. 9). The post-World War image of Canada was that of a white European colony emerging to become a state. The irony was that Canada was on the verge of confronting its own self image. In a renewed analysis, Palmer counters the notion that Canada's 1960s was *sui generis*, that is, a spent generation whose objectives were not obtained (p. 5), and argues that this particular period was characterized with widespread changes in Canada.

Palmer sets the stage by contextualizing events within the broader history affecting Canada in the post-war era. Part 1 begins with the fluctuation of the Canadian dollar and its subsequent inflation in the early 60s. Reflecting on the unstable dollar as an indicator of political and economic ineffectiveness, political blunderings became the backdrop to express (and subsequently elect) needed change in Canada. These episodes quashed Canada's image as one of British dominion, settled by a robust and progressive populace. As well, it severed many historical economic ties with Britain by shifting economic focus to the rise of the imperialist United States.

In Part 2, Palmer tracks the international attention being afforded to Canada through a variety of publicized events and scandals. Emphasizing the role of electronic media in broadcasting and journalism, Canadians became fascinated with sex scandals and political wrangling. From the Munsinger affair wherein a displaced women from World War II came to media attention due to her personal relationships with prominent conservative figures, to the acceptance of the Ali-Chuvolo fight where an underdog boxer survived fifteen rounds with the 'Louisville Lip". The way Canadians perceived sexuality and white-ness was being transformed, paving the way for Trudeau mania. Canadians found themselves elated by the international recognition these events received, though these events flew in the face of Victorian values and conventions.

In Parts 3 & 4, he mentions that the politicization of youth and striking workers lead to the opening of Canada's political organizations for debate. With airwaves and television screens saturated with nationalistic fervour, the unruly, reactive, and openly rebellious youth had moved from the margins of social transformation (paralleling labour) into "the very core of a decade's understanding of social-political meaning" (p. 209). Youth were rejecting integration into family and nation, as represented in the Victoria Day disturbances. Street youth hostility shifted towards the development of subsequent banners of new left radicalism, revolutionary strife in Quebec and Indian Red Power. Alternative identities awoke and broadcasted their displeasure with British Canada. They drew their ideals, strength and support from the pantheon of marginal groups which were reinventing and redefining themselves.

The conclusion ends with the vanguard of British Canada gathering with the world in Montreal's Expo 67, celebrating Canada's arrival into the modern era. With the replacement of the Red Ensign for the Maple Leaf and an army of RCMP keeping the protestors and the FLQ at bay, Canadian identity would remain precarious. Yet, Expo 67 and the Maple Leaf flag would be as unsuccessful at charting a unified path for Canada as the Victoria Day celebrations and Bank of Canada issued currency before it. Palmer's remarks in the introduction are epitomized in this final section in which Canadians "finally extricated themselves from a national identity... [that] so many voices had come to proclaim outmoded" (24).

Palmers understanding and application of historical materialism places increased emphasis on content and examples as compared to theoretical debate (five pages in the introduction are devoted to Eagleson & his theoretical perspective). Choosing to elaborate the historical antagonism bred from exploitation and struggle within Canada, as seen in the dearth of detail, he presents an interpretive history of Canada during the 60s, refocusing the period as a topic worthy of analytical spotlight. Palmer uses this work to 'suggest' (p. 21) the reasons why the past happened as it did, and how the outcome of these events maintained a destabilized Canadian identity. His analytical approach focuses on how the conflicting ideas were critically important to history. Palmer concludes that the dominate relations of class conflict may be seen in the struggle over Canadian identity, an identity which required significant consideration of how gender, race, empire and imperialism, social movements and identity interplay.

The significance of this book lies within its reminder to scholars that the struggles of the 1960s have not completely died, and that this period has made a lasting contribution to Canadian society. The intent is for others to understand the significant impact that 1960s & 70s politics and activism had in the uprooting of Victorian Canada. This book was written for both those who were present during the 60s and those who are interested in the implications of views from this period in Canada. Palmer asserts that what he offers through his work is "not so much a synthesis of the 60s, as suggestion on what destabilized the Canadian identity, rooted in some specifics" (21). The point becomes clear that everything has a history; that before Trudeau, we needed Munsinger; that before Red Power or the FLQ, we needed 'White Niggers of America' and hooliganism; that the transition of the Canadian identity could only occur while being rooted in these events. Reinforcing the point that Canadians have accepted an undetermined identity rather than one passed down from establishment, this book reopens the tumultuous period which was the 1960s for further analysis.

Alternate Routes: A Critical Review, *Vol. 1*, 1977
Clement, Wallace. *Macrosociological Approaches: Towards a 'Canadian Sociology'*. Pp.1-37.
Glenday, Daniel. *The Dominion Government as Gatekeeper to the Canadian Ethnic Mosaic: The Case of Quebec 1867-1885*. Pp. 38-57.
Marshall, Stan. *Embourgeoisement or Proletarianization?*. Pp. 58-86.
Mayer, Jan. *Social Mobility: Current Thrusts (and Non-Thrusts): A Critical Approach to the Analysis of Mobility*. Pp. 87-102.
Smith, Chuck. *Toward a Marxist Theory of Transition*. Pp. 103-130.
Campbell, Ken. *Class Analysis and Technological Determinism*. Pp. 131-141.
Saunders, Eileen. *Implications of the Domestic Role of Women*. Pp. 142-157.

Alternate Routes: A Critical Review, *Vol. 2*, 1978
Special Issue: Carleton University Symposium: Braverman & Beyond
Myles, John. *Introduction to Symposium*. Pp. 1-2.
Burawoy, Michael. *Between Marxist Orthodoxy and Critical Theory: Comments on Braverman's Labor and Monopoly Capital*. Pp. 3-14
Comments by:
Panitch, Leo. Pp. 15-22.
Porter, John. Pp. 23-25.
Swartz, Donald. 26-33.
Nelson, W. Randle. *Science as Capitalist Ideology: The Sociology of Max Weber Reconsidered*. Pp. 34-72.
Denis, Wilfred. *Sociology, Philosophy and Materialism*. Pp. 73-113.
Glenday, Daniel. & Christopher Schrenk. *Trade Unions and the State: An Interpretive Essay on the Historical Development of Class and State Relations in Canada, 1889-1947*. Pp. 114-134.
Mayer, Jan. *Mature Marx: The Case Against an Epistemological Break*. Pp. 135-143.

Alternate Routes: A Critical Review, *Vol. 3*, 1979
Heiple, Phil. *The Politics of Probability*. Pp. 1-24.
Haas, Gordon. *Claus Offe and the Capitalist State: A Critique*. Pp. 25-48.
Ward, Bonnie. *The Myth of Autonomy in Family Farm Production*. Pp. 49-62.
Jhally, Sut. *Marxism and Underdevelopment: The Modes of Production Debate*. Pp. 63-93.
Belkaoui, Janice. *A Critical Assessment of Media Studies*. Pp. 94-127.

Alternate Routes: A Critical Review, *Vol. 4,* 1980

Alford, Robert. *Elections, State Policy, and the Marxian Tradition: An Interview.* Pp. 1-20.

Lord, Stella. *The Struggle for Equal Pay for Work of Equal Value: A Case Study.* Pp. 21-52.

White, Robert. *Knowledge and Power: Determinations of Educational Curriculum.* Pp. 53-86.

Malcomson, John. *The Limits of Keynesianism: Some Theoretical Observations.* Pp. 87-104.

Clarke, Debra. *The State of Cultural Theory: A Review of Past and Present Fashions.* Pp. 105-156.

Alternate Routes: A Critical Review, *Vol. 5,* 1982

Christenson, V. Erling. *Aspects of the Crisis in Petit Commodity Production in the Okanagan Valley.* Pp. 1-26.

Myers, Marybelle. *Beyond the Fur Trade: The Rise and Fall of the Eskimo Cooperative.* Pp. 27-66.

Sansfacon, Daniel. Sujet de driot et sujets de droit: de la pratique juridique au pluriel. Pp. 67-94.

Edelson, Mirriam. *Accountable to Whom? Trends in Management-Labour Relations in Local Government.* Pp. 95-132.

Robinson, David. *Community Colleges and the Division Between Mental and Manual Labour.* Pp. 133-166.

Alternate Routes: A Critical Review, *Vol. 6,* 1983

Special Issue: Feminism

Armstrong, Pat. & Hugh Armstrong. *Beyond Numbers: Problems With Quantitative Data.* Pp. 1-40.

Hamilton, Roberta. *The Collusion with Patriarchy: A Psychoanalytic Account.* Pp.41-60.

Saunders, Eileen. Socialist Feminist Theory: The Issue of Revolution. Pp. 61-86.

Morris, Cerise. *Pressuring the Canadian State for Women's Rights: The Role of the National Action Committee on the Status of Women.* Pp. 87-108.

Bourgeault, Ron. *The Development of Capitalism and the Subjugation of Native Women in Northern Canada.* Pp. 109-140.

Alternate Routes: A Critical Review, *Vol. 7,* 1984

Special Issue: Class and Ethnicity

Creese, Gillian. *Immigration Policies and the Creation of an Ethnically Segmented Working Class in British Columbia.* Pp.1-34.

Blight, Stephen. *Nationalism and Ideology.* Pp. 35-60.

Lustiger-Thaler, Henri. *Nationalism and Class: A Case Application.* Pp. 61-101.

Mannette, J. A. *'Stark Remnants of Blackpast' : Thinking on Gender, Ethnicity and Class in 1780s Nova Scotia.* Pp. 102-133.

Schulze, David. *Rural Manufacture in Lower Canada: Understanding Seigneurial Privilege and the Transition in the Countryside.* Pp. 134-167.

Commentary by:

Russell, Jesse. Pp. 168-172.

Alternate Routes: A Journal of Critical Social Research, *Vol. 8,* 1988

Special Issue: Nation, Race, Gender and the International Division of Labour

Broad, Dave. *Peripheralization of the Centre: W(h)ither Canada?* Pp. 1-41.

Faustino-Santos, Ronald. *A Race of Cuckoos: Chinese Migration, Anti-Chinese Legislation and the Canadian Pacific Railway.* Pp. 42-73.

Bourgeault, Ron. *The Struggle of Class and Nation: The Canadian Fur Trade, 1670's to 1870.* Pp. 74-123.

Mackenzie, Ian R. *Early Movements of Domestics from the Caribbean and Canadian Immigration Policy: A Research Note.* Pp. 124-143.

Commentary by:

Russell, Jesse. *Indigenous Women and Capitalist Exploitation.* Pp. 144-153.

Book Reviews:

Alvi, Shahid. *Justice and The Young Offender in Canada* edited by J. Hudson, J. Hornick, and B. Burrows. Pp. 154-156.

Booker, Doug. *Killing Time, Losing Ground: Experiences of Unemployment* by Patrick Burman. Pp. 156-159.

Allan, Stuart. *Manufacturing Consent: The Political Economy of the Mass Media* by Edward S. Herman and Noam Chomsky. Pp. 159-167.

Alternate Routes: A Journal of Critical Social Research, *Vol. 9,* 1992

Special Issue: Cultural Studies

Vasquez Garcia, Veronica. *Gramci, Women and the State.* Pp. 1-25.

Skinner, David. *Public Broadcasting in Canada: Subordinate Service.* Pp. 26-43.

Shreenan, Paul. *On the Devaluation of Women's Labour: Hegemonic and Local Ideological Practices.* Pp. 44-63.

Hubka, David. *Historical Materialism by Cross-Sectional Survey Design: The Limits of E. O. Wright's Study of Class Structure.* Pp. 64-77.

Book Reviews:

Turcotte, Michel. *Bodies, Pleasures and Passions: Sexual Culture in Contemporary Brazil, Boston* by R. G. Parker. Pp. 78-79.

Fogarasi, George A. *Postmodern Education: Politics, Culture and Social Criticism* by Stanlezy Aronowitz and Henry A. Giroux. Pp. 80-81.

Labelle, Paul. *La Folie au Declin du Moyen-Age.* Pp. 82-89.

Kandrack, Mary-Anne. *Studying Psychotherapeutic Knowledge : Notes Toward a Working Definition of Ideology.* Pp. 90-93.

Alternate Routes: A Journal of Critical Social Research, *Vol.10*, 1993
Special Issue: Communications and Democracy
Introduction: Communications and Democracy. Pp. 1-6.

AR Interview: *Communication, Culture and Power: An Interview with Vincent Mosco.* Pp. 7-26.

Rideout, Vanda. *Telecommunication Policy for Whom? An Analysis of Recent CRTC Decisions.* Pp. 27-56.

Robinson, David C. *Taking "Freedom of the Press" Seriously: Critical Media Sociology and the Challenge of Democracy.* Pp. 57-84.

Behnia, Behnam. *Reflections on the Reproduction of Dictatorship in Iran: Communication and Dictatorship.* Pp. 85-112.

Chunn, Ian. *Canons, Publishers, and Literacy Nationalism: Toward a Sociological Perspective.* Pp. 113-120.

Book Reviews:
Hubka, David S. *Culture, Communication and National Identity: The Case of Canadian Television* by Richard Collins. Pp. 121-123.

Newsforum:
Seminar in Canadian Communication Policy: Publics, Markets, and the State. Pp. 124-126.

Alternate Routes: A Journal of Critical Social Research, *Vol. 11*, 1994
Reimer, Joel. *Future Probabilities for a Somali Nation State: Development and Governance.* Pp. 5-30.

Transken, Si. *Dwarfed Wolves Stealing Scraps from Our Masters' Tables: Women's Groups and the Funding Process.* Pp. 31-64.

Huot, François. *Myths on the Left: The Narrative and Discursive Practices of the ALD-CIO News.* Pp. 65-94.

Hladki, Janice. *Problematizing the Issue of Cultural Appropriation.* Pp. 95-120.

Research in Brief:
Skinner, David & Robinson, David C. *Re-thinking Cultural Policy: Critical Approaches in the Era of Privatization.* Pp. 121-132.

MacDonald, J. Rachel. *Free Trade and Social Policy Reform: The Hidden Dimension?* Pp. 133-146.

Newsforum:
Robinson, David C. *Colloquim: "Zadig's Method," the Historical Sciences, Museums and the Performance of Progress.* Pp. 147-150.

Alternate Routes: A Journal of Critical Social Research, Vol. 12, 1995

AR Introduction. Pp. 1-3.

Abdollahyan, Hamid. *Capital Accumulation, Technology Transfer and the Peripheriliza-tion of Sharecropping Agriculture in Iran.* Pp. 3-23.

Dodd, Susan. *Restitching Reality: How TNCs Evade Accountability for Industrial Disas-ters.* Pp. 23-63.

Dufresne, Todd. *Anthropology and the Invention of Deconstruction: A Brief Survey.* Pp. 63-81.

Commentary:

Deisman, Wade. *Ontological Gerrymandering? Non-Identity vs. Difference, Adorno Con-tra Derrida.* Pp. 81-95.

Feminist Workshop:

Browning, Catherine. *Silence on Same-Sex Partner Abuse.* Pp. 95-107.

Enns, Diane. *The Body Deferred: Reconsidering Feminist Approaches to Embodiment.* Pp. 107-115.

Masson, Dominique. *Reintroducing Politics: Recent Developments in Feminist Theories of the State.* Pp. 115-125.

Book Reviews:

Blair, Derek. *Taking Our Informants Seriously: Being Changed by Cross-Cultural En-counters:* The Anthropology of Extraordinary Experience *by David Young and Jean-Guy Goulet.* Pp. 125-134.

Alternate Routes: A Journal of Critical Social Research, Vol. 13, 1996

AR Introduction. Pp. 1-3.

Hamilton, Sheryl N. *Creative and Cultural Expression" but not Art: Multiculturalism Arts Funding as Cultural Management.* Pp. 3-23.

Reddick, Andrew. *Property Rights and Communication.* Pp. 23-67.

Masson, Dominique. *Language, Power, and Politics: Revisiting the Symbolic Challenge of Movements.* Pp. 67-101.

Wolfman, Oscar. *Homophobia in/as Education.* Pp. 101-119.

Hermer, Joseph M. Please, Bears Don't Talk! The Smokey Bear Performance Rules. Pp. 119-126.

Alternate Routes: A Journal of Critical Social Research, Vol. 14, 1997

AR Introduction. Pp. 1-3.

Drouillard, Lisa. *Miami's Little Havana-A Nation in Exile.* Pp. 3-21.

Bennett, Nicole. *Global Village Chic: "Multicultural Fashion" and the Commodifica-tion of Pluralism.* Pp. 21-45.

Whelan, Emma. *Staging and Profiling: The Constitution of the Endometriotic Subject in Gynecological Discourse.* Pp. 45-69.

Book Reviews:

Shantz, Jeffrey. *Listen Anarchist! Murray Bookchin's Defence of Orthodoxy: Social Anar-chism or Lifestyle Anarchism by Murray Bookchin.* Pp. 69-77.

Sorge, Antonio. *Nationalism by Ernest Gellner.* Pp. 77-83.

Alternate Routes: A Journal of Critical Social Research, Vol. 16, 2000
Johnstone, Rory. *Sexual and Ethnic Scripts in the Context of African American Culture.* Pp. 5-9.
Patterson, Mike. *Where the Forest Meets the Highway.* Pp. 9-42.
Seibert, Anita. *From Matka Polka to New Polish Woman.* Pp. 42-62.
Robinson, Phil. *Resisting Subjection, Subjected Resistance: Sadomasochism, Feminism, Moral Regulation and Self-Formation.* Pp. 62-89.
Book Reviews:
Di Luzio, Linda. *Taking A Stand: A Review of Nancy E. Dowd's In Defense of Single-Parent Families.* Pp. 89-93.
Shantz, Jeffrey, Wally Seccombe and D. W. Livingstone. *Down to Earth People: Beyond Class Reductionism and Postmodernism.* Pp. 93-98.

Alternate Routes: A Journal of Critical Social Research, Vol. 17, 2001
Patterson, Mike. *Millenialism and Y2k.* Pp. 5-29.
Nalaskowski, Lukasz. *Why Communism Lacked "Information Flow": A Theoretical Analysis.* Pp. 31-42.
Vachon, Al. *Horkheimer and Adorno go to Japan.* Pp. 43-53.
Yacoubian, George S. and Blake J. Urbach. *Disproportional Involvement in the Use of Crack and Powder Cocaine: Findings from the Arrestee Drug Abuse Monitoring (ADAM) Program.* Pp. 54-70.
Book Reviews:
Shantz, Jeff. *A Structured Anarchism by John Griffin.* Pp. 71-73.

Alternate Routes: A Journal of Critical Social Research, Vol. 18, 2002
Patterson, Mike. *Walking the Dog: An Urban Ethnography of Owners and their Dogs.* Pp. 5-70.
Provost, Terry. *Bodying Black Goddesses: The Duty of Representation Across Time and Cultures.* Pp. 71-99.
Gwilliam, Janet E. *Dangerous Customs: Censorship in Risk Society.* Pp. 100-126.

Alternate Routes: A Journal of Critical Social Research, Vol. 19, 2003
Miller, Brian P. *Talk of Inventing Tradition: Sketching Limitations of Anthropological Concepts of Culture.* Pp.5-19.
Arnone, Anna. *Being Eritrean in Milan.* Pp. 20-57.
Fish, Kenneth. *Biotechnology and the Society-Nature Relation.* Pp. 58-78.
Martin, Fiona. *The Changing Configuration of Inequality in Post-Industrial Society: Volunteering as a Case Study.* Pp. 79-108.
Smith, Robyn. *The Possibility of Pleasure: Foucault's Philosophy of the Subject and the Logic of an Appeal to Aesthetics.* Pp. 109-122.

Alternate Routes: A Journal of Critical Social Research, Vol. 20, 2004

Godoy-Paiz, Paula. *"Canada's Troubled Troops": The Construction of Post-Traumatic Stress Disorder and Its Uses by the Canadian Armed Forces*. Pp. 6-23.

Herro, Anne. *The United Nations and International Conflict Resolution*. Pp. 24-39.

Vallee, Mickey. *The Secret Musical Self: Nostalgic Reification of Music According to Adorno*. Pp. 40-58.

Goldstein, Hilary. *Tuning into Democracy: Community Radio, Free Speech and the Democratic Promise*. Pp. 59-106.

Quehl, Nadine J. *Queering "Madness": Possibilities of Performativity Theory*. Pp. 107-131.

Tejani, Riaz. *The Vanishing Point: Humanity, Vision, and Value Theory in the Age of Economic Globalization*. Pp. 132-148.

Young, Kevin. *The Other Side of the Market: social governance in neoliberal world order and the economy of passive mitigation*. Pp. 149-177.

Book Reviews:

Joffe, Linda S. *Shakespeare, Einstein, and the Bottom Line: the Marketing of Higher Education by David L. Kirp*. Pp. 178-181.

Alternate Routes: A Journal of Critical Social Research, Vol. 21, 2005

Braje, Todd J. *Deep History: Using Archaeology and Historical Ecology to Promote Marine Conservation*. Pp. 5-17.

Walton, Gerald. *The Hidden Curriculum in Schools: Implications for Lesbian, Gay, Bisexual, Transgender, and Queer Youth*. Pp. 18-39.

Stoddart, Mark C.J. *The Gramsci-Foucault Nexus and Environmental Sociology*. Pp.40-62.

Howlett, Oren. *Racial Origins of Civic Nationalisms: Exploring Race Creation in Australia and Canada*. Pp. 63-81.

Kistler, Sarah Ashley. *Loanwords and Code-switching: Distinguishing Between Language Contact Phenomena in Ch'ol*. Pp. 82-118.

* Back Issues: $3.00 each or 2 for $5.00. Email: editor@AlternateRoutes.ca

New (In)Securities: Empire, Environment & Employment

Spring 2011

CALL FOR PAPERS

We are living in increasingly insecure times. In the face of drastic climate change, global economic uncertainty and imperialist wars with no clear battlefield or determined timeline, a good many social scientists have concluded that insecurity, broadly defined and in its many forms, is the new norm. For our next issue, *Alternate Routes* invites submissions on the various ways in which '(in)security' has manifested in the new millennium. How has state repression been employed and under what pretexts? How does ecological degradation threaten our—food, labour, biospheric, geopolitical and physical—security? In what ways are planetary life and the future of the earth threatened? To what extent has labour market restructuring made work more precarious? What groups and persons are most vulnerable to insecure forms of work and labour? Is the future of unions uncertain? How may we understand imperialism today? What relationships are there between war, terror and foreign policy?

Alternate Routes is also interested in media, arts and cultural contributions with political and/or academic merits. This may include works of poetry, verse, photography, graphic design and media analyses. We likewise welcome reviews of books, theater, art exhibits, documentaries and cinema. Finally, Alternate Routes appreciates rejoinders and/or reflections on previously published material. For information regarding the submission process, see our online policies at www.AlternateRoutes. ca. The deadline for submissions is **1 March 2011**. We look forward to your submissions!

Carleton University, Sociology & Anthropology
1125 Colonel By Drive, Ottawa, Ontario, Canada K1S 5B6
Phone: 613-520-2600 (ext: 8316) • Email: Editor@alternateroutes.ca